8-30-2013

To Doke

My Fellow artist
Capt !

Best Wishes
Capt LeRoy H Brown

FROM CROPDUSTER TO AIRLINE CAPTAIN

The Biography of Captain LeRoy H. Brown

by

LeRoy H. Brown
Captain, National Airlines
&
Pan American World Airways

and

Dr. Leo F. Murphy
Commander, U.S. Navy (Retired)

On the Front Cover:

LeRoy Brown as a young crop duster circa 1945 (left) and as a
senior National Airlines DC-10 captain in 1979 (right).

On the Rear Cover:
National Airlines 5, 10, 15, 20, and 25 year service pins.

International Standard Book Number 13: 978-1-60452-076-7
International Standard Book Number 10: 1-60452-076-0

Library of Congress Control Number: 2013935778

BluewaterPress LLC
52 Tuscan Way Ste 202-309
Saint Augustine FL 32092
United States of America

http://bluewaterpress.com
        This book may be purchased online at -
        http://www.bluewaterpress.com/captain

Leroy Brown
1945
TRAVEL AIR 4000

Introduction

The first entry in my first logbook reads that on July 2nd, 1942 I flew 30 minutes in a Piper Cub with W.I. "Tag" Eure as the instructor. But by far, that was not my first flight in an airplane. Forced to open a logbook so I could get a pilot's license, I had already flown some unlogged flight hours under the watchful eyes of experienced cropdusters who taught me how to control an aircraft cleanly and precisely in the low, slow and steep turn world of their chosen profession. For years, I flew and flourished on the ragged edge of stalls while flying open-cockpit biplanes on dusting contracts throughout the south until the airline industry beckoned me to join. When I closed my logbooks in 1993, I had accumulated more than 35,000 wonderful hours of flight in the air, each new minute airborne more joyous than the last.

The goal of this autobiography is to share some of my aviation experiences in the hope the reader will enjoy my adventures as well as to document an era in flight long past. I have tried to be as accurate as possible as far as names, dates, and events, but at 91 years of age, sometimes the memories have grown dim. Accordingly, any mistakes are the sole responsibility of the author and I apologize to any friend or adversary I may have inadvertently or unintentionally omitted in the telling of these tall tales.

In particular, I would like to acknowledge the assistance of Dr. Leo Murphy, who has turned out to be a wonderful friend. I expect our friendship to last forever. This book would not have happened if

Leo had not helped me to go through all of my papers, pictures and logbooks and pushed me along.

I would like to give credit for all of this to the many people who have helped me along the way, especially those in the late 1930's. They are Jack Faulkner, Jimmy Crawford, Bill Longino, "Stormy" Wharton, R.J. Cardwell, Joe Basso, and J.L. Schroeder. While they have all passed on, they will always be in my memory. I would also like to acknowledge my flight instructors, including Tag Eure, Henry Hein, and Kathryn McJunkin; and the Civil Aviation Administration inspectors who helped me, particularly Samuel Dellinger who gave me my commercial license, and George Sackett, a maintenance inspector, who chastised me into doing better. This is only a partial list of the many people who helped me get through the maze of getting a pilot's license without attending an accredited flight school. There is no way a 15-year old boy in the middle of the depression could have accomplished this alone. I never spent a dime. I will be forever grateful to people of their caliber who would go out of their way to help a skinny kid.

Lastly, this book is dedicated to my talented and beautiful wife, Wanda, and our wonderful children, Charles, Cheryl, and Lori, who have been after me for many years to write this book.

Captain LeRoy H. Brown
National Airlines
and
Pan American World Airways (Retired)
Zellwood, Florida

Captain LeRoy H. Brown and Commander Leo Murphy

Foreword

I first met Captain LeRoy Brown while researching my book on the history of Pensacola International Airport. Knowing that National Airlines had served Pensacola since 1938, I contacted F.A. "Bud" Quick, historian for an association of former National Airlines employees, to find the earliest airline pilot who had flown into Pensacola. Quick said he knew just the man for me.

He placed me in contact with Captain LeRoy Brown, who examined his logbooks and found that his first trip into Pensacola was in February 1952 as a brand new copilot aboard a tail-dragging, piston-powered, propeller-driven 14-passenger Lockheed Lodestar. Fourteen years later he landed a turbine-powered, 130-passenger Boeing 727 jet at Pensacola, capturing the full breadth of flying classic airliners into that airport.

As aviation history enthusiasts, we quickly became fast friends. As he related some of his more exciting stories to me, it soon became evident that Captain Brown needed to capture his own flight adventures in book form. For me, the fun is always in the telling.

But as we thumbed through his worn and battered logbooks, studied his faded photographs, and talked quietly about this wonder called flight, I could not but help but daydream that we could be transported through time where I could fly wingman on his beloved Travel Air 4000 154V as we dusted crop fields in the serenity and peacefulness of the early morning. It has been my honor to help Captain Brown with his biography.

Dr. Leo F. Murphy
Associate Professor of Aeronautical Science,
Embry-Riddle Aeronautical University
Commander, US Navy (Retired)

Contents

Introduction   vii

Foreword   ix

Chapter One — Beginnings   1

Chapter Two — Entomology   7

Chapter Three — Cliff Daniels   27

Chapter Four — Jack Faulkner and Jimmy Crawford   33

Chapter Five — J.L. Schroeder   45

Chapter Six — Journey to a Pilot's License   50

Chapter Seven — Crop Dusting   72

Chapter Eight — National Airlines   100

Chapter Nine — From Two to Four   116

Chapter Ten — Wanda's Story   126

Chapter Eleven — Flying the Line   133

Chapter Twelve — Cucumber Bombers   146

Chapter Thirteen — Jets   163

Chapter Fourteen — Retirement   196

Chapter Fifteen — Final Reflections   214

FROM CROPDUSTER TO AIRLINE CAPTAIN

The Biography of Captain LeRoy H. Brown

Chapter One

Beginnings

I am an aviator: always have been, always will be. When asked at what point I discovered I wanted to fly for a living, my answer is always the same. There is no beginning. I have had a love of flight and all things associated with flying for as far back as I can remember.

I was born on March 5, 1921 in New Hartford, New York, the older of two children born to Arthur LeRoy Brown and Evelyn Bessie Smith. My parents named me LeRoy Harlow Brown, after both my father and his brother. My sister's name was Janette.

My maternal grandparents lived nearby and my grandmother's family came

I was about six years old when I posed for this picture with my sister Janette. Note my flying helmet and goggles. My mother wrote below this picture "LeRoy wanted to be an aviator at an early age."

My cousin Fred Laughlin standing in front of a JN-4 Canuck, an authorized Canadian version of the famous Curtiss Jenny. Most likely assigned to the RFC or the RAF, I was told he served during World War I but I do not know if he saw combat in Europe.

from Oldham, England. My grandfather was a one-half Niagara Indian born in Canada, which might explain my lack of fear of heights. He was a loom fixer and worked in a nearby cotton mill. My grandmother's sisters still lived in Canada and one of my cousins, Fred Laughlin, served with the Royal Canadian Air Force during World War I. I am uncertain as to whether he served overseas in combat operations.

While visiting my grandparents one day in 1928 when I was about 7-years old, I watched the U.S. Navy airship, USS Los Angeles (ZR-3), float directly over their house. I was absolutely astonished and to this day, I can still hear those big airship engines rumbling.

I believe it was a year later when I was in the third grade that we had an assembly period for all twelve grades in our school. The speaker was an aviatrix of some note during this period by the name of Amelia Earhart. I do not remember her talk at all, but upon concluding, she walked down the front row containing all the young children and stopped and shook hands with some of them. I guess it was my lucky day as she reached down and shook my hand. Little did I realize how much it would later mean to me, when in 2009, both Amelia and I were inducted into the Florida Aviation Hall of Fame in the same ceremony. She was certainly more famous than I will ever be, but I treasure her memory. While I was cropdusting in Ft. Pierce, FL, I met her stepson, who owned a hardware store, and on rare occasions, we talked about Amelia.

During World War I, my father enlisted in the aeronautical division of the U.S. Army Signal Corps. He went through Kelly Field in Texas for training before shipping overseas to serve in an aviation unit assigned to France. I still have one of his 1917 flight charts, marked restricted, indicating various aeronautical information, including enemy anti-air gun emplacements. I have never been able to confirm whether he flew as a pilot, or an observer, or if at all. A machinist before the war, he returned home in 1919, a year after the war ended, to become a furniture maker like his father before him. While I was growing up, he never expressed any particular interest in flight and certainly never shared any stories of his adventures during the war, which to my regret, I never thought to ask about.

My father's mother was Louise Kimball Doyle and she was the daughter of Oscar E. Doyle and his wife Mary. Mr. O.E. Doyle was a photographer of note in the late 1800's and early 1900's. I still have a collection of his early glass plate negatives. O.E. Doyle was born in Turin, NY and many of those glass plates are of that area along with Sylvan Beach, located on Oneida Lake. There are rumors the Doyle side of the family was related to Arthur Conan Doyle, the noted author.

My paternal great-grandparents were William and Julia (Morse) Brown, who were the parents of Roth Brown, a balloonist. Julia Morse is supposedly a descendant of Samuel Morse, inventor of the telegraph.

My great-uncle Roth Brown flew, although only for a few brief moments and not necessarily with the benefit of an airplane. In addition to being an aeronaut, he was also a parachutist and at local county fairs, he would get his hot air balloon from that era as high as it would go and then jump out. When I was about 10-years-old, I attended a county fair in Oneida County, New York where he performed, although I do not recall actually watching him jump.

At this particular county fair, they were also selling rides in an old biplane. My grandfather Brown wanted to take me for a ride in the airplane, but my mother put her foot

My father, Arthur L. Brown, served overseas in Europe in a field signal battalion from 1918 to 1919.

down and said she did not want me killed and would not let me go. I think I was mad the rest of the day, even though I watched a car race that reached the then blazing speeds of nearly 60 miles per hour.

At this point in my life, I was fascinated with everything associated with aviation. I built hundreds of paper gliders and rubber-powered balsa airplanes. I often begged my father to take me to Marcy Airport near Utica, New York, where I would just sit and watch various airplanes takeoff and land. There was also a Buhl AirSedan offering sightseeing rides, but once again I was not allowed to go.

In 1934, my family moved to Oakland Park, Florida. I was a sickly young boy growing up in New York, often confined to bed for months at a time with colds, pneumonia and other lung diseases. Our family doctor eventually told my dad and my mother that if they did not move to either Arizona or Florida, I would not live. They decided on Florida and during the trip, our car broke down in Daytona Beach. This was at the height of the Great Depression and our family was completely out of money. We were sitting on the side of the road wondering what we would do when a passing car stopped to help us. Chuck Culver, a kind, US Coast Guard pilot, and his wife, Ann, came to our rescue. We lived with them for two or three months before we were able to continue on to Oakland Park. Due to my illness, I never had the chance to talk with Chuck about flying and I regret this missed opportunity to this day.

Shortly after we moved to Oakland Park, Florida I was in our backyard when I heard the sound of airplanes approaching. An engine on one of the airplanes was making a loud cracking and popping noise. Soon a Curtiss Shrike passed overhead very low and crash-landed, not too far from where I stood. Another airplane continued flying on without stopping. I ran to the accident site, which was just west of the Seaboard Airline Railroad tracks, and saw that the pilot was safely out of the

The Buhl AirSedan was a 5-place, cabin biplane introduced in 1927. The most celebrated of these aircraft was the Miss Doran, which disappeared over the Pacific Ocean during the ill-fated 1927 Dole Race to Hawaii. I was not allowed to take a passenger ride in one for fear that I would be hurt.

My great-grandfather Oscar Doyle, who was a professional photographer, took this photograph of my great-uncle Roth Brown inflating his balloon at a county fair, in 1928 or 1929.

wrecked airplane with a lot of people gathered around him.

He told them that he was 2nd Lieutenant Livingstone, from Barksdale Field and that he had to get to a telephone. Some in the crowd pointed to the nearby Seaboard Airline Railroad Station and he then began walking down the railroad track by himself carrying his parachute.

I hurried along beside him and asked if I could carry it for him. He looked at me in surprise and said it was pretty heavy for a small boy, but he handed it to me anyway. It did weigh a lot and I managed to carry it for only a short distance before he recognized my distress and took it back.

I continued to the station with him where he apparently called Barksdale Field with the accident report. They put a guard around the airplane to keep people away and, with nothing further to be done, I went home.

I was obviously thrilled to death about being able to talk to a real live aviator. I shall never forget him, nor will I ever forget how heavy that parachute was.

This was the first time I had ever met a pilot in person and I was destined to soon meet another aviator who would have an extraordinary influence on my life and my career ambitions. Thanks to my mother, who kept a diary her entire life, I know the exact date I first met Cliff Daniels, crop duster.

A photograph from the official U.S. Army Air Corps report on the Curtiss A-12 Shrike accident I witnessed as a young boy. An accident investigation revealed that the engine failed due to a cylinder head being blown off. The airplane overturned after landing in a furrowed bean field and the pilot, 2nd Lt. Richmond A. Livingstone, was trapped under the wreckage and drenched with gasoline. He was eventually freed by local bystanders who rushed to the scene and his fellow crewmember, Sgt. J.D. Stephenson, who had managed to crawl to safety.

Chapter Two
Entomology

Bug's eye view of a crop duster with his wheels barely skimming the tops of a field of peppers.

Since cropdusting became an integral part of my life from the moment I meet Cliff Daniels, I would like to digress for a moment and provide the reader with a broad overview of the cropdusting business.

While simple in concept, cropdusting is complex in its execution. Effectively combating crop-damaging pests requires the collaborative effort of researchers, scientists, farmers, chemical suppliers, and aviators. This endless battle of the bugs also encompasses several variables, including entomology, expert knowledge of the effects of various herbicides, insecticides and fungicides, chemical compatibility, airplane performance, dispensing equipment, meteorology, and most important of all, pilot judgment and skill.

Entomology

Entomology is the scientific study of insects. Within the context of farming, entomologists study the various insects, pests, fungi, weeds, viruses, and bacteria that can harm or kill crops. As an experienced cropduster, my expert knowledge of entomology was gained by on the job training and years of experience dealing with both preventive and corrective infestation measures.

Preventing crop damage, no matter how slight, is one of the most critical elements in successful farming. At worst, pest infestations can kill an entire crop or reduce the crop yield so much that a farm cannot survive financially. This is precisely what happened with the first appearance of the boll weevil in Texas in the late 1890's. Feeding almost exclusively on cotton plants and advancing 40 to 160 miles a year, by the early 1920s, it had infested virtually the entire Cotton Belt, devastating cotton production. The first effective insecticide to combat the boll weevil, calcium arsenate, was not developed until 1918, but it was costly and therefore not affordable by most farmers. I would witness several similar severe infestations during my cropdusting career, including blight on tomatoes, which could destroy 100 acres of this crop overnight.

At best, however, a mild disease might only lower the quality of the produce, which the farmer could still bring to market. However, American consumers are fickle and they will only buy fruits, vegetables, or flowers that are unblemished. While perfectly edible, a housewife is not going to buy corn that might have a worm in it. Nonetheless, the farmer must weigh the benefits of cropdusting against the cost of treatment and the amount of money earned by selling his crops.

A misconception of cropdusting is that it involves the indiscriminate killing of all insects in the treatment area. Nothing could be further from the truth. Cropdusters recognize there is a delicate balance in nature and that non-selective killing of all insects may also inadvertently eliminate a beneficial insect that feeds on plant eating pests. Moreover, even a 100 percent kill of the targeted pest is not necessary. In many cases, only a 20 percent reduction in the insects may be enough to make a substantial difference.

At first, cotton crops were devastated by the boll weevil. But farmers soon learned that preventive measures could control infestation.

An additional false impression is that it only requires a single treatment to rid a farm of a particularly harmful insect. In some instances, this may be true. For example, defoliation required only one treatment. In reality, however, to combat most pests multiple applications across days, weeks or months are required until the insect is under control. Corn, as an illustration, required dusting with DDT once a day during its final productive cycle to kill earworms. As I will discuss later, even though the government banned DDT, I feel it was unfairly maligned.

Whether insects can develop resistance to a specific insecticide with prolonged use is a common question. Consensus among entomologists is that the targeted insects as a whole are not developing resistance. Rather, in a Darwinian survival of the fittest illustration, those insects that have a natural resistance to the insecticide survive and reproduce.

Development of Aerial Cropdusting

The first insecticides, which were nearly always in powdered or granulated form, were spread by farmers shaking gunnysacks over the plants. Later, farmers developed hand carried sprayers and animal-pulled dusting equipment. But the process is slow, impracticable for large acreages, and it is difficult to treat the tops of tall crops or penetrate the thick leaves of fruit trees or closely spaced fruits or vegetables.

With technical advances in aviation after World War I, it was a logical progression to consider airplanes for use in agriculture. An airplane could accomplish in minutes what would have taken hours using other methods.

The U.S. Department of Agriculture at the U.S. Army's McCook Field near Dayton, Ohio is where the first actual experiments with aerial application of insecticides took place in 1921. A Curtiss Jenny JN-6H biplane, supplied by the War Department and flown by U.S. Army pilots, was modified to carry chemical dispensing equipment. Officials deemed the tests successful and additional testing at

The U.S. Army conducted the first experiments with the aerial application of insecticides. The pilot flew from the front seat and in the back seat was the dust dispenser. It was hand-cranked by a second operator who stood behind the equipment. Eventually, this second operator was replaced by a handle operated by the pilot.

the U.S. Department of Agriculture Delta Laboratory at Tallulah, Louisiana further refined the equipment and procedures necessary to make the aerial application of insecticides a practical and effective method of pest control.

Civilian Cropdusters

With the military aviators successfully pioneering the principles of cropdusting, the stage was set for the entrance of commercial operators into this potentially profitable business.

In 1923, George B. Post, an airplane manufacturing executive from New York, visited Tallulah and learned of the ongoing aerial application experiments. Convinced this meant a new market for his company's airplanes, he convinced the two chief executives of the Huff-Daland Aero Corp, Thomas Huff and Elliot Daland, to form a subsidiary agricultural firm to fly the company's airplanes.

Initially based in Macon, Georgia, the company became known as Huff-Daland Dusters, Inc. Later, company officers moved the headquarters to Monroe, Louisiana. Cotton dusting operations began in 1924 and by 1925, 18 aircraft, 12 pilots, and 20 mechanics were dusting cotton, peach trees, and pecan orchards from nine locations throughout the South. Within a few years, the organization's name changed to Delta Air Service and eventually, the company gained an almost complete monopoly of agricultural dustings. Eventually, Delta Air Service transitioned into passenger transport operations and is now known as Delta Air Lines.

The airplanes used by the company were their own biplanes, upgraded to 400-horsepower Liberty engines giving the airplane the ability to carry 1,000 pounds of calcium arsenate dust. The dust was loaded into a compartment in front of the pilot and came out of a chute in the bottom of the airplane in great clouds. This allowed a uniform dispersal of chemical over the crops as they flew about three feet above the ground dodging trees, poles, birds and anything else that might be sticking up in the air.

The airplane was soon nicknamed the "Puffer," for obvious reasons, and their pilots were soon called duster pilots and sometimes various other names. These were highly experienced aviators. Dusting was a hazardous job, which required very skilled pilots.

Delta Air Service dusters operated in the Pompano area in the 1930's and were quite successful dusting vegetable crops. They used a landing strip located in Hammondsville owned by the Hammond Development Company. Delta also operated off the Pompano Navy field immediately following WWII.

I often worked near the "Puffer" pilots and they were fine fellows, but I was not a big admirer of their airplane. It did not have any trim tabs and all the control cables were mounted outside the airframe, making them susceptible to corrosion.

Dusting Equipment

Typically used for coal or grain, a hopper is a container for bulk material that tapers downward to discharge its contents under gravity through

True to its name, a Huff-Daland "Puffer" lays a trail of dust over a cotton field. An experienced crop duster, however, will note that this pilot is wasting insecticide by not shutting off the hopper before reaching the field boundary.

For Stearman
$650.00

This advertisement from a 1959 magazine shows a chemical spreader for Stearman biplanes.

a dispensing tube controlled by a moveable plate.

The mechanics and pilots mounted the first hoppers used to store cropdusting insecticides in a biplane's rear cockpit. Capacity varied per aircraft and among the first airplanes I flew, a J-3 Cub could carry about 500 pounds, a Travel Air 4000 model could hold 700 pounds, and a Travel Air B4000 carried 1200 pounds.

The pilot primarily flew from the back cockpit for reasons concerning the airplane's center of gravity. This also gave the pilot some relief from the heat thrown off by the engine. A hand operated sliding door placed across the bottom of the hopper, jokingly known as the "money handle," metered the amount of dust distributed

Dust was loaded into the hopper by way of a covered opening accessed through the top of the airplane. When I first started cropdusting, supply stores delivered chemicals in 50- or 100-pound metal containers and later, in paper bags. The loaders filled the hopper by hand. Later, we used tractors with mechanical loaders and a hopper could be filled in only a few seconds with a single dump. In either case, it was important that the staging area be located as closely as possible to the treatment area to avoid wasted transit time. For most of my career, the staging area was no more than two or three miles away.

The U.S. Army aviators first attempted to dispense dust through a single opening drilled directly into the bottom of the airplane. The first airborne tests of this system found that the powerful airflow underneath the bottom of the fuselage interfered with the flow of dust from this hole.

This was corrected by using an hourglass shaped spreader connected perpendicular to the hopper. The constriction of the discharge tube took advantage of the Venturi effect: when air is channeled into a constricted opening, its speed increases and air pressure drops. This lower pressure generates suction, pulling the dust from the hopper and minimizing backpressure on the airplane dust exit point.

We soon discovered an additional problem: dust tended to clump inside the hopper and we needed to develop a method to keep the dust mixed to ensure an even distribution. This led to the development of agitators, either wind-powered or motor-driven, to meet this need for an even flow of material.

When liquid chemicals became available, we modified the airplanes to accommodate spraying nozzles with their associated airplane systems. Most airplanes remained capable of dispensing either dust or liquid, with only a few simple field changes. We also put out fertilizers, grass seed, and rice.

Airplane Types

The first airplanes used in agricultural operations were modified versions of existing civilian and military aircraft. Early cropdusters favored single engine airplanes such as Waco's, Command Aire's, and Travel Air's. These airplanes were generally easy to handle, carried a fair amount of chemical, and when equipped with more powerful engines, provided a great safety margin for low altitude operations.

Biplanes were preferred for cropdusting duty because air spilling from the lower wing assisted with the spreading of dust on the ground by stirring up the leaves on a crop. This made the dust more effective in reaching the lower branches. The high wings of monoplanes flew out of ground effect making them slightly less efficient.

Theoretically, we were limited to a 10 percent weight overload for disposables but this was seldom adhered to. Rookie cropdusters often made the mistake of assuming the airplanes could accommodate full hoppers, full fuel tanks, a hefty pilot, assorted equipment, and still remain within the airplane's authorized weight and center of gravity limits. They usually learned differently when they tried to take off, particularly on a hot day with a high air density altitude.

When former military training biplanes like the Stearman and the N3N aircraft became available, pilots quickly purchased and modified them for cropdusting use. Equipped with powerful engines with airframes nearly indestructible, these airplanes became the workhorses of cropdusting, and their use continues to this day.

Today, instead of using former military airplanes, there are plenty of aircraft specially designed for agricultural use, such as the Cessna AgWagon, Piper Pawnee, Grumman's AgCat, and Leland Snow's Air Tractor. These were built with improved pilot safety and comfort systems, increased hopper capacity, higher dispensing speeds, and strengthened structures.

Aircraft Registration Number

An aircraft registration number is a unique alphanumeric string that identifies a civil aircraft. In the United States, all aircraft registration numbers begin with an "N" in accordance with an international identification agreement. This is followed by a

Close up of one of my airplanes modified to accommodate spraying equipment for liquid insecticides.

hyphen and unique identity letters, numbers or combinations of both. Many in aviation often refer to this as an "N-number," "side number," or "tail number," as this number is required to be displayed on the tail or aft fuselage of the aircraft.

Prior to 1948, a second letter followed the N letter and used to indicate the aircraft's airworthiness category. Two examples of these, "C" for commercial and private aircraft, and "R" for restricted aircraft like cropdusters, will be seen in photographs of airplanes I have included in this book.

Swath

A swath is defined as the width of one sweep of the airplane as it passes over a field. The aerodynamic forces created by an airplane as it moves through the air are mostly responsible for the distribution of a chemical on the ground. Vortices generated at the end of the wings by the production of lift usually limit the spray swath to the width of the wing tips.

Marking swaths to prevent gaps in treatment, or to avoid wasteful overlapping runs, really depends on pilot skill in keeping track of where he has flown or what the agricultural operation can afford in terms of extra men stationed on the ground to guide the pilot.

During most of my career, I dusted alone, using a prominent landmark on the horizon to maintain orientation of what I had just covered. Once dispensed on plants or trees, dust or liquid sprays are very difficult to see unless they are colored. I have also used flagmen, who stood among the crops, marked each of my runs, and then indicated the direction of the next swath. Today modern electronic navigation systems make marking covered areas much easier.

Application rate is defined as the total quantity of chemical applied per unit area. In farming, this measurement was usually the desired amount of active ingredient in pounds per acre.

As a cropduster, the farmer would usually tell me the specific chemical and the application rate he desired for his crops. Occasionally, I would be solicited for my opinion on which chemical was the best to use for a recurrent or new problem. If I didn't know the answer from firsthand experience, I could find out from my contacts in the industry. It was a rare occasion during my career to find me stymied as to the best treatment chemical.

Often a farmer would ask me to determine how bad his crop was infested. A good example of this is the degree of infestation by boll weevils.

Boll weevils infest cotton via the cotton plant's flower bud, or square, as the farmers call them. The female eats a tiny hole in the square and then pushes a very small egg deep into the hole. This square is now doomed and will never open into a beautiful showy, off-white flower from which a boll of cotton emerges and which is harvested.

About three days later the egg hatches and a tiny larva appears that begins to eat the cotton plant from inside the square. After eating away for several days, the larva changes into a pupa. Three to five days later, the pupa sheds it skin, cuts a hole in the square, and emerges to the outside world as an adult boll weevil. The cotton square turns yellow and dies.

About five days after it has left the square, the weevil, if a female, begins to lay eggs in other squares and creates the next generation, all within a two to three week time span. There are several generations born during the warm season each year and during winter, the adults seek shelter in dead grass, fallen leaves, moss, or trash. This explains why several applications of insecticide are necessary during the growing season to control the boll weevil.

To determine the degree of boll weevil infestation, I would walk diagonally across the farmer's field, opening the squares to judge the number of infestations. I would pick 100 squares. If 10 percent were infested, then there was a 10 percent infestation.

Of interest, most farmers did not want fields sprayed on Sunday, their only day of rest.

Chemicals

By FAA definition, cropdusting chemicals are any substance or mixture of substances intended for preventing, destroying, repelling, or mitigating any insects, rodents, nematodes, fungi, weeds, and other forms of plant or animal life or viruses.

There are three basic forms of chemicals used for cropdusting: dust, granules, and liquid sprays. Normally, we discharged dust and granules through a spreader mounted on the bottom of the airplane. Liquids, however, required the use of spray booms, nozzles and atomizers to set droplet size and ensure even distribution.

There are also several types of chemicals: insecticides used against unwanted insects; fungicides for germinating fungus spores that cause diseases, we used herbicides for weeds, defoliants to strip leaves off of a crop to ease harvesting, desiccants were drying agents, fertilizers to nourish crops, and seeding to quickly plant new crops.

Spraying groves makes keeping track of swaths much easier. In this 1978 photograph, I am dusting my own citrus grove north of Orlando in a Cessna AgWagon.

Most of my cropdusting work involved the use of insecticides, classified as either inorganic or organic depending on how they are made.

Inorganic insecticides are of mineral origin and have been in use as early as the 17th century. Predominantly in dust form, these include compounds of arsenic, copper, and sulfur, which was the insecticide of choice when I first starting cropdusting.

The danger of sulfur dust was that it was highly explosive. I lost several good friends when a spark from an engine ignited the trail of sulfur flowing from the airplane, immediately engulfing both the plane and pilot in flames.

Accordingly, when the hopper was open and dispensing sulfur dust, you never touched the throttle for fear of generating a spark. When the swath was complete and the hopper closed, the procedure was to look back and check the color of dust trail behind you. If it was yellow, all was well. But if it was black, the dust was on fire and you

had only a few minutes to land and get out. If there was no suitable landing area close by, the emergency procedure was to climb as fast as possible and immediately bail out. I never experienced a sulfur fire, but I still wore a parachute my entire dusting career in case of such an emergency, except when I was flying J-3 Cubs. The cockpit was just too small to accommodate both pilot and parachute.

During World War II, we developed highly toxic organic and chlorinated hydrocarbon insecticides, including parathion, hexaethyl tetraphosphate, and DDT. This also marked the first increased use of spray application.

Personal Safety

Some of these chemicals are dangerous, not just to pests, but also to the pilots and ground handling personnel coming into contact with them. Chemicals can be accidently ingested through the mouth, inhaled into the respiratory system, or absorbed by the skin. This can result in acute poisoning, perhaps from a single exposure to a toxic chemical, which has been accidentally spilled; or chronic poisoning, which is caused by the repeated intake of small seemingly harmless doses.

Symptoms include headaches, dizziness, nausea, chest pain, anxiety, and tears. As a general rule, during my later career, we knew which chemicals were potentially harmful and we would take special precautions by wearing protective clothing such as gloves, respirators, and full body suits.

In the early days of my dusting career, though, I worked in the cropdusting environment without any protection whatsoever. Dropping dust from a biplane was particularly messy and I would always be covered in dust from head to toe due to the material being sucked into the cockpit. I would literally be eating and breathing the dust the entire time I was flying.

Sulphur dust in particular caused me to tear up. When I landed to reload the hoppers, the support crew could see that I was crying from the tears streaking down my stained face from under my goggles. Every time I landed, they asked me why I was crying and I always gave them the same answer, "I was thinking of my poor grandmother."

I never heard of a cropduster getting sick from any of the insecticides we used, despite all the ominous warnings from the government. I have probably eaten more toxaphene, BHC, and DDT than anyone I know yet I am almost 92-years-old and in good health, despite all the published articles about the dangers of exposure to insecticides. In fact, most of my duster pilot friends lived into their 80's and 90's. Old cropdusters tend to die of old age, more than anything else.

So much for the environmentalists and their scare tactics about DDT and other chemicals. The public would see us dusting corn with DDT and be horrified of all that dust. They did not realize that the dust only contained 3 or 5 percent DDT and the rest was talcum or Fuller's earth to make the swaths visible. Therefore, there was very little insecticide in the mixture.

In the 1970s, however, the emergence of the environmental movement and the creation of the U.S. Environmental Protection Agency (EPA) banned some chemicals such as DDT, which I thought was the best insecticide ever made. In my opinion, these people made some ill-informed decisions. I ingested more DDT than most people have seen with no harmful effects. In fact, during my airline career, I passed more than 60 flight physicals with no problems.

I should mention, however, that some chemicals are highly corrosive and not very friendly to metal airplanes. The fabric airplanes I mostly flew were safe from corrosion, as were those metal airplanes equipped with anodized aluminum hoppers, as long as the crews kept them clean. Some newer dusting airplanes, however, are made of metal and were more subject to corrosion.

Editorial

A SLOGAN FOR THE INDUSTRY

California's Agricultural Aircraft Association, Inc., is searching for a slogan for dusters and sprayers. In keeping with other industries which strive to keep their services and products before the public with a short, crisp message such as "Make Mine Milk" for the milk industry, and "Ship by Truck" for the trucking industry, California operators sense the value of a good slogan.

Submitted to date are the following:

"DO IT BY AIR"

"FARM BY AIR"

"QUICKER BY AIRPLANE"

"FASTER BY AIR"

"WEED 'EM AND REAP"

The California Association wants everyone to join the search and to send in slogans. The NATIONAL DUSTER believes this movement is meritous, that a search as this could well be national, and that the use of a good slogan nationally would be another forward step by the industry.

We suggest this search be broadened, that the operators in all the other states give thought to this important subject, and send their slogans to the Agricultural Aircraft Association, Inc., Route 3, Box 1142-B, Sacramento, California.

The next time you have a pencil in hand, place your slogan on a piece of paper and send it in.

This editorial from the October, 1954 National Duster Journal highlights just how new the crop dusting industry was: we didn't even have a slogan. I do not recall what was finally adopted but my personal slogan was "When the bugs begin to bite, let us spray."

Pay

Unlike other industries, there are no set rules governing a pilot's pay in cropdusting. Income depends on whether the pilot is working for an agricultural operation, or whether he is working as an independent cropduster.

The bottom line, however, is that dusting contracts are the lifeblood of an agricultural operator. An established, reputable firm might average 100,000 acres a year in dusting contracts and use two to three airplanes to complete the treatments in a timely manner. A new operator, however, might only have a few contracts as he builds his business. Thus, there is always the danger of a new competitor appearing in the area and undercutting the incumbent's prices, leaving little work for treatment by other dusters.

Competition is always keen in the cropdusting industry, but due to the sheer volume of work during the growing season, it is not unusual for a farming area to have several agricultural operators working in close proximity to each other, with everyone earning a respectable living. I soon recognized, however, that towards the end of the growing season, the dusting contracts start falling off, and that it was time for me to move on to more fertile areas.

While rare, there were cases where the farmer refused to pay his bill for a dusted field. Maybe it was because the treatment was ineffective and the farmer felt he had been duped. Or, perhaps there was never any money to begin with and the farmer was just hoping to hold on until he could sell his crop. Either way, both the duster pilot and the agricultural company suffered. During my cropdusting career, though, I never experienced an instance of someone not paying.

Fees

The fees for cropdusting were many and varied, but all within a certain range that primarily benefited the farmer. Usually it was so much a pound per acre with the farmer purchasing the insecticide. For instance, the normal going price in the '40s, '50s, and '60s was three to five cents a pound. Corn, for example, required 30 pounds of DDT per acre, which at three cents a pound would be $.90-$1.50 an acre, and the pilot usually got 30 percent of this, which netted him in the neighborhood of $.30 to $.40 an acre. Thirty pounds per acre of DDT resulted in approximately one pound of DDT insecticide spread over the entire acre with the rest of the mixture being Fuller's earth or talcum, both inert ingredients mixed in for a carrier. To put this in perspective, if you put two or three shakes of salt on your eggs for breakfast, this would amount to several tons of salt per acre. I have never heard of a duster pilot becoming ill from daily exposure to DDT.

Using the prices for dusting mentioned above, in Florida if you dusted 500 acres a day you made out fairly well. In contrast, tobacco farms in Georgia were under the control of the USDA with the size of tobacco acreage on an allotment basis based on the farmer's total acreage planted. It was not unusual to have to dust a tobacco patch of only one or two acres in total size, with hardly any patches more than 10 acres. For this, we charged $5 an acre for the application with the pilot getting 30 percent. For spraying, they usually charged a set price per acre with the price being similar to dusting. You could spray liquids most of the day in light wind.

So, paychecks varied. On large tomato farms, which were usually 100 to 150 acres with no obstructions, it would take about two hours of actual work and dusters were still paid per acre. The best job was a corn contract because the corn required dusting 21 days in a row to have worm free corn.

While running one's wheels on peppers could be done without danger, cotton was a different story and could throw an aircraft to the ground if the pilot was not careful. In this 1937 photograph, Bill Longino is spraying peppers in Oakland Park, Florida.

Nowadays, however, the cost per acre is considerably more.

A cropduster had a couple of options: flying for an agricultural operation or flying as an independent contractor. When I first started dusting in 1944 for R.J. Cardwell, he offered me a $200 base salary or 25 percent of the gross, whichever was greater.

As an independent cropduster, I kept all the money for myself. When I retired in 1975 as an independent duster, I was usually pocketing about $12 to $14 an acre, depending on whether I was responsible for purchasing the chemicals or not. My rule of thumb regarding distribution of cropdusting fees was 30 percent of the gross for the pilot, 30 percent for airplane maintenance, and 40percent for supplies and miscellaneous items.

There are advantages, however, to flying for an agricultural operation. They absorb all the ancillary expenses associated with operating the business. For example, fuel costs, equipment, maintenance, repairs, storage, and more. Often, I was required to travel several hundred miles to complete a dusting contract and the company paid for my living expenses. There is no health care for the cropdusting pilot and his family. Nor was there any insurance to protect the pilot in the event of damage to the aircraft, loading equipment, or lawsuits emerging from claims of drift or damage to power lines or telephone wires.

The amount of acreage treated at a time is limited by the maximum payload of the aircraft. An airplane with a relatively small application load will take much more flying time to treat a field than an airplane capable of carrying a large application load.

Chemical prices also vary, so the profit margin is tighter for some chemicals than others are in order to keep the prices affordable for the farmer. It does the farmer no good to treat a field for $10.00 per acre when the crop itself at harvest only brings $5 per acre.

To earn a paycheck as a cropduster, there is only one rule: you don't fly, you don't get paid. It was not unusual for me to make several flights in the early morning and then return for several more flights in the evening if the winds died down. Examining my logbooks at the height of my dusting career, I can see that I was flying nearly every day, including all the major holidays. Pests never take a break so neither can duster pilots.

Dusting is also seasonal, peaking during the growing season and virtually disappearing during the fallow season. There were months of incredibly high income, equaled by months of absolutely no earnings at all.

In my case as a Florida-based cropduster, it was possible for me to chase various crops' growing seasons up the eastern seaboard. I would dust truck crops such as citrus, carrots, corn, and celery in the south during the winter. Then I treated cotton and peaches in the Carolinas and peanuts, sunflowers, corn, and cotton in Georgia during the summer. Some fellow Florida cropdusters even traveled as far north as New England to dust potatoes, but I never traveled

Piloting Skills

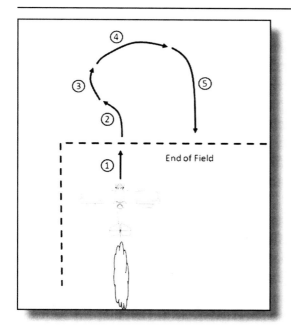

The typical procedure turn made at the end of one swath to line up properly for the return to the next swath. At Point 1, the pilot anticipates the end of the swath run and clears ahead for any obstacles. At the end of the swath run at Point 2, the pilot closes the hopper, applies power, climbs to clear any obstructions, and turns steeply 45 degrees off original course. At Point 3, a level turn adjusted for wind effects is begun in the opposite direction and at Point 4 power is reduced and the rate of turn adjusted to line up for the next swath. At Point 5 the airplane is descended, power adjusted to maintain a steady airspeed over the field, and the hopper opened when crossing the field boundary.

further north than North Carolina or west of El Paso, Texas. Chasing growing seasons also means long absences from home, which is why I had no desire to go too far north. I also noticed that traveling over any swamp area to a dusting site meant the engine would go to automatic rough.

All cropdusting pilots develop their own techniques and preferences for treating a field, but each variation is fundamentally based upon the same principles: be attentive to environmental conditions, treat a field in the minimum number of passes necessary, and don't stall the airplane in the turn. The primary factors I considered when preparing to dust a field were field dimensions and wind direction and speed.

The dimensions of the field determine the number of turns that the pilot must make to treat the entire field. A rectangular field is most desirable, providing the pilot with nice long runs over the field before turning. The longer the runs, the quicker the field can be treated. Tomato fields were the easiest to dust, as they were invariably straight and level with no obstructions on the field. Irregular field dimensions, however, can be a challenge. Peach groves in the Carolina's were always the most difficult to dust due to their uneven rows.

A procedure turn is simply the method the agricultural pilot uses to reverse course to return accurately to the next swath when reaching the boundary of the field. It is also when the largest percentage of accidents occur in cropdusting, usually when the pilot accidently stalls the airplane.

I really learned to fly an airplane on the ragged edge of stalls all the time. I could tell a stall was coming just by the seat of my pants. I didn't need to have the stick go shaking or the airplane quiver. I could sense what the airplane was doing by the sound of the wind in my wires.

Pilots would have to repeat procedure turns, interspersed with frequent returns to the staging area to refill the hopper, hundreds of times on each job. As the old saying goes, "when you're turning, you ain't earning," so every cropduster's goal is to make these turns quickly, efficiently, and most of all, safely. Procedure turns are fast, steep course reversals and the pilot must maintain adequate power and airspeed to avoid a stall. While there is more danger in turning a heavily loaded airplane rapidly than a lightly loaded one, I have known duster pilots who have stalled in both configurations with very unpleasant results.

My personal priorities prior to entering a field were to scan for obstructions and establish wind speed and direction, by possibly observing a puff of smoke from a nearby home's chimney. My next goal was to establish a steady airspeed as I approached my first swath and then descend to just above crop height at the field boundary.

Once over the field, I would open my hopper and concentrate on flying a straight swath by selecting a reference landmark on the horizon. I was always careful to maintain a constant airspeed and altitude. Dust follows an airplane so I had to be careful to close my hopper before reaching the field boundary, or else I would waste insecticide or accidently treat an adjacent field.

Low and slow was my crop dusting technique. This is Bill Longino dusting the other direction from the previous photograph.

Approaching the end of the run, I would close the hopper, open the throttle, and pull the nose up at a 45-degree angle to my run. With my airspeed decreasing in the climbing turn, I would kick the rudder to bring the nose of the airplane around to line up for my next swath. After completing my runs, I always made a mop-up or clean-up swath around the perimeter of the field to ensure no areas were missed from having closed the hopper a little too early when I commenced my procedure turns.

Altitude, Airspeed, and Weather

The three primary variables influencing the proper distribution of chemicals applied by cropdusting are airplane altitude, airplane airspeed, and weather conditions at the field.

Often, I was asked what altitude I flew at as a cropduster and my joke is that I took off and descended to my operating altitude of only a few feet above the crop to be treated. However, the optimal height for cropdusting has always been a subject of much discussion. I was trained to fly with my wheels virtually touching the crops or the tops of trees. At this low altitude, the swath is about the same width as the wingspan and the chemical is driven downwards with some force. I found that increasing my altitude higher did not usually increase the swath width. Critics of low flying, however, state this reduces the width of the chemical distribution swath.

Correspondingly, flying too high can also reduce the swath width and worse, can result in an uneven distribution of the chemical. Additionally, releasing a chemical too high increases the time required for the chemical to reach the ground, making it more susceptible to wind drift. Cropdusters always achieved the best results by keeping the discharge height at the minimum altitude necessary to achieve the optimum swath width.

Airspeed is also a critical element of successful cropdusting. Delivery of the chemical required a specific airspeed to provide a uniform distribution and desired application rate. Accordingly, this airspeed should be established and maintained without change during the swath run. Flying faster than this airspeed decreases this application rate and flying slower than the reference airspeed dispenses too much chemical. Surprising to the novice, low airspeeds provide greater swath widths than high airspeeds due to aerodynamic vortices and downwashes created by the wings as they develop lift. A pilot has to maintain a uniform altitude and airspeed throughout the swath to insure uniform distribution and penetration of the chemical.

Most chemicals are also very sensitive to weather conditions and cannot be applied if the crops are damp or wet or the temperature and humidity are not within limitations. High winds are the cropduster's primary foe due to drift concerns. We would always start our swaths on the downwind side of the treatment area to avoid flying through our own dust or spray.

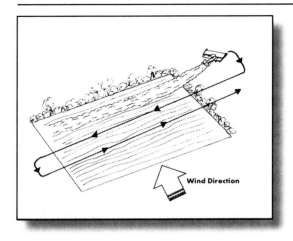

Typical crop dusting patterns. When strong winds are present, application begins on the downwind side of the field to avoid flying through the previous swath.

Obstacles

Descending and ascending over obstacles such as trees, wires, or poles when working a field is certainly one of the more exciting aspects of cropdusting. Additionally, the low-altitude environment of cropdusting is fraught with unseen perils and the art of cropdusting requires an innate ability to make instant decisions, abrupt changes in altitude, and sudden steep turns at low speeds. The pilot must minimize such maneuvers when laying a swath in order to prevent an uneven application of the chemical. One can gain comfort in this demanding flight environment only with experience. I became quite at ease sideslipping into fields, flying under wires, or executing a quick wing dip to avoid an obstacle on the field.

Obstacles take many forms and shapes, including electric wires, telephone lines, trees, buildings, hills, sloping terrain, birds, and livestock. While wires themselves may be invisible from the air, the location of telephone poles or towers often gives away their location. The ability to survive a collision with any of these items is directly related to the point of impact, strength of the airplane, and the pilot's good judgment.

One would think a cropduster would conduct a thorough and careful inspection of every field from the ground to scan for obstacles before flying to it, but the business of cropdusting often just doesn't permit the time. I would rely on the experience of fellow cropdusters or the reports of contact men to alert me, although as I will relate later, not all contact men tell the truth.

Frost Flying

But even the best of us get caught napping sometimes. Frost flying was used by farmers to protect crops if frost was predicted for the early morning in Florida. Frost would kill tomatoes and in this particular case, Roger Brandenburg contacted me to protect his 150-acre tomato crop.

If the frost forecast predicted a temperature inversion near the ground, we would fly there to disturb the air pushing the warmer air towards the crop. If there were no temperature inversion, we would fly a little bit lower and the wind generated by the airplane would keep the air moving to prevent frost from forming.

I rose well before morning, dressed warmly, and proceeded to fly my Travel Air in the dark back and forth across his field at a height of about 20 feet. There is always a horizon visible no matter how dark it is and I was familiar with the field, after having dusted it several times throughout the growing season. So I knew where I was at all times.

Suddenly, a loud "bang" with wood shattering and exploding all around me interrupted the peacefulness of my runs. The explosion announced that I had just had a mid-air collision. But the airplane kept flying. Something had happened but it was so dark I couldn't tell what I had hit. The airplane flew normally, so I kept making my runs.

After I landed, I found out that the Seminole Indians who were working for Brandenburg had piled tomato crates in the middle of the field and that is what I hit head on. There were splinters of wood all over the area and only my dry cleaner knew how much the impact scared me.

Drift

The primary effect of wind on cropdusting is the unintentional drift of the chemical to areas not meant to be dusted. This is potentially disastrous because some chemicals may kill or damage crops other than those for which they were intended, or the chemical may endanger humans. An

In my dreams, I am skimming across the top of a patch of peppers at 80 miles per hour in my favorite Travel Air biplane on a nice cool Florida morning. Ever alert for obstacles in my path, I am anticipating the moment when I will simultaneously close the hopper door, sharply apply power, pitch up, and kick my rudder over to commence a steep turn. Mild "g" forces pin me to my seat as I evaluate the effect of winds on my turn radius and calculate the precise moment when I will simultaneously roll out, descend, level out, reduce power to establish a steady airspeed, and then open the "money handle" for my next run. I allow myself to relax only for a few moments before I refocus my energy to repeat the maneuver. I am in hog heaven because I am doing something that I love to do.

additional problem with drift is that the area to be treated may be missed. Any application errors committed by the pilot will soon become patently obvious by uneven growth, dead or discolored crops, patchiness, and one angry farmer. Farmers have sued for ineffective treatments and there have been many lawsuits involving unintentional drift onto people, cattle, and pastures. I never experienced such a thing in my cropdusting career.

To avoid drift, cropdusting is normally only done in the early morning or late evening when the surface winds are light. Therefore, on a typical working day, my morning began with breakfast well before dawn and I would start flying as soon as it was light enough to see.

Cropdusting with airplanes was always a real pleasure and fun flying for me. But flying the airplane was secondary, properly applying the chemical was always my primary concern. I took pride in my work and if I did my job right, when I was done with a field, it would look like I had dusted each plant with a powder puff.

However, I knew none of this back in 1935 when, as a 14-year old kid, I walked up to Cliff Daniels' dirt field. To my delight, I was about to meet one of the original pioneers of the cropdusting business.

Chapter Three
Cliff Daniels

Since there were no schools in Oakland Park, I was enrolled in a school in Fort Lauderdale, about a five mile school bus ride from my home. One day when I was 14 years old, my school bus driver, Max Christian, mentioned that an airplane was flying out of a small pasture just north of Oakland Park on the west side of the Old Dixie Highway. I arranged for Max to drop me off at the field and it was November 16, 1935 when I first became acquainted with Cliff Daniels, one of the local area's very first crop dusters and a pioneer in the field.

1935 photograph of the author LeRoy Brown (right) and Cliff Daniels standing beside a Waco 10 used by Daniels for crop dusting in the Oakland Park, Florida area. Faintly visible on the side of the airplane is the logo of his crop dusting company, the Atlantic Air Service. As we posed for the photograph Cliff whispered to me "You know that I am only letting you lean on the airplane because they are taking a picture." I never did it again for fear of tearing the fabric.

He owned a 1929 Waco 10 (correctly pronounced Wah-Koe), powered by a 220 horsepower Wright Whirlwind J-5 engine. The aircraft did not have a side number on it so it was probably not registered with the U.S. Department of Commerce, a common practice in those days. In fact, I do not even know if Cliff had a pilot's license, which was first required with the passage of the Air Commerce Act of 1926. But I cared not as I thought him an incredibly skilled pilot. As will be discussed in a later chapter, I myself flew without a pilot's license for many years.

The Waco had been converted to a crop duster. The pilot sat in the rear cockpit and the two side-by-side passenger seats in the front cockpit under the upper wing had been removed and replaced with a dry insecticide dispenser known as a hopper. This hopper held approximately 1,000 pounds of dry insecticide. The pilot operated a lever from the cockpit that opened or closed a sliding gate that metered the amount of insecticide, pesticide, or fungicide to be spread in an even swath of dust flowing from a Venturi device protruding into the airstream from the bottom of the airplane and gravity fed with chemicals from above.

The pilot knew how many pounds of insecticide per acre were required and flew mostly in the early mornings with cool temperatures and little wind to minimize chemical drift. The pilot would reduce airspeed over the intended drop area, drop to about three feet above the ground with the aircraft's wheels almost touching the

crops, and adjust the lever to achieve a fairly uniform spray that extended just beyond the wing tips. This would be done while dodging trees, poles, birds, wires, and anything else that might be sticking up into the air to ensnare an unwary pilot while preparing for a sharp pull up at the end of the field and course reversal to get in the proper position for the next run.

In retrospect, I do not know much about Cliff Daniels' past but I do know that he traveled with the various growing seasons. During the summer he dusted potatoes in Long Island and cranberries and other crops in New Jersey and then traveled south in the winter to dust the various crops growing here.

From the first moment I saw Cliff's operation, I spent nearly every day at his field, at first just sitting and looking at that wonderful biplane and imagining that I was flying it. Cliff couldn't help but notice me and one day he walked over and asked me what I was doing. I told him that I was just looking and he offered that perhaps I could help him. Soon I was picking up trash, loading chemicals, and wiping his airplane down of grease and oil.

A few weeks later, on Saturday, December 14, 1935 (according to my mother's diary), I traveled to Miami to watch the All-American Air Maneuvers. Accompanying me was my boyhood friend Chuck Robinson, who lived at Fort Lauderdale-By-The-Sea. Wow! As I watched those skilled aerial stuntmen perform their unbelievable aerobatics, I knew right then and there that I wanted to be an aviator, specifically a "duster pilot" like Cliff.

I later found out that Cliff lived in a house directly behind ours. One day when I was in my backyard trying to make one of my models fly correctly, I noticed him in his own yard talking with two other men. I approached Cliff asking for help with my model, which he ably provided. The two other men I later found out were also pilots: Jack Faulkner and Jimmy Crawford, both of whom I will talk about later. About this time, I also saved enough money to purchase a simple $1 Brownie camera that I used for nearly five years to document my early aviation adventures.

Accidents

One day, a pilot by the name of Joe Marks landed at Cliff Daniels' dusting field in a nice looking Travel Air 4000 equipped with a 220 horsepower Wright J-5 engine. Apparently, he intended to stay a while and he told me that if I would help keep his airplane clean he would take me for a ride. Boy was I happy because it was such a beautiful airplane! I wiped it down a few times but never got the free ride because only a few weeks later he was dead.

On New Year's Day in 1936, he killed himself during a landing attempt when he collided with the telephone lines that crossed the eastern approach end of the grass strip. Whether he was drunk, suicidal, or just simply careless was the subject of much speculation by the local aviators. What is known is that his fatal accident severed the main transmission line (there was no television at the time) from Miami for the only radio broadcast for the Orange Bowl football game between Catholic University and the University of Mississippi. Basically the entire United States north of the accident site could not hear the game,

Bystanders examine the wreckage of Joe Marks' Travel Air 4000 in which he died when he struck telephone lines during a landing attempt. Telephone repairmen can be seen in the background restringing the wires.

Cliff Daniels and his wife Josephine standing beside their wrecked Waco 10 crop duster. Cliff emerged unhurt after a wheel axle broke during the takeoff roll, causing the aircraft to overturn.

Visiting Dinner Key

The first commercial airliner I ever saw in my life was when I visited Pan American Airways' operation at Dinner Key, Florida on February 3, 1935. Little did I know when looking at those flying boats that several decades later I would be a "Clipper Captain" for Pan Am. As I look back upon that journey, it is almost like a perfect dream that I have not awakened from.

When my Dad told me that we were going to Dinner Key to look at airplanes, I could hardly believe it. We drove to Dinner Key in my Dad's 1931 Hudson Straight 8 and even though it was only 30 miles, it seemed like it took forever for us to get there. When we walked into

bringing much displeasure to both local and national fans.

I cannot begin to explain how upset I was when I first saw the wreckage. I had never seen an airplane accident before and it was a terrible thing for a child to be told of his new friend's death. Yet he would be but the first of many of my close friends who would be killed or severely injured over the years in airplane accidents caused by their own neglect, other's carelessness, or simple misfortune. Learning of their deaths, even to this day, has never gotten easier.

Cliff had a less serious airplane accident of his own when a broken axle caused his left wheel to come off during the takeoff roll, causing the Waco to overturn. The aircraft was quickly repaired and returned to service.

I was 14 years old when I took this photograph of a Pan American Airways Sikorsky S-40 approaching Dinner Key, home base to Pan American Airway's flying boats. I could never have imagined that several decades later I would be a Pan American captain.

Pan Am's office building and looked at that big globe of a world, I could not comprehend the fact that this was what the world really looked like.

Later as I watched some of the flying boats take off, I could only imagine what the captain was thinking as he flew passengers to other parts of the world. It must have been a real thrill for the flight crews to accomplish such a feat. Little did I know what this skinny, sickly, little 14-year-old boy had in store for his future. My wildest dreams would become a miracle.

My First Flight

During this same period, I took the first airplane flight of my life. I found out that a very wealthy and famous aviatrix by the name of Annette Gipson was offering barnstorming flights in a Waco 10. The price was $2 and she flew from a cow pasture then known as Merle Fogg Airport and now known as Fort Lauderdale International Airport.

Times were tough, however, and for Chuck and me to get the necessary $2.00 for an airplane ride it was going to be even harder. So on January 11, 1936 I officially became a bean picker, paid at the handsome rate of 7 cents a hamper.

I took the first hamper I picked, which seemed to take forever, to the straw boss for my first chit (you got one chit for each hamper filled and you were paid at the end of the day by turning in your chits).

The straw boss looked at me and said, "Boy, is that hamper full?" I said "Yes, Sir." He then took the hamper, set it down, and pressed the beans down with both hands until it was only half-full and said, "Go fill it up!" It took me 8 days of hard labor to get my $2, so I guess I was a bean picker even before I moved to Pompano, the bean capital of the world.

With our $2 in hand, on Sunday, January 19, 1936 Chuck and I walked to Merle Fogg Airport and went for the first airplane flight in our lives in Annette Gipson's beautiful red Waco. It was actually piloted by a Lieutenant Livingstone who was working for her that day and I am not certain if this was the same Livingstone who crashed his Curtiss Shrike near me as related in the previous chapter.

This particular Waco was equipped with a big siren that blared as we flew down the beach, attracting the attention of all who could hear us. What a thrill! I was now hooked good as a future pilot but I never wanted to do anymore bean picking. It seemed like it took 10 million beans to make that $2.

So every day on the school bus ride home I would have the driver drop me off at Cliff Daniel's duster strip where I performed whatever chores he would dream up. Other airplanes frequently landed and I became well acquainted with more and more of the local duster pilots and visiting aviators.

One day I arrived at the field and I noticed an airplane on the far end of the field with smoke rising from it. I asked Cliff about it and he told me that it was a Curtiss Robin that had landed and burned up. I was completely amazed but they would not let me go down and look at it.

I later pieced together what had

happened from the conversations of the other pilots at the field. This was the prohibition era and the airplane was loaded with liquor brought in from the islands. The pilot landed, offloaded the liquor, and then burned the airplane to hide any evidence. No one would tell me the name of the pilot.

I worked free for Cliff, although I would have gladly paid him for the right to be around his airplane. Cliff did employ a young mechanic's helper by the name of Aubrey "Red" Iley and on Sunday, March 8, 1936, he asked us if we might like to go for an airplane ride. We immediately scrambled aboard the biplane and sat in the dust hopper. With no restraints of any sort, we launched into a clear-blue summer Florida sky.

It was a nasty experience for these young boys as we quickly were covered in swirling chemical dust. But we were happy as larks as Cliff overflew the miles and miles of crop farms that surrounded the area at that time. The farms were quite large and covered an area from South Florida north to West Palm Beach.

I flew again on March 12th and I probably made another two to three sightseeing flights on an irregular basis, although my mother would have killed us both had she known, as she was terrified that I might get hurt.

Aviation Ground School

Unfortunately for me, Cliff Daniels and his Waco left at the end of the growing season, so that ended my flying career for a while. At this point, though, programs under the Works Progress Administration, an emergency work relief program formed during the Great Depression, were in full swing. I found out that they conducted an aviation ground school at no cost in Fort Lauderdale at the high school.

I enrolled on October 8, 1936 and finished on November 19, 1936. I was 15 years old at the time and was the youngest member of the class, as nearly everyone else was in their 20's. I learned about engines, aerodynamics, air navigation, and meteorology. I never flew, however, and I did not take any formal licensing examinations. But the immeasurable value of this course was that it gave me familiarity with a broad range of complex aviation-related concepts, which later helped me pass the commercial pilot license examination.

Move to Pompano

In February 1937, my father moved our family to nearby Pompano, which was about four miles north of Oakland Park. I desperately wanted to remain behind because I did not want to leave Cliff Daniels, who would shortly return for the fall dusting season with his wonderful airplane.

The move, however, ended up working out quite nicely for my aviation ambitions. Soon after we arrived at our new home, I found out that there was another airfield nearby. I immediately walked about a mile south of Pompano on the Old Dixie Highway to see what aeronautical wonders it held. I was not disappointed.

Chapter Four
Jack Faulkner and Jimmy Crawford

When I walked up to the new dusting field in February 1937, I found to my delight a solitary airplane sitting there. I later learned that it was a Pitcairn PA-5 Mailwing (serial number 27) that had been converted to cropdusting duties. The Pitcairn series of Mailwing airplanes were developed by Harold F. Pitcairn to transport airmail for the U.S. Postal Service.

Courtesy of my trusty $1 Brownie camera, this is the wondrous sight I beheld when I first walked to the crop dusting strip near my new home. It is a Pitcairn PA-5 Mailwing converted to crop dusting duties.

Never in my wildest imagination could I ever envision that many years later I would end up owning the remnants of that airplane. In 1938, a little more than a year after this picture was taken, a cropduster by the name of Joe Toth was preparing to launch from a dusting strip in Woodstown, New Jersey in this Mailwing when nature called. He climbed out of the cockpit and left the J5 engine idling at a very slow idle speed, which was a routine practice at isolated dusting fields.

While Joe was temporarily

Curtiss Robin equipped with a Curtiss Challenger 185 horsepower engine owned by Jack Faulkner and converted to duster duty.

indisposed, passing mechanic Mike Brago noticed gasoline leaking from the carburetor. Sensibly, he shut the engine down and turned the gasoline supply off to avoid a fire. Irresponsibly, he failed to find Joe and notify him of this event.

When Joe returned to the airplane, he cranked the engine up and made an immediate takeoff, not realizing the gasoline supply had been turned off. There was just enough fuel left in the lines for him to fly to the scene of his accident. The engine failed, Joe crashed, and the airplane, fully loaded with fuel and highly combustible chemicals, exploded into flames.

Joe survived unscathed but the Pitcairn was abandoned in place. Joe would move on to a successful career as an engineering test pilot for Eastern Air Lines. Many years later when I became a vintage aircraft enthusiast, I thought it would be nice to have the original registration paperwork for this airplane, as it had served as one of the original airmail airplanes. In 1988, 50 years after the accident, I discovered the Pitcairn's wreckage still lay where it had crashed. I purchased the rights to the airplane and sold it to a restorer from Illinois. He recovered the charred remains from the field and is in the process of restoring it.

Faulkner Air Service

Returning to the events of 1937, the new dusting airfield was located on the outskirts of Pompano and it sat at the entrance to an abandoned harness racing track. To gain access to the field, you had to travel along an old dirt road with tall trees bordering the south side and a fence to the north. The rocky road that served as the actual landing strip was rather narrow. From the air, a pilot could easily identify the landing strip by two small, distinct buildings located on the Old Dixie Highway. The buildings marked the entrance

The Pelican logo later painted on the tail of Faulkner's Curtiss Robin by mischievous loaders. It was a spoof on the old limerick "A wonderful bird is the pelican. His beak can hold more than his belly can. He can hold in his beak, enough food for a week. But I'll be darned if I know how the hellican!"

to the old racing track. It was, and still is called, "The Dusting Field," by those who remember these operations. Today this is the entrance to John Knox Village, with its main thoroughfare still named, "Airport Road."

The land was owned by Bud Lyons and was leased to a true gentleman named Jack Faulkner and his wife, Jessie Lee, who operated a cropdusting business named Faulkner Air Service. Even though I was only 15-years-old at the time, Jack let me hang around the field and get in the way until I started learning the ropes. I learned later from Jessie Lee that Jack thought an awful lot of this skinny kid. He kidded with me endlessly and took me everywhere with him on his travels.

Cropdusters normally work in the early morning when the wind is not blowing. I wanted to be there when they were dusting, so my mother would wake me up before dawn and I would walk in darkness to the field, which was about a mile away, to watch them. Sometimes they would let me sit in the cockpit on cold mornings with the motor running to warm up the engine oil before flying to prevent clogging. I could pretend to my heart's content that I was a veteran pilot about to take off on another dusting job before the real cropduster arrived to relieve me of my seat.

At a certain time, however, school would beckon and I would reluctantly trudge off, smelling of the insecticides, which at that time, were mainly sulfur dust. After school, I would head back to the field to see if the dusters were there working on their airplanes or perhaps returning from some unknown destination. Since this was also the Prohibition era, I strongly suspected that they were hauling whiskey and rum out of the Bahamas in the afternoons and

While I might appear as a dapper pilot standing beside Jack Faulkner's Waco 10 ASO, tail number R634N, if you look closely you will see I have a rag in my hand. I am admiring my work after wiping down the Waco 10 before I head to school. I had yet to control an airplane.

evenings. However, I never personally witnessed such activity.

Jack had several dusting airplanes at the field and he built a rather large shade hangar for them as well as a small tool shed. The five airplanes based at the field at this time were a large 420-horsepower 1928 Stinson Detroiter owned by Archie Wilson, the previously mentioned Pitcairn Mailwing (side number N5808), a Curtiss Robin (side number 700M), a Waco 10 ASO straight wing, and a 1929 Stinson Junior (side number 469H). Other pilots flying a variety of airplanes frequently flew in to help with the dusting for a few days, including one memorable day when I saw a Pitcairn autogiro arrive for a dusting mission.

The 1928 Stinson Detroiter was a six-seat cabin monoplane built by Edward "Eddie" Stinson's company in Detroit, Michigan, hence the name Detroiter. It boasted a heated, soundproof cabin, electric starter, and Harley-Davidson wheel brakes. This airplane was designed for airline and industrial use and had been converted to duster duty.

In comparison, the 1929 SM-2AB Stinson Junior was a 4-seat high-winged monoplane built for private owners and featured seating for four and a fully enclosed cabin, which was unique for its time. The story told to me was that this particular airplane had been specifically built for Eddie Stinson's personal use and was the only model that incorporated a control stick instead of a control wheel. It had not been converted into a cropduster and Jack Faulkner and his crew used

Jimmy Crawford (standing) sneezed just as I took this photograph of him and Jack Faulkner (kneeling) in front of Jack's Waco 10 ASO. In typical crop duster fashion, Jack was diagramming directions in the dirt for Jimmy to follow to find the next field to be dusted. Jack's dog, named Contact, had also been paying close attention to the directions.

it for business travel. They would fly to such places as Palm Beach, Miami, or Homestead and pretty much every time that passenger Stinson went somewhere, I was onboard. One of my most memorable trips was flying over my house at 11th Street and Kester and taking pictures to show my parents.

Jimmy Crawford

One of Jack's pilots was a man by the name of Jimmy Crawford, who hailed from Martin, Georgia. Jimmy would become my life-long friend and he and Jack, in my eyes, were both top-notch aviators. Jimmy had taught himself to fly in an airplane he had built himself from plans in Popular Mechanics and which his son still owns. Jimmy later hired on with Eastern Air Lines and flew for them until his mandatory retirement at age 60. He then returned to his home in Martin, Georgia where he continued in aviation by building airplanes until he passed away.

One day, Jimmy came back from dusting in the Waco 10 with the left landing gear dangling from the airplane. He had hit a stump in the bean field he was dusting and the landing gear was hanging on only by its cables. He flew low over us at the strip and we heard him holler, "Fort Lauderdale." We all jumped in the car and raced to Fort Lauderdale's Merle Fogg Airport. Jimmy had picked the Fort Lauderdale airport, which was about 7 miles away, for the emergency landing because it had a larger landing field than the narrow cropdusting field.

When we got there, Jimmy had already landed, initially touching down on the good wheel before flopping to a stop. Due to Jimmy's exceptional piloting skills, there was very little damage to the airplane. We lifted up the left wing and placed an empty gasoline drum with cushions under it.

Jack Faulkner then arranged for the chief welder from Pan American Airways' operation in Miami, a gentleman by the name of Mr. Legg, to weld the landing gear back in place. As the airplane was nothing more than wood and fabric, bunches of wet towels were draped over the airplane near the welding site to prevent the airplane from burning.

I watched every move that was made and within two days, the Waco was back in service. It is impossible to describe the excitement of a young boy who was in love with aviation being

The year is 1938 and standing in front of this Stinson Junior from the left is Stanley Hampton, Jimmy Crawford, Aubry "Red" Iley, and Joe Toth. This was the first airplane that I ever controlled in flight.

at the center of all these wondrous activities. Many years later, when I was a National Airlines captain, I was reviewing the passenger list before a flight and noticed a young lady with the name of Legg. It is an unusual name so I asked if she was related to the welder and she was in fact, his daughter. She remembered the incident well.

While at Fort Lauderdale, I had the opportunity to meet a really nice guy by the name of Joe Mackey, who was an aerobatic air show performer. He kept four airplanes at the field, including a Waco Taperwing open cockpit biplane with its namesake tapered wings, two straight wing Waco's, and a Stinson Trimotor. Joe flew the Taperwing for his aerobatic air show and if I remember correctly, the sign on the side of his airplane read Linco Flying Aces. This name referred to a formation aerobatic team contracted by the Ohio Oil Company, a manufacturer of Linco brand gasoline and motor oils, to perform at air shows. During World War II Mackey would rise to the rank of colonel in the U.S. Army Air Corps and after the war, he founded Mackey Airlines, which would later merge with Eastern Air Lines.

Another aviator celebrity I met at Fort Lauderdale was Clarence Chamberlain, who barely missed crossing the Atlantic Ocean before Charles Lindbergh's successful attempt. I had flown into Fort Lauderdale with Jack Faulkner and Chamberlain was there carrying passengers in a Curtiss Condor, a twin-engine biplane. If you bought a flight and you were a student pilot, he would let you sit in the copilot's seat. I was waiting in line for my turn to fly when they stopped flight operations due to darkness. I would meet Chamberlain again in 1948 when I was cropdusting in Okeechobee, Florida. I was reloading and refueling my 1929 Travel Air 4000 at the airport when he landed and taxied in to shut down beside me. While chatting, I asked him about his 1927 Atlantic crossing from New York to Germany. He had made this flight only weeks after Lindbergh's crossing and had bettered Lindbergh's record for distance travelled. He told me there was nothing to it, he just headed east and hoped the engine kept running long enough to run into land somewhere. He had written a book about his adventures and he provided me with a signed copy from a stock he had in his airplane.

My First Time at the Controls

On one trip in the passenger seat in the Stinson, Jimmy let me fly copilot and handle the controls. While I thought I was doing pretty well, after a bit he took them back saying that I was making him airsick.

Before I was allowed even to think about learning to fly, however, I spent a lot of time loading airplanes with insecticide. I also began to work on them, particularly the Wright J5 engines that needed a check every 20 hours of flight time. This air-cooled engine was unique in that the rocker arms and push rods were completely enclosed, but still required manual greasing of all fittings. I was soon

This photograph of me striking a casual pose in front of a Stinson Detroiter was taken in 1937. The Detroiter had been converted to a duster and was owned by Archie Wilson who was assisting Jack Faulkner during that dusting season. My first dusting experience was operating the hopper in this airplane.

responsible for performing this lubrication, which involved removing the rocker box covers, taking the rocker arm out, removing the push rods, cleaning and lubricating them with Texaco Marfax Grease Number 3, and then reassembling all the parts. I also performed other routine engine preventive maintenance tasks such as oil changes.

It took two people to dust using the 1928 Stinson Detroiter, with the pilot flying the airplane while the copilot operated the dusting apparatus. The crew sat side by side, in what used to be the passenger front seat, with the hopper located where the back seat used to be.

Climbing into the front cockpit was always an awkward adventure as the passenger access door had been removed and access was gained only through the trap door. Much later, I heard that two fellows were killed in that same airplane when it crashed and they could not get out of the airplane.

First Cropdusting Experience

After much begging and pleading, in the spring of 1937 I finally got the chance to serve as the hopper operator. It was an absolute pleasure knowing I would be dusting beans by air rather than picking them by hand on the ground. I was only 15-years-old at the time and my total flight time was as a passenger. The pilot, Stanley Hampton, was not jumping for joy at the thought of having a skinny, untested kid operating the dusting mechanism. After some brief instructions by Stanley on what to expect, I got in, sat down, and fastened my safety belt. On command, my responsibility was to open the dust hopper door and simultaneously turn on a Chevrolet starter motor that would activate a device in the discharge throat of the hopper known as an agitator, which helped to release the dust uniformly.

I was all smiles as we took off. The excitement level was extremely high and I could barely restrain myself at the thought that I would actually be cropdusting. I was probably the youngest cropduster and the only one who didn't know how to fly. I was on top of the world, but I would soon fall off for a different, sadder reason.

Suddenly we were at the field to dust! The pilot pointed the nose down and we dived into the field leveling off at two or three feet above the crops and he gave the command, "Open hopper!" Wow! I was so excited I could hardly do my job and then he ordered me to close the hopper while he pulled up sharply, made a steep turn, dived back into the field, and again yelled, "Open hopper!"

This went on for maybe two or three more times, but this young boy was turning green and swallowing hard to keep from heaving my insides out. I certainly could not let him know how sick I felt because I feared he would never let me fly again. I was seriously beginning to doubt whether I really wanted to be a duster pilot.

But I hung in there and I soon overcame the airsickness caused by the abrupt steep turns, swift pull-ups and quick dives back into the fields.

I dusted several more times after

that first flight, but all too soon, the big Stinson left and I never had the chance to dust in it again. My parents would have had a fit if they had ever known I was flying in such a manner, so I never told them. And certainly none of the cropdusters at the field wanted to face my Mom.

First Near Accident

One day, one of the helpers named Walter Berg, a Swede who was Jack's brother-in-law, and I were alone at the field. For some forgotten reason, Walter wanted to move the Pitcairn about 40 feet straight ahead. He and I tried to push the airplane by hand to no avail. He then suggested that I sit in the cockpit while he hand propped the engine to start it so we could use engine power to move the plane. It seemed like a good idea at the time.

Inasmuch as I was more or less familiar with the cockpit controls, I knew enough to keep the throttle closed to keep the engine at low power. I also knew this airplane did not have any brakes and that only throttle control could be used to slow or stop it.

We got the engine running and he came back to the cockpit and told me to open the throttle a little bit to taxi the airplane where he wanted it. He stood off to the left of the airplane and motioned me to move forward. Not knowing what a little bit meant, I moved the throttle forward too far.

The airplane immediately jumped forward and headed straight for a nearby loading truck. I was absolutely terrified and closed the throttle. In a dream sequence where everything moves in slow motion, out of the corner of my eye, I noticed Walter jumping up and down waving his hands. But I was absolutely powerless to stop the inevitable collision.

The airplane slowly stopped moving, but not before the wing gently kissed the truck. I turned the engine switch off and hopped out to find there was no damage to the truck or airplane, not even a single scratch on the wing. I don't know who was more scared or relieved, Walter or me. Anyway, Walter moved the truck out of the way and nothing was ever said to anybody. From that moment on, I knew that a little throttle did not mean half way.

J.B. Starling sitting in the cockpit of his Fairchild KR-31 in which we made many flights together. I severely damaged this airplane showing it off to my friends.

J.B. Starling

While Faulkner was still operating from the duster field, a well-off playboy by the name of J.B. Starling bought a Fairchild KR-31 biplane from Stanley Hampton, which he kept at the field. Originally produced by the Kreider-Reisner Aircraft Company as the Kreider-Reisner Challenger, it was redesignated the Fairchild KR-31 when Kreider-Reisner was taken over by the Fairchild Aircraft Company. This biplane had two open tandem cockpits and was powered by a 90 horsepower OX-5 engine.

I was standing around watching Starling preflight one day when he asked me if I would like to go for a ride. I immediately agreed, as I was happy to get any airplane rides. After we landed, he offered to give me flight lessons in exchange for cleaning his airplane. After the cropdusters left at the end of the dusting season, he had the only airplane at the field and we flew quite a lot together. He was a great guy, but a terrible flight instructor, as he barely knew how to fly himself. I never soloed and I later discovered he was subject to epileptic fits. I never noticed anything unusual myself, but if something had happened in flight, I would have learned to fly a lot sooner than I actually did.

Eventually, it became obvious the Fairchild needed to be recovered, so he took the wings off and brought it down to a workshop in downtown Pompano. One afternoon after school, I was showing the airplane to about a half a dozen friends when the ill-conceived thought came to me that it would be a good idea to demonstrate how the engine ran. I properly chocked the wheels, closed the throttle, and as the choke in the updraft carburetor was broken, I stuck a rag in there so gasoline would be sucked into the carburetor instead of air.

I then hand propped the engine and it was running wonderfully, the wooden propeller just clicking over in slow motion. I noticed the rag was still in and pulled it out. What a mistake. That engine immediately went to full power. The chocks prevented it from moving forward so the airplane promptly stood up on its nose and then fell over on its side, the wooden propeller splintering and kids scattering everywhere. I managed to turn the engine off but I never saw or spoke to J.B. Starling again. To my knowledge, he just left the demolished KR-31 in that shop.

Kindness

I was there every single day when Jack's group was dusting. One morning, as I walked to the landing field in the dark, Jack and Jimmy drove by, saw me walking, and picked me up. They were on their way to breakfast before heading to the field and stopped at Angelo's Restaurant in Pompano.

I sat down with them as Angelo took their order and then Angelo turned to me and said, "What do you want to eat, boy?" I told him that I didn't have any money. He looked at me and said, "I didn't ask you if you had any money." I was soon treated to a fine breakfast of eggs and sausages.

Only hours after we had flown together on a beautiful Sunday afternoon, I awoke to find this terrible headline. Nothing since has affected me as sadly as Jack Faulkner's passing.

Jessie Lee Faulkner, with her dog Contact at her feet, stands beside her company's Pitcairn Mailwing converted to duster duty. She continued to operate the Faulkner Air Service's crop dusting business after her husband Jack's untimely death.

Angelo, bless his heart, couldn't see a young boy go without food. I will never forget his kindness.

After I finished my work at the dusting field in the morning, I would walk to school where I was disinterested in my studies, as my grades reflected. My passion was flying and every day my routine was the same: walk to the dusting field in the dark to work and fly, go to school, and then return to the dusting field to work and fly some more before heading home.

Tragedy

I loved working with Jack and Jimmy and all was going well at the landing field. Then disaster hit and I fell off the top of the world. On Sunday, March 21, 1937, Jack, his wife Jessie Lee, their daughter Lenore, and I flew to Homestead in the passenger Stinson. We arrived back in Pompano in the late afternoon and my parents picked me up and took me home.

The next day I awoke to find newspaper headlines that announced that Jack had been killed in his automobile on his way home to Fort Lauderdale after our trip. He had rolled his Hudson automobile, with his wife Jessie Lee and daughter Lenore inside, off the Old Dixie Highway Bridge into the Cypress Creek Canal. The car flipped upside down and although his family managed to escape unharmed, Jack drowned in the wreckage.

To this day, nothing has disturbed me more in my life than when I found out about Jack's death. He is buried in an unmarked grave in Fort Lauderdale, a sad tribute to such a fine man.

Jack was only 36 years old when he died. Although I had known him for only two months, I was taught an awful lot about flying from this kind man and the experienced duster pilots who worked for him. I learned not only basic airmanship skills but also critical aeronautical decision making skills that were passed down from pilot to pilot through informal "hanger talk" sessions. Listening attentively to one of these discussions saved my life many years later when I had an engine failure at night, which I will discuss in a later chapter.

Jessie Lee continued to operate Faulkner Air Service after Jack's death. But cropdusting is migratory work. When the Pompano season was over in the spring of 1937, Jessie Lee took Faulkner Air Service back north as usual to Bridgeton, New Jersey to dust cranberries and other crops for Seabrook Farms.

Once again, I thought my flying ambitions were stopped. But in the fall 1937, dusting season another important cropduster entered my life.

Chapter Five
J.L. Schroeder

Dawn Patrol Fights On Food Front

THE DAY'S WAR PLANS against insects are discussed before dawn by J. L. Schroder, center, and Tom Ewing, left, and Al Reilly, right, pilots. Two mechanics look on.

In 1941 the Miami Herald wrote an article about crop dusting operations in Pompano. I am one of the unidentified mechanics, the third person from the left wearing the flight helmet. J.L. Schroeder is in the middle wearing the hat. Such is the life of those who work behind the scenes.

When Jessie Lee returned to Pompano with her Faulkner Air Service in the fall of 1937, she found that her old dusting strip, which ran east and west, had been leased to another dusting operator. So she built a new landing strip running north and south just across the street from the old strip and west of the Florida East Coast Railroad tracks.

While Jessie Lee preferred to drive from New Jersey to Florida, several crop dusters who worked for her flew down, including Jimmy Stewart and Joe Toth. I appeared at the field shortly after they arrived and I was soon put to work helping to load and maintain the airplanes. This field would only be used for one year. Jessie Lee departed in the spring of 1938 to return to her home base in Bridgeton, New Jersey and never returned to Pompano. I heard later that her crop dusting business eventually ceased operations but I do not know why.

J.L. Schroeder

The new crop dusting company that worked from the airfield previously used by Faulkner Air Service was owned by Joseph "J.L." Schroeder. J.L., a true gentleman in every sense of the word, hailed from Houston, Texas where he owned the Main Street Airport.

He began his crop dusting business in 1924, which was certainly among the first in the duster field. He appropriately named his dusting service J.L. Schroeder Incorporated and although J.L. knew how to fly, he never did any dusting himself.

Even though the two dusting companies operated adjacent to each other, there was more than enough dusting work for both. In fact, within five miles of each other there were four dusters flying in the area: Faulkner Air Service, J.L. Schroeder Incorporated, Cliff Daniels' Atlantic Air Service, and Delta Air Service Incorporated.

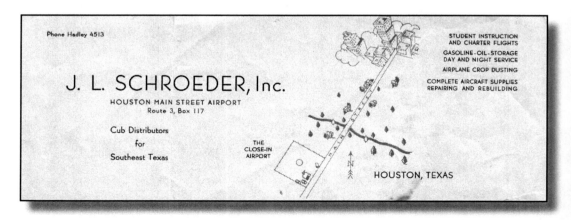

Schroeder owned Houston, Texas' Main Street Airport, which consisted of two L-shaped sod runways. Today it is completely covered by housing and there is no trace of the airfield.

Relationships between the four dusting companies are best described as a friendly rivalry. I never personally heard of any physical conflicts between the two groups of duster pilots or of any duster trying to undercut another with lower prices. I do know that J.L. charged 3 cents a pound of dust dropped and pilots typically received 25% of the gross charged amount.

In my mind, airplanes and motorcycles were equals when it came to pure fun, and in 1937 at the age of 16 I bought my first motorcycle, a 45 cubic inch Harley Davidson, for which I paid $50. I would ride the motorcycle to school and many times, I picked up J.L.'s son, Joseph Laurie, when he needed a ride. Throughout my flying career, I always owned a motorcycle and I finally sold my last one in 1995.

J.L., whose middle name was also Laurie, lived next door to me in Pompano and it wasn't long before he took a liking to this skinny kid. When Jessie Lee did not return for the fall 1938 dusting season, I started working for J.L. loading dust, greasing engines, changing oil, and gassing up his airplanes.

The first airplanes J.L. used in the Pompano area were called Command Aire's. These dusters were built in the late 1920's and early 1930's in Arkansas and had 185 horsepower Curtiss Challenger engines. The Command Aire was a very good dusting airplane with a normal load of dust weighing 400-900 pounds.

J.L. also operated Travel Air 4000's, three place open cockpit fabric biplanes converted to duster

2593
RESIDENCE POMPANO: PHONE 4482   OFFICE PHONES 361 AND 341

J. L. SCHROEDER, Inc.

Airplane Crop Dusting Since 1924

Pompano, Florida

Although based in Houston, my lifelong friend J.L. Schroeder dusted crops extensively in the Pompano area.

duty. Powered by an extremely reliable 220 horsepower Wright J-5 Whirlwind engine, the same type of engine used by Charles Lindbergh on his flight across the Atlantic, this was my favorite duster of all the models I have flown.

J.L. Schroeder poses with duster pilot and later, Braniff Airlines Captain Bill Longino in 1937.

The flight line at J.L.'s dusting strip near Pompano. On the left are two Command Aires and on the right is a Travel Air, my favorite airplane.

In my opinion, Pompano was the best place in the world and I felt like I was on top of it. Pompano was a great farming area at that time and I met many of the local farmers as they visited the dusting strip to discuss the various insecticides and fungicides they wanted applied to their fields by airplane.

At the conclusion of the Pompano dusting season in the spring of 1939, J.L. returned to Texas to dust cotton. With no airplanes left at the field, I reverted to a projectionist job at the local movie theater. J.L. returned in the fall of 1939 and once again, I was helping him and his duster pilots with their airplanes.

This cycle of J.L. arriving in the fall and departing in the spring repeated itself from 1939 to 1942. J.L. hired several different duster pilots and I became associated with all of them.

Among them were John Riley, W.I. Eure, Sim Speer, and Tom Ewing, to name a few. There are different stories to be told for each one of these and they were all my friends.

One of J.L.'s most popular duster pilots was Bill Longino. Although he was only 21 years old at the time, he was an excellent pilot and duster and well liked by everyone. It has been said that farmers had their fields dusted just to watch Bill fly. Bill loved to fish on his time off and usually went with one of Pompano's finest fisherman, John Whitmer. Longino later left to fly for Braniff Airlines, where he stayed until mandatory retirement at age 60. I am sure that Bill's experiences would fill many books.

J.L. used several additional types of dusting airplanes, eventually switching to J-3 Piper Cubs, which

Bill Longino, one of Schroeder's most popular crop dusters with farmers and the local girls, stands beside a Command Aire about 1937.

made for an economical duster. It could carry as much as 500 pounds of insecticide with only a 65 horsepower Continental engine.

A & E Certificate

In 1942 during the fall of my senior year at Pompano High School, we were told that as part of the war effort we could go to Miami and attend an aircraft and engine (A&E) school. Upon successful completion, we would

be awarded our high school diploma. As I was now 21 years old and not doing particularly well in school, I immediately volunteered. I completed the course in time to graduate with my Pompano High School classmates in the spring. For my efforts, I received a certificate that stated I had completed the A&E course of instruction, but not a license.

After my Pompano High School graduation ceremony in 1942, I promptly got on my motorcycle and rode straight to Houston to work for J.L. It was time that I became a pilot.

10. *LeRoy Brown* (Signature of student)		
Aircraft Engine Mechanics		
11. (Occupation for which training was given)		
3-12-42 VOCATIONAL TRAINING RECORD 110		
School years 12	Units of training (Preparatory—Extension) 13	Clock hours of training 14
	Aircraft Engine Mech.	470

Certificate of completion I received from Technical High School in Miami, Florida. My instructor was Bruce Hadley and I received 470 hours of training on aircraft engine mechanics.

My second motorcycle, a 1931 Harley-Davidson 74. The year is about 1939 and I am 18 years old.

Chapter Six
Journey to a Pilot's License

My new home: Houston's Main Street Airport owned by J.L. Schroeder. I made my first legal solo flight from this field in a Piper J-3 Cub on October 16, 1942.

When I arrived at Main Street Airport in Houston, I found that J.L. had about 30 airplanes that he used for flight instruction, crop dusting, and rentals. I was hired as a mechanic and general gofer, but in the evenings, it was my responsibility to taxi back the various Porterfields, Rearwin Sportsters, J-3 Cubs, and Taylorcraft into the hangar, which was pretty heady stuff for a non-pilot.

I was usually by myself and while the straight-line distance from their parking spaces to the hangar was only about 50 feet, I started taking a more circuitous taxi route around the grass strip runway. I would then taxi back daringly fast and sometimes the airplane accidently got a few feet off the ground, fully airborne if even for a few brief seconds.

How not to perform an annual inspection on a Piper Cub. Taken in Schroeder's hangar in Houston, I am on the left, duster pilot Emil Eubanks is on top, fellow mechanic A.C. Howe is next followed by George Bischiff who was just passing by.

Now when J.L. was about to get serious he had a certain mannerism that involved him clearing his throat a few times before he spoke, indicating that he was about to make an important point, to which a young man might want to pay particular attention. So after one of my long distance, high speed, low altitude taxies he approached me out of nowhere, cleared his throat a few times, and then said to me, "Taxiing kind of high aren't you?" I wasn't given a chance to reply and he followed with, "You might not want to do that anymore or I will blackball you with the CAA."

That was enough to scare the wits out of me and I never made any further flight attempts. But I learned how to fly tail wheel aircraft by taxiing them on the ground in various wind conditions, which explains why I have never groundlooped an airplane. I also met some interesting people at J.L.'s airport in Houston, including Howard Hughes, who was not very friendly, and Gene Autry, who was a pure gentleman.

I was quite proud of my work as a mechanic and one day a Civil Aeronautics Authority (CAA) maintenance inspector by the name of George Sackett observed me overhaul an engine and asked me a lot of questions. He never provided me any feedback but several weeks later I bumped into him and he muttered to me without explanation, "You are never going to amount to anything."

I was deeply hurt by his remark and many years later when I was with National Airlines I noticed that he had been assigned to Tampa. I called him and asked if he remembered me. He said that he sure did and asked me what I was doing. I informed him that I was now a captain with National Airlines. There was a brief silence and then he congratulated me and told me he was glad that I had settled down. We chatted very pleasantly for a while before we hung up.

Flight Lessons

Finally, in the fall of 1942 I realized that it was time for me to start flying legally if I ever was going to achieve my ambition of becoming a crop duster like my heroes. Although I had many hours in the air at this point, I had never flown solo and I did not have a logbook.

So I purchased one, and my first logbook entry states that on July 2, 1942 I flew 30 minutes in a Piper Cub with W.I. "Tag" Eure as the instructor. Many years later when I was with National Airlines, I got Tag a job with the airline and even checked him out in a Lockheed Lodestar. We also crop dusted together many times during our careers. Small world.

A review of my early logbook entries reveals that I rarely flew with the same pilot twice as I begged any instructor to take me flying in between our other responsibilities. I flew in a wide variety of aircraft and

these flights were usually very short. Many times these flights were less than 15 minutes as an instructor took me on a few quick circuits of the field before both of us returned to work. Courtesy of J.L., all these instructional flights were also free, so I was earning dual time without having to pay for my lessons.

Finally, on October 16, 1942, with a grand total of 8 ½ hours flight time in my logbook, I soloed in a Piper Cub side number NC-40640. Cecil Beyette was my instructor and he flew me around the patch once before turning the airplane over to me.

I wish I could relate how exhilarating it was to finally fly solo but that would be untrue. I had flown so much by that point that I can only remember feeling relieved that I did not need to have an instructor aboard with me anymore. Cecil then signed my logbook.

Accordingly, my formal flight training essentially stopped at that point because I felt that I already knew how to fly. My true flight instructors were the experienced duster pilots who taught me how to feel comfortable in the low, slow, steep turn environment of crop dusting. Since my primary goal was to start building flight time so that I could apply for a commercial pilot's license, I just did not see the need to apply for a private pilot's license.

While J.L. let me fly any airplane on the field, I wanted my own airplane. So I traded my motorcycle for my first airplane, an Aeronca KCA. This airplane was a high wing, single engine light airplane that featured side-by-side seating for two people. On December 24, 1942, I made my first flight in an airplane that I actually owned.

First Airplane Accident

I had also decided that it was time for me to leave Houston and return to Pompano and try to join one of the duster outfits there. I now had 46 total logged flight hours and I intended to fly my Aeronca KCA cross-country.

I was told by everyone not to fly to Pompano without a license because I would most certainly get caught by a CAA flight inspector during an enroute fueling stop. So I found a private pilot by the name of Wheeler who volunteered to fly my airplane for me. I would serve as his copilot.

We departed Houston for Pompano on a nice clear cold December day. After we were airborne for quite a while, I asked him if we were lost, because at this point I was pretty sure that we should be seeing the blue waters of the Gulf of Mexico on our right.

At almost that exact moment, over the piney woods of what I later learned was Livingston, Texas, the engine quit. We began to descend fairly rapidly towards what I was certain would be a horrible crash when a narrow fire lane carved out of the woods suddenly came into view.

Wheeler was on the controls and he immediately turned towards it. Then he turned to me and shouted, "You gotta help me." The only thing I could say was, "I can't land it for you but you better slow this airplane down."

He didn't and we came across

My Aeronca KCA sits forlornly at Houston's Main Street airport where I abandoned her in place after my accident.

that road at about 90 miles per hour, which was pretty close to that Aeronca's cruising speed. Wheeler slid that airplane right between two big pine trees, which we hit while still airborne. The wings smoothly folded backward and in what seemed like slow motion the airplane gently slid down to the ground.

Miraculously unhurt, we walked to a nearby manned fire tower for help and we arranged for a truck to find us, load the airplane, and return us to Houston.

I left my broken airplane sitting forlornly outside one of J.L.'s hangars and I caught a ride in a truck bound for Pompano with spare parts for J.L.'s

Instead of flying to Pompano in my beautiful Aeronca KCA I rode in this truck.

dusting operation there. The vehicle was driven by Hubert Sessions, one of J.L.'s mechanics who was also a pilot. I never saw my first airplane again.

Return to Pompano

When I arrived in Pompano in January 1943, I once again ended up working as a mechanic, fueler, and loader for J.L.'s crop dusting operation. Unfortunately, I did not have any opportunities to fly but I was still happy to be around the duster operation. When J.L. left at the end of the dusting season in the spring of 1943, I moved to Hollywood, Florida to work as a general mechanic for anyone who needed work on their airplane.

It was there that I met a young lady by the name of Kathryn McJunkin, who was the daughter of a rich local farmer. I was immediately attracted to her as she owned a Taylorcraft and she was serving as a flight instructor out of the Hollywood Air Park. She would give me flying time in exchange for my maintaining her airplane.

My Second Airplane and First Biplane

In June, 1943 I learned that a Fairchild KR-34 biplane side number 292K, the same type as J.B. Starling's biplane that I had accidently ruined a few years back in Pompano, was available. It was owned by W.W. Brown who owned the Brown Dusting Company. I paid him $500 for the biplane, jumped in, and flew back to Hollywood.

According to my logbook, I had flown it only five times before a CAA inspector stopped by one day and thumped the fabric to test its strength. He turned to me and said, "There's something wrong here. This airplane needs recovering. There are five layers of fabric here. You can't fly this airplane like that." So I did not and instead flew Kathryn's Taylorcraft. There will be more about this biplane a little later in this chapter.

Second Airplane Accident

I was having a grand time flying Kathryn's Taylorcraft, sometimes with her for some flight instruction, but most times solo for my own enjoyment. I must have impressed some people with my skills because one day a military man by the name of Lowrey Woosley, who already had a private license, asked me for some flight instruction. Although I had a grand total of 172 hours in my logbook, I still did not have a pilot's license, not to mention a flight instructor's certificate. Yet I could not in good faith turn down a paying customer and I agreed. I would regret this decision.

So on July 6, 1943 at Hollywood, Florida while giving this gentleman a flight lesson, I experienced my second airplane accident. My logbook simply reads, "Spun in."

Jack Faulkner had told me once that you could not consider yourself a good pilot unless you had wrecked two or three airplanes. I was about to meet that criterion.

Barely visibile in the remarks section of my logbook for July 6, 1943 is my simple entry "spun in." I was severely injured.

We were flying in a rented J-3 Piper side number NC 27015 when, almost immediately after takeoff, at about 300 feet the engine quit. The student pulled back on the stick in fright and the airplane immediately stalled and started spinning toward the ground. I immediately grabbed the controls and tried to recover the airplane but we didn't have enough altitude and impacted the ground at a diving attitude of about 65 degrees.

I have no memory of the actual crash, but I do recall seeing the top of a pine tree go by just before we impacted. I was in the front seat and unbeknownst to me my right fist impacted the gas tank, my left thumb was nearly severed where I was holding on to the throttle, and my head smashed into the instrument panel. My back was also broken from the impact of the rear control stick.

When I regained consciousness, two fellows were carrying me under each arm to a waiting ambulance. I told them to turn me loose and advised them that I was all right and could walk fine by myself. They refused to let me go and then I passed out again.

The impact hole where my head hit the instrument panel is clearly visible.

Wreckage of the Piper Cub in which I was severely injured on July 6, 1943.

My student was uninjured. Although I was wearing a lap belt, the airplane was not equipped with shoulder harnesses, which would have protected me from being thrown forward into the console. Instead, I ate the airspeed indicator and I can emphatically state that it didn't taste very good.

When I came to in the hospital, I found that when I opened my mouth my whole jaw fell down. An orthodontic specialist was brought in and he told me that he needed to operate on me but that it was going to hurt me real bad because he could not give me an anesthetic.

His assistant then held the top of my head while the doctor shoved my jaw back up into my head to realign it properly. I could hear my bones crunching as he manipulated it into place.

I thought the worst was over until he informed me that he needed to hurt me really bad again. His assistant then held my mouth shut while the doctor drew brass safety wire between my top and bottom teeth and tightened it up, all without an anesthetic.

I was initially fed intravenously and later sipped various concoctions with a straw through one of my missing teeth. After 30 days, the doctor removed the safety wire holding my jaw in place with cutting pliers. He told me that I could now eat a steak dinner if I wanted but he bet that I couldn't open my mouth. He was right. It took a long time for my jaw muscles to finally relax enough for me to eat normally.

I have always felt that these severe facial injuries changed my appearance. Looking in the mirror, I didn't look the same after my accident as I did before. I had also cracked all the teeth in my upper jaw and a few years later, they had to replace all of them with false teeth. This often confuses my new dentists who cannot understand why my bottom teeth are so perfect yet all my upper teeth are false. I have to explain to them that they were knocked out.

During my recovery, I was flat on my back in a special bed for three months. Rather than remain hospitalized this entire time, Kathryn kindly let me stay at her family's home and their maid took care of me until I recovered. I was initially told that I would never walk again but I fully recovered and to this day, I have never had any back problems.

When I was released from bed rest, the doctor wanted to put me in a protective cast for a year. I told him that I didn't need one and that I felt fine. He then said, "Well, I am going to wash my hands of the whole affair." And he did. I never saw him again.

The very next day I got on a Greyhound bus and rode to Panama City, Florida, to pick up my motorcycle that I had loaned someone. I then rode it back to Ft. Lauderdale without incident.

The Civil Aeronautics Board was not too kind in their accident report. They pointed out that I was not a qualified flight instructor and the investigator noted that the accident was due to the poor judgment of two students pilots flying together who had little knowledge of each other's flying ability. Still, I maintain that if

I had been given another 50 feet of altitude I would have been able to recover the airplane and land safely.

Return to Houston

Kathryn and I were married in October 1943 and with few prospects in the Pompano area, we drove to Houston. Huburt Sessions, owner of Sessions Aircraft Service and who performed all the aircraft maintenance for Cliff Hyde's Flying Service, found jobs for both of us.

I was hired by Huburt as a mechanic while Kathryn worked for Cliff Hyde as a flight instructor. He had a contract with the military to train pilots for the War Training Service. Under this plan, the first eight hours were flown in light airplanes.

I had applied for the aviation cadet program myself soon after the war began but I was turned down due to my childhood asthma. Subsequently, crop dusting was designated as an essential occupation and I should have received a deferment but to my delight, I received a draft notice for the Army. I failed my physical, however, due to my broken back and I was classified 4F.

After we had been in Houston for only a few months, Huburt was killed by a train in November 1943 and we quit, too upset by his death to continue with the company.

Irwin Newman Company

Our next job was working together again for the Irwin Newman

Company, which manufactured hangars. This company bought George Cunningham's airport, which was not too far from Schroeder's Main Street Airport, after Cunningham was killed in a Piper Cruiser at Schroeder's airport.

Ernie "Pop" Gaither, one of J.L.'s original duster pilots, was manager of all the maintenance. I had met Pop in Pompano years ago when he was crop dusting there. The other crop dusters used to laugh about the way he flew a Command Aire because he would make flat turns using rudder only and not use ailerons to put the wing down. He simply skidded around his procedure turns. Pop never called me LeRoy, he always called me either Boy Scout or Cowboy.

So I walked into Pop's office and he said, "Cowboy, what are you doing?" I told him, "Nothing" and that I was looking for work. He asked if I could recover and repaint airplanes. I said, "Kind of," and buffaloed both Kathryn and myself into jobs for $20 a week each.

It didn't take Pop long to figure out that we didn't know much about paint and fabric, but he kindly showed us what to do. We became quite proficient and a Piper Cub would be rolled into our hangar on Monday morning and we would be done by the following Saturday, including all the rib stitching.

Years later, when I was dusting in Navasota, Texas, I was sitting on the ground waiting to be reloaded when a Travel Air circled and landed. The pilot called me to the cockpit and to my surprise, it was none other than Pop Gaither. So Pop says to me, "Hey, Cowboy, how are you doing?" Still in shock because I thought Pop had grounded himself because of vision problems, I answered, "Fine."

He then asked me, "Is this Navasota?" I managed to blurt out a "yeah" and then he said, "Well, I'm in the wrong place. Will you point out the direction of the runway so I can take off?" His vision was so bad he couldn't see the runway yet he was still managing to crop dust somewhere out in the wilds of Texas.

Third Airplane Accident

Just before Kathryn and I moved to Houston, I took the wings off my grounded Fairchild KR-34 side number NR292K and hired a fellow to put it on a flatbed truck to transport it to Houston. I rode with him and I must say the trip took forever: that fellow would not drive over 30 mph the entire way.

I never repaired that particular airplane but in October 1944, I heard of another Fairchild KR-34 side number NC299K that was available in Charlotte, North Carolina. I do not recall how I got to Charlotte, but I purchased that biplane from "Red" McChord and intended to fly it home with Henry Hein, one of my flight instructors. Henry was a former U.S. Army aviator of German descent and spoke with a thick accent. One of Henry's claims to fame is that he crashed an airplane onto the top of J.L.'s hangar in Houston.

We launched out of Charlotte and made fuel stops in Atlanta, Georgia

I am being advised by E. Eubanks as I dismantled Henry Hein's airplane that he crashed into J.L. Schroeder's hangar.

and Meridian, Mississippi. By the time we left Meridian, it was nighttime and we were tracking the lighted airway in total darkness when the engine suddenly failed. This was my second engine failure, but the first at night and it is always a real shock to lose an engine when you have but one.

It was at that precise moment that I remembered a hangar-flying session with Cliff Daniels and his crop dusters. One of the older pilots advised that if ever caught with an engine failure at night, head towards the darkest area on the ground and not towards any lights for fear of being caught in power lines or telephone cables.

I turned the Fairchild toward the darkest area, trimmed the biplane for best glide angle and held on. Before long, I heard something slapping against the bottom of the wing. We had landed upside down in a cornfield. I later found out that we were in Columbus, Mississippi, which is about 100 miles north of New Orleans.

Henry and I emerged unharmed and we were soon greeted by an unhappy farmer who demanded payment for the damage we had done to his corn. To add to his displeasure, gawkers soon arrived to stare at the biplane and trampled his corn further.

Henry and I decided that discretion was the better part of valor so we hightailed it out of there, abandoning the Fairchild in the field and catching a bus back to Houston. Once back home, I arranged for the biplane to be dismantled and trucked to Houston. I never did receive a bill for damages from that farmer.

Flying the Stinson Tri-Motor

I now owned two airplanes, both Fairchild KR-34's and neither of which was flyable. In November 1944, however, Henry Hein and a gentleman by the name of Charlie Toce approached me with a business proposition. Charlie was not an aviator but rather a well-known inventor who had created flashing stop signs for highways. He seemed to me to be somewhat the shyster and full of baloney and later I was not proved wrong.

Nonetheless, they had heard about a Stinson Tri-motor SM-6000B side number NC11167 that was available in Dallas, Texas. The Stinson SM-6000B was originally designed for airline use and was powered by three Lycoming 215 horsepower engines. It featured an enclosed cockpit with two pilot seats side by side and the spacious cabin with seating for 10 passengers.

Charlie had figured out that he could make money by hauling U.S.

Army personnel from nearby Ellington Field to wherever they needed to go. To purchase the Stinson they needed a loan from a gentleman by the name of Tom Collins who was in the finance business and wanted collateral for this risky venture.

So Henry and Charlie asked me if they could use my two dismantled Fairchild KR-34 biplanes as security against their loan. In exchange, I would get to fly the Stinson and share in the profits. It seemed like a good deal to me so I agreed. Tom Collins approved their loan and to my knowledge, no one ever inspected the airplanes upon which this agreement was based.

So in November 1944 Charlie and Henry asked me if I would like to accompany them to Dallas to pick up the Tri-motor and bring it back to Houston. When we arrived, we found the Stinson to be in pristine condition with Toce-Hein Flying Service painted on the side.

It had been completely recovered by Pop Van Cleve, an old friend of Bill Longino's, who told us that he had used more than 20 barrels of dope on the fabric. In addition, the three engines had also been overhauled. Henry asked me if I wanted to fly it back with him and I jumped at the chance. So we flew it back to Houston, with me sitting in the copilot seat.

Soon after our return, Charlie and Henry received a contract from the U.S. Army to transport ten navigators who had just completed navigation training at Ellington Field, to Roosevelt Field, Long Island, another U.S. Army

training base. Roosevelt Field was the site of Charles Lindbergh's departure for his famous non-stop New York to Paris flight in 1927.

Henry offered me the copilot seat as he and Charlie owed me money for my airplanes. I eagerly accepted. But I didn't have any nice looking clothing so Henry loaned me a pair of his old U.S. Army trousers known as "Army pinks," although they were really more tan in color. Henry always treated me like a young gentleman and I learned a lot about flying from this experienced aviator.

So the evening of December 3, 1944 ten navigators boarded the Stinson, placed their duffel bags in the storage room in the back of the airplane where a bathroom use to be, and settled in for a long trip. And what a journey it would be.

Henry and I intended to fly the more than 2,000 miles between Houston and New York straight through, with nine planned fuel stops and without stopping for sleep. We taxied out at approximately 10:00 PM, Henry opened the throttles on the three engines, and we were soon airborne.

Almost immediately, Henry screamed, "Help me, LeRoy, help me push this yoke forward!" I got on the controls but we had so much weight in the tail that it was nearly impossible to get the nose down.

Henry yelled over the engine noise for the navigators to drag their duffle bags forward as if their lives depended on it, which it did. Meanwhile, the tower was observing our odd maneuvers as Henry and I

The Stinson SM-6000B that I flew as copilot on a roundtrip charter flight from Houston, Texas to Long Island, New York. I did not yet have a pilot's license.

fought to keep the Tri-motor from stalling. They kept calling us to ask if anything was wrong but we didn't have time to reply. The navigators scrambled to move their duffel bags forward and Henry and I slowly regained control of the Tri-motor. We finally began a slow climb and eventually got the proper weight and balance established on what surely was an overloaded airplane.

As Henry and I reoriented ourselves and started heading outbound to pick up our first lighted airway beacon, I couldn't help but wonder what those poor navigators thought they had gotten themselves into after those first few terrifying minutes of what would eventually be a 20-hour trip. There was still a little more excitement to come for them.

There is nothing more peaceful than following lighted airway beacons at night with the engines humming in perfect strength and harmony. This was before the age of electronic navigation and pilots navigated at night by following a string of powerful rotating beacons mounted on tall towers and normally spaced ten miles apart. These beacons formed various lighted airways and flashed identification marks in Morse code enabling the pilot to pinpoint his exact location. Depending on weather conditions and terrain, usually two or more beacons were visible in the darkness. Different colored beacons also marked civilian or military landing fields along the route.

We flew through the bitter cold night at an altitude of only a few thousand feet and at a groundspeed probably averaging 90 miles per hour, requiring us to make frequent stops for fuel. My logbook shows that we refueled at Lake Charles, Louisiana; Jackson, Mississippi; Birmingham, Alabama; Atlanta, Georgia, where daylight finally dawned; and Charlotte, North Carolina. During the next fuel stop at Greensboro, North Carolina, Henry told me that he just couldn't keep his eyes open any longer and asked me to fly the rest of the way.

He then told me to trade seats with him, keeping with the time-honored tradition of the pilot-in-command sitting in the left seat. I had perhaps 300 flight hours in my logbook, no license, and I was now sitting in the left seat of a Stinson Tri-motor. I was now captain of an airliner with 12 souls on board who were depending upon my aeronautical knowledge and sound judgment to get them safely to their destination. Henry had already fallen sound asleep in the seat to the right of me. I was in heaven.

So I made the takeoff from Greensboro and headed towards Richmond, Virginia, our next scheduled fuel stop. Enroute I noticed that we were getting extremely low on fuel and could not make Richmond so I headed for the nearest field in sight, which turned out to be a U.S. Army Air Force base named Blackstone Field, just 60 miles short of Richmond.

Henry was still sleeping as I made what I thought was a perfect landing, considering that I did not even awaken him. I taxied in to what I thought was base operations and shut the engines down.

The navigators remained in their seats as I stepped through the rear door of the tri-motor and noticed that there was a whole bunch of P-40's flying around us. An officer whom I assumed to be the Commanding Officer of the base, drove up to me and shouted, "Get that damn thing out of here. "I explained to him that it was an emergency and that we were out of gas. But he was resolute and said, "I don't care what you are out of, get that damn thing out of here. I am trying to do some training here."

Well at this point Henry finally woke up, came outside and asked me, "What's going on?" I told him that this fellow was giving me a hard time because I landed here. Henry said to me, "Well, this fellow doesn't know the rules."

He then turned to the Commanding Officer and said, "You gas this airplane up. This is an emergency and we don't even have to pay for the fuel." And we didn't. The Commanding Officer left, we gassed it up, the navigators re-embarked, Henry went back to sleep in the right seat, I made the takeoff essentially solo, and shortly thereafter we landed in Richmond.

Now refreshed, Henry returned to the left seat and we landed at Wilmington, Delaware and Newark, New Jersey for refueling before finally arriving at our final destination, the U.S. Army Air Force base at Roosevelt Field, Long Island. I logged 21 hours of flight time in the Stinson Tri-motor during this phase of the trip. Since I didn't have a pilot's license I could not log it as pilot-in-command time and instead logged it as dual instruction under Henry.

Our charter complete, we didn't have anything to do and Henry tried without success to find passengers for our return trip. After three days, we departed Roosevelt Field empty for our flight back to Houston.

At night outside of Charlotte, it started snowing and the weather slowly deteriorated and kept getting worse until our visibility was about zero. I advised Henry that we were getting low on fuel and he told me, "I can't find the airport. I guess we are going to have to land anywhere. Throw out the flares."

The Stinson had three parachute flares mounted on the outside rear of the fuselage. Release cables ran to three individual switches mounted overhead the co-pilot's station. When released, the parachute flare would ignite and float slowly downward, brightly illuminating an area of about 1 mile around the flare for about three minutes. Henry's intentions was to circle the three flares hoping that they would cut through the snow and clouds enough for him to find a suitable emergency landing spot.

Well, this really shook me up. I pressed the release switches to put all three parachute flares out but nothing appeared outside. I then informed Henry that maybe they had ignited but hadn't released and we might be on fire.

Now Henry was really shook up. We kept flying ahead and I called Charlotte tower to ask for assistance in locating the airport. A controller answered and said that he had heard an airplane overfly the airport a few minutes ago.

Henry immediately executed a 180-degree turn to go back to the field but he told me that even if we couldn't find the airport we had to get on the ground while we still had power to control the Stinson.

We let down through the swirling snow and thick clouds, bracing for the worst. Suddenly, we broke out into the clear and Charlotte's runway appeared directly in front of us. Just flat out crap house luck.

We landed safely and when we later examined the flare dispenser, we found all three flares safely attached to the fuselage. It turned out that the reason the flares didn't ignite and launch was because in my excitement I failed to turn the master switch on. This unintentional mistake on my part actually saved Henry and me from making a forced landing.

In the terminal building at Charlotte, we were approached by a gentleman named Haskel Deacon, who owned a little airport not far from Charlotte called Plaza Airport. He asked us to bring the Tri-motor to his airport to provide rides. Having nothing else to do and with the potential of finding paying customers we agreed and shuttled over there for a day or two of sightseeing rides.

We were greeted at Plaza Airport by none other than "Red" McChord, who had transported my Fairchild KR-34 that I landed in a cornfield after having an engine failure at night. We also picked up a paying passenger who needed transportation to Shreveport and we dropped her off there before heading back home to Houston.

Henry and I logged an additional 20 flight hours on the way home, bringing my seven day trip total to 41 hours in the Stinson Tri-motor. All of this without a license.

Henry and Charlie never did pay me wages for the trip but I was smart enough to put a labor lien on the Stinson and I flew two more charters with them. I finally figured that the only way I was going to get my money out of this deal was to push the Stinson out of its hangar and fly it myself, charging the gasoline to them.

I flew several hours alone in the Tri-motor but business was bad for Henry and Charlie and they finally couldn't pay their hangar rental fees. So airport management tied the Stinson down outside and that's where that airplane died. It never flew again.

Charlie, Henry and I parted ways and I later found out that on July 13, 1947 Henry was killed in a DC-3 crash near Melbourne, Florida. He was flying for Burke Air Transport, a small, nonscheduled airline, on the return leg of a roundtrip flight from San Juan, Puerto Rico to Newark, New Jersey when the DC-3 flew into the ground. The subsequent accident investigation revealed that in a period of 38 hours Henry was airborne for more than 23 hours without rest. All the evidence indicated that the exhausted pilots had probably fallen asleep.

First Commercial Pilot License Attempt

In January 1945, shortly after my return from the Stinson cross-country trip, I felt confident enough in my piloting skills to apply for my commercial pilot's license. J.L.'s flight instructors gave me some free extra instruction for the maneuvers I would be required to demonstrate and I felt pretty prepared. I was about to find out that was not entirely correct.

At the CAA office at Hobby Airport in Houston, I took the written examination, which in those days was completed in long hand with fill-in-the-blanks answers, not online and with multiple-choice questions like today. I failed the navigation section, retook it successfully, and was given credit for the examination and permission to take the flight test.

For the flight test portion, Beach Mott loaned me his J4 Piper Cub Coupe, side number NC27832. My appointment for my check ride was at Hobby Airport with S.C. "Nelly" Fox. He examined my logbook and said, "So, you don't have a private license?" Unconcerned, I replied, "No," and he responded, "Well, you are kind of low time." At that time, I had a total of about 360 flight hours in my logbook.

We got airborne and I completed all the maneuvers satisfactorily. Fox then told me to set 1200 engine RPM and land. Well, I thought this was a test to see if I was dumb enough to try to land with that much power. So I calmly flew right over the airport while maintaining altitude and demonstrating what I thought was fine aeronautical sense.

Fox then turned to me and said, "I have a good mind to file a violation on you for buzzing the airport." Shocked, I said, "You told me to do it." He replied, "I told you to land." That busted me right there. Fox failed me and I was so upset that I never bothered to apply for a retest.

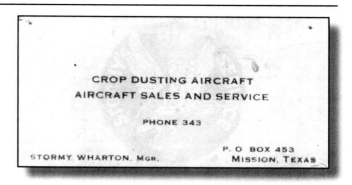

CROP DUSTING AIRCRAFT
AIRCRAFT SALES AND SERVICE

PHONE 343

STORMY WHARTON, MGR.

P. O BOX 453
MISSION, TEXAS

Faintly visible in the center background of Stormy's business card is his logo: "Stormy's Air Service" featuring a bug wearing a flight helmet and shooting an old fashioned bug sprayer.

"Stormy" Wharton

Nonetheless, I continued to build flight time in Houston by flying for fun in Beach Mott's Piper J-4 and keeping up with my work in Pop Gaither's paint and fabric shop.

In February 1945 a gentlemen by the name of "Stormy" Wharton flew into Houston with two Travel Air 4000's that he owned that were equipped with J5 engines. Stormy flew one of the airplanes and a duster pilot by the name of Tommy Saffold flew the other. Stormy was using the Travel Airs for crop dusting and wanted Pop Gaither to work on them. I was tasked with repainting them orange under the direction of Mr. Gaither.

Stormy and I got to talking one day and I mentioned that J.L. had transitioned to Piper Cubs for dusting duty and he was making more money with them. The Cubs were proving to be more economical because of the greater amount of dust they could carry and the lesser amount of fuel they used. Stormy then said to me, "If I give you the money, will you buy a Cub for me, turn it into a crop duster, and then fly it for me?" I couldn't agree to these terms fast enough.

So Stormy gave me the money and I went to a military surplus auction field near Beeville, Texas. I picked out an L-4-B, a military version of the Piper J-3 Cub. On February 15, 1945, I flew that L-4 back to Houston via Corsicana, Bryan and Navasota, Texas to show Stormy his new airplane.

I then began all the work necessary to turn a people carrier into a crop duster. Modifying the L-4 into a duster required me to make a wooden frame for the hopper that would be placed in the rear cockpit. In those days, a heavy canvas bag was used as a hopper, filled with dust and then placed inside the frame. If the dust was not coming out right, the pilot could just reach back and beat the canvas until it did.

I also had to cut the control stick out of the back seat to make room for the hopper and reattach the aileron cables. I made a Venturi for the bottom of the airplane, a sliding door, hopper

Notice the stylish white scarf, leather helmet, goggles, and embroidered name over my left pocket. I have achieved my childhood dream of becoming a dashing crop duster pilot.

handle and connections between them as well as a dust loading door on the top of the fuselage.

I built all of these from hand, as there was no place to order such parts. I did buy a gearbox with a 48:1 ratio for the agitator from the Boston Gear Company that was attached to a propeller taken from a Model A Ford engine fan. When placed into the airstream the propeller would turn 48 times to turn the agitator once.

I completed all the modifications necessary to the L-4 on April 1, 1945. I said my goodbyes to J.L. and Pop, both of whom were supportive of my new job with Stormy. I was about to achieve my childhood goal of becoming a true crop dusting pilot.

Mission, Texas

On April 9, 1945 I flew the L-4, now redesignated as Piper J-3 side number NR 50699, to Mission, Texas where Stormy was crop dusting. Mission is located about 350 miles southwest of Houston near the Mexican border. Stormy had told me to hurry down because one of his pilots, Tommy Saffold, whom I had met on Stormy's original visit to Houston, had recently been killed when some sulfur dust he was laying exploded, engulfing poor Tommy and his airplane in flames.

After my arrival, I learned that at an adjacent airport, a famous Texas crop duster pilot by the name of "Slats" Rogers was working. Slats is credited with building the first airplane in Texas' history and I had the chance to get to know this unique individual. His biography, Old Soggy No. 1, is hard to find but it is a worthwhile read.

Kathryn soon joined me in Mission and we lived with Stormy, as there was no other place for us to live. There was quite a bit of work to be done so I was able to keep pretty busy dusting with that Cub.

My First Dusting Flights

On April 9, 1945, I made my very first solo dusting flight in the J-3 that I had modified myself to be a duster. At least that's what it says in my logbook. Before I ever kept a logbook, I had a one-time only solo crop dusting escapade that almost ended tragically.

Back in 1941, I was working for Schroeder in Pompano cleaning, loading and fueling the J-3 Cubs that he was using at that time. J.L. was away from the field one day and I casually mentioned to Clive Ricks and Tag Eure, two of J.L.'s more experienced duster pilots, that I wished I could dust.

Well, they said go ahead and dared me to take a light dusting load to Mr. Smokes' place to dust some beans.

Now I had no license, no logbook, and had never flown solo. But I thought I knew what to do because of my flight experience flying in the big Detroiter and operating the hopper controls.

So I hopped in the airplane, which was carrying only about 150 pounds of dust, and headed to Mr. Smokes' farm, which was only a few acres. Now in the Cub the hopper handle was located on the same side of the cockpit as the throttle. So when you got to the end of your swath you had to simultaneously open the throttle and close the hopper with the left hand and pull the stick back and make your turn with your right hand. It is easier said than done.

I successfully found Mr. Smokes' farm but on my very first swath while I fiddled with the hopper handle and the throttle I hit the top of a banana tree, leaves scattering everywhere in an explosion of branches.

This scared the heck out of me and for the first time I realized that this dusting business was a little bit more serious than I thought it was. I immediately headed home and landed with banana leaves on the landing gear, my friends asking me in amazement what had happened. When I told them, they didn't want J.L. to find out so they quickly pulled the debris off the airplane and we all took a vow of silence.

I was a little bit more prepared, but not by much, to crop dust for Stormy. So I started my professional crop dusting career for Stormy without any

This endorsement by the CAA examiner overlooks the fact that I never held a private pilot's license although I had nearly 450 hours when I took my commercial pilot check ride. I probably had several hundred more flight hours but I had never kept a logbook to document them.

My first pilot's license. It took two attempts to get it and it was followed only a few years later by my air transport pilot's license. I never held a private pilot license.

formal training, everyone assuming that I knew what I was doing.

Stormy did get after me one day for making high nose turns back to the field. After watching me fly one day, he told me that I would get in trouble making turns in such a manner with the dusting load I was carrying. The J3 Cub had a 500-pound load and he was afraid I was going to stall out on the turn.

From that very first dusting flight in April 1945, I flew multiple flights in that Piper Cub nearly every day for several months. Then fate, in the form of a kindhearted CAA inspector, intervened.

Getting a License

Stormy had warned me several times that I should think about getting a pilot's license because there was a lot of talk going around the other dusters that I didn't have one. I remained unconcerned until one day when I was walking back to the hangar after a crop dusting mission. I was greeted by a stranger who asked me, "Were you flying that airplane alone?"

Covered in dust, I knew right away that only a CAA inspector would ask me that question and I answered, "Yes," truthfully. He then asked the fateful question, "Do you have your license?" I quietly responded, "No," and he said, "I could cause you a lot of trouble for flying without a license."

Form ACA 663
(Rev. 11-1-40)

UNITED STATES OF AMERICA
DEPARTMENT OF COMMERCE
CIVIL AERONAUTICS ADMINISTRATION
WASHINGTON

CERTIFICATE OF WAIVER OF AIR TRAFFIC RULES   № 30954

ISSUED TO: LeRoy Harlow Brown

ADDRESS: Box 453, Mission, Texas

The application attached hereto, bearing the above number, having been considered, and its proposals and facts investigated, and it being believed that the public safety, the safety of those engaged in aeronautics, and the encouragement and development of Civil Aeronautics require the waiver of certain sections of the Civil Air Regulations, the provisions of the following listed sections of the Civil Air Regulations are waived as to the operations in the areas and during the times set forth in such application. This certificate is applicable only to the aircraft and pilots specifically listed in the application, subject to the standard and special provisions incorporated in this certificate and strict observance of all other requirements of the Civil Air Regulations not specifically waived by this certificate.

List of waived rules by section:

60.3502 is waived to permit operation at an altitude below 500 feet to permit dusting of crops.

60.347 is waived to permit dropping of insecticides and dusts.

STANDARD PROVISIONS

1. Civil Air Regulations applying to: Weather minimums, lights and signals and the use of parachutes will be strictly observed.
2. This certificate is not valid in the event that it conflicts with any local law or ordinance, and does not constitute authority to fly below the minimum prescribed altitude over property, the owners of which have not granted such permission.
3. No person, other than the members of the crew essential to the operation, shall be carried in any aircraft during its participation in any event or operation for which this certificate is issued.
4. This certificate shall be presented for inspection upon the request of any authorized officer or employee of the Administrator, and of any State or municipal official charged with the duty of enforcing local laws or regulations involving Federal compliance.

THE FOLLOWING PROVISIONS 5 TO 8, INCLUSIVE, APPLY TO AIR MEETS ONLY

5. The air meet shall be conducted in accordance with the Civil Air Regulations.
6. No event of the air meet shall begin or be permitted to continue during the period beginning 10 minutes before the arrival, and 10 minutes after the departure of any air carrier aircraft engaged in scheduled air transportation.
7. The air-meet officials shall require that all participants in races occurring in the air meet using fast, specially built racing aircraft shall be qualified on such aircraft and the course to be flown.
8. The applicant, sponsors, and management of the air meet shall be held jointly responsible for the strict observance of all rules and regulations, including the terms of these provisions, by all participants.

SPECIAL PROVISIONS

(Special Provisions Nos. .... to ...., inclusive, are set forth on the reverse side hereof)

This certificate is effective from ......June 13, 1945.......... to ......June 13, 1946.........., inclusive, except that it shall immediately expire at any time an authorized inspector of the Administrator shall demand the surrender of such certificate after inspection or examination.

By direction of the Administrator:

Leslie I. Hables

Aeronautical Inspector Region IV
(Title)   (Region number)

Date ......June 13, 1945......

16—15751   (OVER)

After obtaining my pilot's license, the next step in establishing my legal crop dusting career was obtaining this waiver to fly below 500 feet.

I knew very well that he could but I was young and brash and I countered with, "Aren't you the man who gives licenses? Couldn't you give me one?" To my complete surprise, he agreed.

He told me to meet him at nearby MacAllen, Texas, on May 3, 1945 and rent an airplane there. He said that he would give me a check ride and that if I did well, he would give me a license.

In the meantime, he told me not to fly any more. I said, "Yes, Sir." At this point, I had about 440 total flight hours in my logbook.

This inspector's name was Samuel Dellinger and at 0800 on the appointed morning, I met him at the airport with a rented J4 Cub Coupe all preflighted and ready to go. I could have easily borrowed one of Stormy's Cubs, but I had promised not to fly solo and I didn't.

Dellinger had me don a parachute and then told me to take the airplane up and give him a turn and a half spin in each direction. He would stay on the ground and watch me and emphasized that each spin had better come out on point.

I was quite nervous but I got airborne, and performed a spin in each direction. Somehow or another they both came out on point. Quite proud of myself, I then landed but I could not find Dellinger anywhere. I asked a lady at the FBO where the inspector was and she told me that he had told her that he was going into town to have breakfast.

I quietly waited and just as he returned, a Fairchild KR-31 flown by two sailors in uniform landed. The airplane was in terrible shape and I would not have sat under it for fear that it would fall on me.

Dellinger walked over and said to them, "Are you guys actually flying this wreck?" They replied yes and he told them he wasn't going to do anything about it but they were to get it out of his sight immediately. He walked away shaking his head.

He then turned to me and said, "How did the spins come out?" I told

Standing in front of a Piper Cub I used for dusting circa 1946.

him pretty good so he said, "Ok, well let's go for a flight then." After we leveled off at altitude, he asked me to do some S-turns across the road. I had never heard of that maneuver so he took the controls, demonstrated it to me, and then had me do it. He then asked me to do eights on pylons. Same thing, I had never heard of that maneuver either so he took the controls again, demonstrated it to me, and then had me perform the maneuver.

This give and take repeated itself for several additional maneuvers and he never lost his temper or expressed his frustration at my not knowing the performance maneuvers required for a commercial pilot's license, which I should have had memorized.

We finally returned for some spot landings and after about an hour and a half in the air he told me to come in for a final landing. Walking back to the office, he said, "Well, the way you fly you are going to kill yourself." I was somewhat of a smart aleck and replied, "Well, that's encouraging."

He then surprised me by saying, "But what I am going to do is give you your license. Do you hear what I said? I am going to GIVE you your license."

I understood his meaning clearly that I had not earned my license from my performance on the flight test. He then said, "The next time I see you, we will go for a ride. If you have not improved, I will take your license away from you."

Despite his comments, there is no way to explain how happy and relieved I was. I thanked him to no end and we parted with him advising me to, "Be careful."

I now owned commercial pilot certificate number 366103. Sadly, Dellinger was killed three months later while performing in an airshow during an airport dedication in Mexico City.

For me, the fun could really begin. I had been breaking the law of gravity and the laws of the CAA my entire flying career and finally I was licensed. My logbook shows that the very next day I went back to crop dusting for Stormy.

Legally.

Chapter Seven

Crop Dusting

Taken in 1945 in Bryan, Texas, my first wife Kathryn is holding my oldest son Neville in front of my favorite duster, a Travel Air 4000. This particular airplane was owned by R.J. Cardwell and although it had only a 175 horsepower engine, it could still carry 700 pounds of dust. Kathryn and I were married for 12 years before we divorced, and we had four children, Neville LeRoy, Paul Cirrus, Don Leslie, and Mary Louise.

Now that I held a commercial pilot's license, nothing could hold me back in the world of aviation. But in June, 1945 the dusting business got slow with "Stormy," and I decided that it was just about time for me and my family to leave Mission, Texas for opportunities elsewhere.

Flying for R.J. Cardwell

Nearly coincidentally with this decision in early June 1945, a gentleman by the name of R.J. Cardwell approached me as I stood by a Piper Cub at Stormy's dusting field. I had never met him before and after some casual conversation, he asked me if I could fly his Travel Air duster. The Travel Air is an open-cockpit biplane whose front cockpit could seat two people side by side in the passenger configuration. Cardwell owned three E-4000 versions of the Travel Air equipped with J-6-5 Wright 175 horsepower engines that he had converted to duster use for his business. Approximately 85 4000's were built in the 1920's by the Travel Air Company owned by Walter Beech, Lloyd Stearman, and Clyde Cessna, who all went on to form their own successful airplane companies. My immediate response to Cardwell

then and as it would be in the future whenever I was asked if I could fly a particular airplane, was a confident, "Sure." It didn't matter, of course, that I had never flown a Travel Air but I was not about to give up such a spectacular opportunity.

Satisfied with my answer and not at all doubtful of my piloting abilities as he knew I was dusting for Stormy in Piper Cubs, R.J. offered me $200 a month plus a very small commission to crop dust for him. So I left Stormy with his blessing to fly for R.J. and on June 20, 1945, I made my first flight ever in a Travel Air.

I picked up R.J.'s Travel Air 4000 (side number NR611K) at Edinburgh, Texas where R.J. was working a dusting contract, and flew it to Robstown, Texas, for an additional dusting contract, stopping in Alice, Texas for fuel. I almost, but not quite, ground looped the airplane landing on the pavement. This was the only time I ever did such a thing.

A ground loop occurs when an airplane violently swaps ends after

Business end of the Travel Air 4000 I flew for R.J. Cardwell in 1945. The agitator's propeller is clearly visible on the left wing.

Leroy Brown
1945
TRAVELAIR 4000

I am about to take off on another dusting mission for R.J. Cardwell in his Travel Air 4000.

landing, sometimes severely damaging the wings, tearing off the landing gear, or overturning the aircraft. A ground loop typically begins when a sudden gust of wind causes an airplane to swerve or the pilot does not maintain directional control after landing or while taxiing. If the pilot does not immediately stop the turn with rudder, one wingtip will drop and dig into the ground and the pilot will be powerless to stop the airplane from swinging violently around. To avoid ground loops, taildragger pilots tend to have what is known as "happy feet," as they constantly step on the rudder pedals to keep the airplane straight and on the runway.

Despite this excitement, it was still love at first flight for me in that Travel Air. I consider the Travel Air to be the best duster I have ever flown in terms of controllability, maneuverability, and payload. I could carry 700 pounds of calcium arsenate in this particular model of the Travel Air, although during my career I probably killed more boll weevils with my propeller than I ever did with actual insecticides. I later owned several Travel Air's myself, selling my last one in 1962. But more about those airplanes later.

Travel Air Adventures

While still in Robstown, I had some unwanted excitement when R.J. sent me to dust for the King Ranch. Flying alone from a small pasture, I launched one morning with a full dusting load and the engine quit almost immediately after takeoff.

I made a routine emergency landing on the flat prairie and rolled to a stop. I immediately drained the gascolator, which serves as a strainer for the fuel system, and checked for water contamination. I did not find any water in the fuel, however, or anything else obviously wrong with the engine.

So I hand propped the engine by myself and the engine immediately coughed to life. Hand propping is used when an airplane does not have an electric starter and the pilot manually starts the engine by grasping the propeller and swinging it downward rapidly, creating an ignition spark that fires the engine. The engine ran normally so I took off and once again, the engine died as soon as I was airborne.

This sequence of the engine running fine on the ground and then shutting down once I was in the air repeated itself for several more emergency landings. Despite my best efforts, I could not isolate the problem, so I called Cardwell and asked him to send me a mechanic as quickly as possible as I still had a full load of dust aboard the airplane that I did not want to lose. Dust is very sensitive to moisture, which causes it to clump and become unusable.

The mechanic soon arrived and decided that the problem was most likely the ignition switch. So he replaced it and we ran the engine on

the ground and it sounded all right. So I took off and the engine failed again as if it was hitting a magic wall once we were airborne.

The mechanic chased me down the field for each emergency landing and he kept at it, trying every possible adjustment he knew to try to make that engine fly. The oddest thing was that the engine run ups and performance during takeoff rolls were normal. But every time that airplane rose a few feet above the ground, that engine would just come to a sputtering stop.

After several more skips and hops, I had had enough, so I called Cardwell and told him that I would not fly this airplane again until a new engine was installed. So he gave us permission to send to Houston for a new engine. Houston was less than four hours away, so a new engine that had recently been overhauled was soon delivered to us.

The mechanic and I installed the new engine and ran it for a while on the ground to break it in. It worked perfectly and I was feeling pretty good about the whole thing until I took off and that engine failed too.

Now the blame shifted to me and when the mechanic caught up to the airplane he shouted angrily at me, "What in Sam Hill are you doing?" I told him that all I had done was open the throttle for takeoff and before I had time to do anything else, the engine stopped once I pulled back on the stick. Still staring at me suspiciously, he made some additional adjustments to the new engine and told me "Try it one more time."

Page 8

FAMOUS LAST WORDS
By BOB BUNCH
Safety Chairman, California AAA

THESE ARE CLASSIC SAYINGS — famous last words said by pilots every day. How many have you heard and said to yourself?

"I've never ground looped one yet."

"I'll wheel land it hot, I've got to save time."

"He might have five years more experience than I do, but I'll show him how to dust."

"These chemicals can't hurt me — I've used them for years."

"What! Me fly with a hard hat? I'm no sissy."

"Oh, I'll try it. I think there is enough clearance under those wires.'

"Oh heck, fill it up. I'll take it all in one load."

"That's enough gas to finish this last load, I guess."

"The boss said not to try it, but I'll show him it can be done."

"It's running a little rough, but it will keep running long enough to finish this last load."

"I know you have never done it before, but anyone can work the throttle and switch while I prop it."

"Oh, quit shaking in the turn! I'm not horsing you around too tight. Woops!"

"I'll roll the wheels in it and show him what a good duster pilot I am."

"Come on, hurry it up! I've got a date in in town. Boy, what a doll she is."

"Oh, I can relax now. All I got left is to border up."

"Watch me beat that car under the wires and across the road."

"Darn, got to remember to fix that hopper leak in the cockpit when I finish today. You know, that spray is cool though."

"ME look at the field from the ground? It's just another job, and I've done hundreds of them. That field-inspection stuff is for the new boys."

"Watch these field laborers get out of that field when I dust them off."

"Oh, I'll use this road for a strip this time. It will save ferrying. It's narrow and rough, but after all I'm good."

"Who is tired? Making this kind of dough I can fly twenty more loads."

So I did, and the engine failed again on schedule right after takeoff. I was now convinced that this airplane was jinxed and I did not want to fly it any more. Suddenly inspired, the mechanic got a flashlight and looked inside the fuel tank to make sure we had enough gas, which you might have thought would have been our first troubleshooting step.

We had plenty of fuel, of course, but as the mechanic was staring into the fuel tank, he noticed a large beetle floating in the gas.

We finally figured out that once I became airborne the gas would swirl downward to the bottom of the fuel tank. The beetle would be sucked down and block the gas line, effectively shutting off the fuel supply to the engine.

Once I made an emergency landing and the airplane came to a stop, the suction would be released, the beetle would float up to the top, and normal fuel flow would be restored in time for our engine checks. It took him a while but the mechanic finally fished the beetle out of the fuel tank and we had no further problems.

I should have kept that beetle as a rare example of the capture of an airplane Gremlin. For those readers unfamiliar with these mythical creatures, they were first imagined by British aviators during World War II as the source of any unexplained malfunction aboard an airplane. I would be forced to deal with many mischievous Gremlins during my long crop dusting and airline career when mechanical, electrical, or electronic problems would be encountered in flight that could not necessarily be duplicated on the ground.

Dusting contracts complete, on July 11, 1945 I flew the Travel Air back to R.J.'s home field at Bryan, Texas, which is located about 120 miles northwest of Houston, and Kathryn joined me there. R.J. had some very good dusting contracts in Navasota, Texas, which is about 30 miles southeast of Bryan, and my logbook shows that I flew nearly every day for the next several months. This new job was working out pretty well for me as far as pay was concerned.

The Germans

One day towards the end of the war, I was dusting a field and as I was reloading, I noticed there were several German prisoners under guard picking cotton. Few Americans realize that during World War II, nearly half a million German and Japanese prisoners of war were held in the United States. Texas held more prisoners than any other state and many were employed as farm laborers.

Well, one of the guards came over to me and said, "Two of those men over there say they used to crop dust in Germany and would like to come over and look at your airplane if you don't mind." I told him that I had no objection at all.

They came over and inspected my airplane very thoroughly, talking quite a bit amongst themselves. They spoke very little English at all and I do not speak any German, so I really don't know what they thought of my dusting airplane. But I did feel a common bond with these enemy aviators from afar.

Black Annie

In addition to his commercial dusting contracts, Cardwell was also working with the Agricultural Experimental Station located at College Station, Texas. Part of the Texas A&M

In this 1945 photograph I am laying a swath of cyanamid in support of tests conducted by the Agricultural Experimental Station at College Station, Texas. Notice that the dust is black in color, earning it the nickname, Black Annie.

University system, this facility was established to conduct research on methods to improve crop and livestock operations in Texas.

The scientists were experimenting with a new method of defoliating the cotton to make it easier for machinery to pick the crop. They were testing cyanamid powder, and were trying to determine the most effective treatment amount.

I was assigned by Cardwell to

fly these experiments. I made three flights in one day, which proved to be very successful. The powder was easy to apply by airplane but it was black in color and produced big dark clouds behind the airplane. I got it all over myself and some pilots eventually nicknamed it Black Annie.

It also had a very unusual side effect. If you accidently ingested any and then drank a beer, it would completely throw you for a loop.

Return to Florida

At the end of the fall dusting season in 1945, Cardwell's dusting contracts slowed down and I wasn't flying quite as much, which meant low pay.

One day, a gentleman by the name of Joe Basso, who was one of Huff-Daland Dusters' original dusting pilots and now worked for Delta Crop Dusting, visited me. He said, "You're a Travel Air pilot, right?"

"You bet," I instantly replied.

He then asked me if I would be interested in flying one of his Travel Air's to Dania, Florida to dust there for him. I could not believe my ears. Dania was located only 20 miles south of Pompano, my hometown, and I was more than ready to return to Florida.

He then offered me 25% of the gross in commission and $200 a month. It turned out that Joe had married a local girl and her brother, a gentleman by the name of Biaggio "Brazos" Varisco, owned a large cotton farm in Mudville and several airplanes for crop dusting. Joe must have gone into

business with him, which explains why he was approaching me with this crop dusting opportunity. Sadly, Joe would be killed many years later crop dusting in Delray Beach, Florida when he had a mid-air collision with a flock of large cranes.

Joe told me that his company's Travel Air was located at Mudville, Texas on the Brazas River and if I wanted the job, I was to come over to his field and pick the airplane up. It would be fully fueled and I could leave for Florida the next morning.

I immediately accepted the job and on September 18, 1945, I found myself flying from Mudville, Texas to Dania, Florida in Joe's Travel Air B4000 (side number NR6283). Equipped with the more powerful Wright J-5 220 horsepower engine, this Travel Air, in my humble opinion, was one of the best dusters ever made and carrying 1200 pounds of dust in it was a breeze.

I undertook this 1200 mile cross country without charts. I simply flew east along the Gulf Coast until I needed fuel. Then I would land at the nearest airfield in sight, refuel, update my position, and continue.

This airplane could really perform and as I sped along, I thought I was in high heaven and marveled at my good luck. That is, until I encountered a heavy rainstorm in Louisiana and discovered that the J-5's magnetos, which are mounted on the front of the engine, were not fond of being wet. They operated intermittently, but I managed to stay airborne until I could find a suitable airport to make an emergency landing and let them dry out. In all, I made

I am standing in front of Joe Basso's 1929 Travel Air (side number NR6283) in Dania, Florida. My first solo long cross country flight, I flew from Mudville, Texas to Hollywood, Florida without charts. I refueled at airports of opportunity as needed.

refueling stops at Lafayette, Louisiana (where I stayed overnight); Gulfport, Mississippi; Pensacola, Florida; and Gainesville, Florida; before landing 17 hours of flight time later at Hollywood.

I now had nearly 770 total flight hours of which only 29 were flown during nighttime and none on instruments. I was pretty much a day, VFR, fair weather pilot.

Sunrise Dusting Company

In October 1945, Joe sent me to Ft. Pierce where I flew his Travel Air to help the Sunrise Dusting Company catch up on their tomato dusting, which required lots of copper insecticide. The pilots and operators of this service were a great bunch of guys

and pilots and we all got along great. For the record, their names were Jim Morris, Cliff Cooner, Jack Pollenger, and Tex Ethridge.

At this time, they were flying military surplus U.S. Army PT-17 Stearmans and U.S. Navy N3N-3's (Yellow Peril). My trusty Travel Air would outperform both of these airplanes.

The Stearman, for instance, was designed as a training plane for the military and the design of the wings was not made for carrying heavy loads. The N3N, on the other hand, carried a much better load and as far as I was concerned, it flew very well as a crop duster, even though it was rather heavy on the aileron controls. I enjoyed flying the N3N.

Later, the dusting community as a whole installed Pratt and Whitney

R985 engines, which doubled the horsepower on both airplanes. Various companies also made replacement all-metal high lift wing kits to replace the original wood and fabric design. These modifications made these airplanes respectable dusters.

However, I personally preferred the Travel Airs and the 1929 Straight Wing Wacos. For instance, my 1929 Travel Air could carry up to 1200 pounds on 220 horsepower whereas a 450 horsepower Stearman would struggle with a 1000-pound load. I know that many duster pilots of this era would disagree with me, as after World War II they started using war surplus Stearmans because they were plentiful and cheap to buy. So perhaps they never had a chance to fly the old biplanes.

Crop dusting in the Ft. Pierce area from a pilot's standpoint was really great. The fields of tomatoes were usually in 100 acre or more blocks with no obstructions. All I had to do was take off with a heavy load, fly to a big tomato patch, descend to a cruising altitude of three or four feet, dispense the copper or insecticide, pull up at the end, turn around, and once again descend to cruising altitude to lay another swath of dust. This was repeated many times until I had the dusted the whole field.

The swaths were usually 30 to 40 feet wide and my goal was to have the dust descend gently onto the tomato plants. I knew that if I had done the job properly, it would look like I had dusted all of the plants with a powder puff. I thought it was a great way to fly and make a living.

There was another crop dusting company in the Ft. Pierce area owned by J.R. McDaniel. At that time, he was using Command Aires, and his two pilots, Chuck Stone and Tommy Shaw, were good guys also. As time went on, Chuck and Tommy formed their own company and in later years acquired the Sunrise Airport and McDaniel's crop dusting business. They were very successful but Tommy died prematurely leaving Chuck Stone alone to run the business. Chuck Stone turned this dusting company into a huge success.

I continued to fly in a variety of Joe's Travel Air's until the Ft. Pierce season ended in November 1945. His contracts slowly fell off and there was not enough work for me.

Return to J.L. Schroeder and Cubs

By this time, J.L. had returned to Florida for his spring dusting contracts so I left Joe in December 1945 to fly Piper J-3 Cubs for J.L. for a 30 percent commission.

I was not particularly fond of dusting in a Cub with its small, cramped cockpit and underpowered engine. In fact, there is a short entry in my logbook dated May 20, 1946 that laments "Travel Air is tops." Nonetheless, I was enjoying flying from my old home field of Pompano and J.L. kept me fairly busy during the holidays.

The Cubs were making us money because we could land anywhere, including dirt roads and highways, to reload and refuel. This is why I almost got a speeding ticket in a Piper Cub.

While we were using some of the lesser traveled roads to operate from in the Pompano area, a highway patrolman drove up and threatened to give us speeding tickets for exceeding the speed limit while operating from the road. Apparently not familiar with the performance characteristics of a J-3 Cub, he soon discovered that with a takeoff speed of about 45 miles per hour we left the ground prior to the posted speed limits. The same for landing.

But he did not give up. Instead, we were ticketed for exceeding the maximum width of a vehicle allowed on a highway. He had us there with a wingspan of 35 feet but this whole affair turned out to be a futile effort on his part as nothing happened to us and we just kept on using the road.

Business slowly picked up after the New Year and by springtime it was booming, so much so that my two-week check in March 1946 was for $377.10, the most money I had ever made in my life. This would be equivalent to about $4,674 in today's dollars.

R.B. Rocker

In early 1946, a gentleman by the name of R.B. Rocker from Portal, Georgia worked a deal with J.L. Schroeder to operate two or three of Schroeder's airplanes in a revenue splitting deal. Rocker was not a pilot but a contact man and he was fairly successful at obtaining crop dusting contracts from the farmers.

So I flew dusting missions from either Schroeder's or Rocker's side of the fence. It didn't really matter to me as I got the same pay.

Rocker was a large man and also a very smooth talker, but every so often his exaggerated manner would annoy me a bit. He owned a 1941 Chevrolet business coupe with a big bull's eye painted on the top so we could tell which car was his when we were dusting. Well, one time when I was flying, he had me so aggravated that I decided to have some fun with him when I noticed that he was driving down the road.

What I did was to approach his car from the rear and slow the Cub down to match the speed of his car. Then I dropped down behind him so low that my wheels were nearly running on the road so that he could see me coming in his rear view mirror.

R.B. Rocker (right) was my contact man for many years. Bill Hope is on the left.

Whether he actually saw me or not, I do not know, but I picked up a little speed, bounced my wheels off the top of his car, and then kept on going.

Even though we aggravated each other at times, Rocker was really a very nice guy. He was really a jolly fellow and we shared many a laugh between us. By chance, his wife attended the same school in Pompano as I did and we met frequently at school reunions. Their son Bobby and I stay in contact with each other to this day.

I also doubted Rocker's business abilities. One time in 1948, we were in Statesboro, Georgia preparing to dust peanuts with sulfur dust. I went with Rocker to the fertilizer place that sold insecticides, as he wanted to be sure that they had enough. The proprietor asked Rocker how much sulfur he expected to use and Rocker told him a million and a half pounds. Well, I knew that number was preposterous but that proprietor believed him and went out and bought as much sulfur dust as he possibly could. I am sure that some of that sulfur dust is still sitting there waiting to be used.

Mysterious Loss of Lift

One time in 1946 I took off from our dusting strip in Holly Springs, South Carolina and I got about 15 feet in the air when my Cub just plopped to the ground, engine and propeller running normally. I have no other way of explaining this accident other than to say that the airplane literally stopped flying. Rocker saw me go down and came looking for me and I could hear him huffing and puffing around the tall corn stalks. But I was irritated with him for some forgotten reason and I wouldn't answer his calls. Instead, I just let him wear himself out until he found me.

When we returned to the dusting field, we found out that the same phenomenon had happened to four other airplanes flying in the same area as me at almost exactly the same time. Two Stearmans and a N3N had crashed, as well as a Cub, whose pilot, a man by the name of "Speedy" Goza, was killed. No one could explain what happened.

I continued to fly for Rocker until August 1947 when I decided to end our professional relationship. We remained good friends, but I much preferred dusting for J.L. and the Sunrise Dusting Company, flying a Piper Cub and N3N biplane.

Dusting in the Carolina's

In May 1946, J.L. sent me north in Piper J-3 Cub NR 33037 to chase profitable dusting contracts throughout South and North Carolina. I flew from several different sites, including Fairforest, and Inman. In one week alone in July, I made $683.53 (equivalent to about $8,475 in today's dollars). But I was earning my pay, coping with various engine failures and dodging telephone cables, power lines, and other obstacles in small, tightly enclosed fields.

Mostly Avoiding Wires and Cables

During one slightly terrifying flight on May 24, 1946 I clipped some

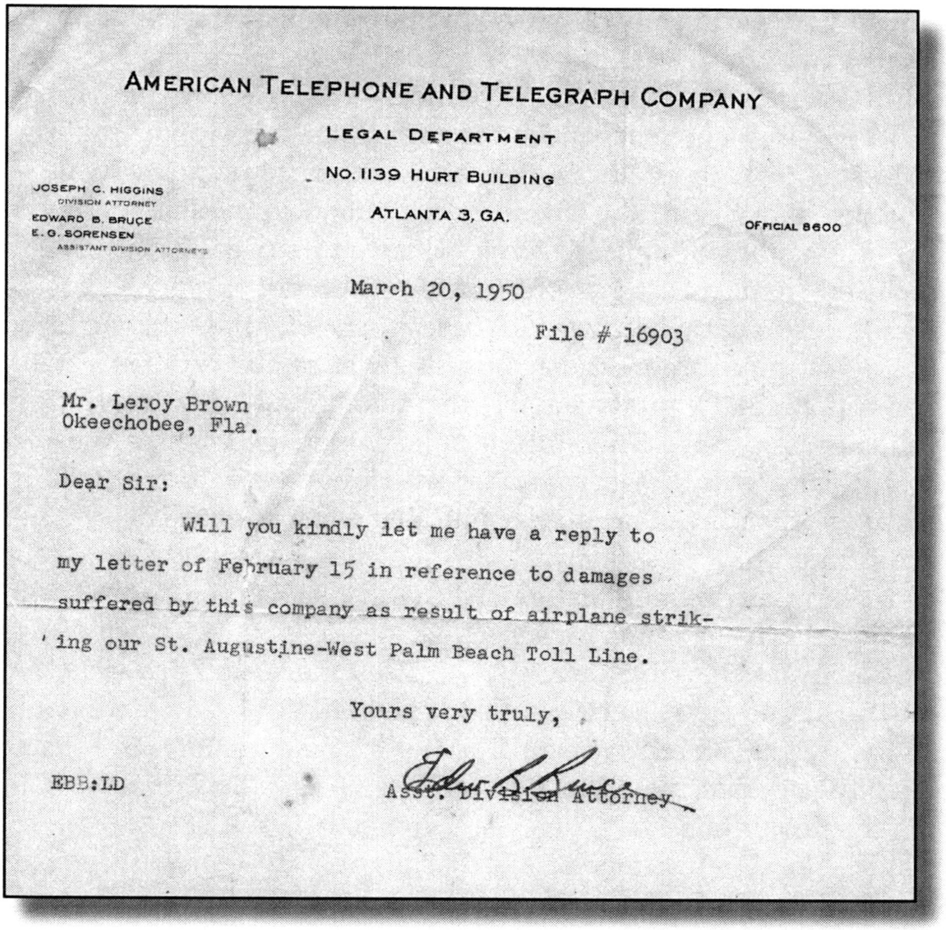

AMERICAN TELEPHONE AND TELEGRAPH COMPANY

LEGAL DEPARTMENT

No. 1139 HURT BUILDING

ATLANTA 3, GA.

JOSEPH C. HIGGINS
DIVISION ATTORNEY
EDWARD B. BRUCE
E. O. SORENSEN
ASSISTANT DIVISION ATTORNEYS

OFFICIAL 8600

March 20, 1950

File # 16903

Mr. Leroy Brown
Okeechobee, Fla.

Dear Sir:

Will you kindly let me have a reply to
my letter of February 15 in reference to damages
suffered by this company as result of airplane striking our St. Augustine-West Palm Beach Toll Line.

Yours very truly,

EBB:LD

Asst. Division Attorney

During my crop dusting career I estimate that I hit about 15 or so power or telephone lines. Some breakages resulted in letters such as the one above, which I ignored.

peach trees as I abruptly nosed down to avoid colliding with an unexpected wire that stretched across the width of a field I was dusting.

What happened was that Rocker had secured a contract to dust some peach orchards that belonged to Mr. Ponder, the owner of the Ponder Ice Cream Store. I asked Rocker if there were any wires at the field and he told me no, that the field was nice and clear. Lie.

I got half way across the field and there were some big wires staring at me. Well, I quickly dropped into the top of the peach trees and fortunately did not hit any of the wires. I somehow managed to escape without damage to me or the airplane although I did fly back with a lot of peach branches stuck in my landing gear.

Three days later, I was not so lucky and did hit a high line, which thankfully broke. I once again avoided serious damage to the airplane, but the event frightened me so much that I wrote "scairt to hell" in my logbook.

I estimate that during my 30-year crop dusting career from 1945 to 1975, I probably broke about 15 telephone lines, power wires, or suspension cables. Most of the time, the wire would entangle itself in the fixed landing gear and then simply stretch off the pole and snap.

Smaller wires usually break fairly easily, but if you hit a large wire on a high-tension pole, that's pretty much where you are going to stay. Therefore, we were always very cautious around high-tension wires. But one day I nearly got strung up.

I was dusting an unfamiliar field and pulled up out of some peach trees to find myself looking directly at a great big, brand new, steel high-tension wire tower. The only reason I lived to tell tale is that they had not yet strung the power lines.

Of course, the greatest fear of all duster pilots is that a wire does not break and throws the airplane to the ground. The steel propeller on the Travel Air was capable of snapping most wires, but the Cub had a wooden propeller and was not quite so strong.

For example, a duster pilot friend of mine by the name of John Riley was dusting in Pahokee, Florida when he hit a wire and it wrapped around his wheel. But the wire did not break and instead was winding him around the pole as he helplessly circled in an ever-tightening ring. He finally cut the throttle and intentionally crash-landed to avoid a midair collision into the pole. Thankfully, he walked away unhurt.

I nearly encountered a similar fate myself when dusting in a Cub in Spartanburg when I hit a wire that immediately wrapped around my wheel. The wire did not break and instead starting slowly pulling itself off a sequence of poles while slowly stretching. I immediately applied full power and I was able to fly straight ahead but my airspeed was slowly decaying. Helpless to do anything else, I was on the verge of a stall when the wire finally broke off the third pole. I managed to fly the airplane very slowly back to the airport with all that wire dragging behind me.

God Bless Piper Cub NR33037

The Piper Cub I primarily flew for J.L. was NR33037, which was equipped with a Continental 65 horsepower engine. I first flew that airplane on March 8, 1946 and accumulated nearly 700 flight hours in it between then and July 31, 1947.

J.L. sent me all over the south in NR33037, including 1900 mile trips as far west as Fabens, Texas to service dusting contracts and 700 miles trips as far north as Inman, South Carolina. If we were flying somewhere where we needed loaders, I would let them sit on the struts and hold on to the inside. Later I let them sit on the doorframe with their feet inside and we looked like very good friends gathered around a card table. So much for weight and balance concerns.

I knew that airplane like it was part of me. In fact, I flew it so much that they had to replace the rudder pedals, which I had completely worn down, and the strut that I grabbed

My trusty companion, Piper J-3 Cub NR33037, which had been converted to duster duty. Owned by J.L. Schroeder, this airplane and I shared many crop dusting adventures together as I flew it nearly 700 flight hours between March 8, 1946 and July 31, 1947.

to climb into the airplane. But it was aging badly. I was flying NR33037 one time when the right wheel fell off. I managed to land on one wheel and gradually slowed the airplane down until the right wing gently touched down. There was only slight damage to the propeller and it was soon back in the air again. Another time the rudder completely fell off, hanging on only by its cables and banging against the tail.

My final engine failure in NR33037 was not my first in that airplane. While crop dusting in Inman, I could tell the engine was sick and not running right. I advised J.L. that it was time for an engine change. He told me to keep flying and on July 17, 1946, the engine failed while I was making my first dusting pass. I managed to land without damage in the shortest cow pasture you have ever seen. I got out and walked back to where Schroeder was standing. As I got close to him, he cleared this throat and said, "Ahem, I will sell my half out cheap." I burst

out laughing and a day later, I was back in NR33037 behind a new engine.

A really serious problem was that the Cub's fabric was wearing out. Finally, it got so bad that I told Schroeder I could not fly it anymore because the fabric was too rotten and I was afraid that it might fail. He told me to take it to Hendersonville, North Carolina to have it recovered. On my flight up, there was a sudden explosion and the airplane shuddered. One of the sections of fabric between the ribs had blown out. While I was dealing with that problem, there was an additional series of detonations and I lost two more sections. The airplane was hardly flying but I kept it in the air and barely made it to Oscar Meyer's airport at Hendersonville. There A.C. Howe, who had previously worked for Schroeder as a mechanic, recovered the whole airplane and in due time it was back in service.

My Next Airplane

A simple entry in my logbook on October 29, 1946 summarizes it best: "The Browns bought a Vultee BT-15 today. Army surplus. $200."

I purchased the BT-15, which was built mostly out of plywood and equipped with a Wright 440 horsepower engine, from surplus military sales in Jackson, Tennessee. Getting used to that powerful 440 horsepower engine after flying nothing but 65 horsepower Piper Cubs was exciting.

My logbook notes that when I tried to fly that airplane back to Ft.

This is a Vultee BT-15 Valiant, a World War II basic training airplane, similar to the one I purchased in 1946.

Pierce the day after purchasing it, I flew "all over hell." What happened was that I was accompanied on this airplane-buying trip by a fellow crop duster by the name of Cliff Cooner. He bought a BT-13 because he wanted the Pratt and Whitney engine, which he considered more reliable than the Wright engine I purchased. He would soon regret this decision.

We had one map between us for the return trip so I told Cliff to take it and I would follow him. It was nighttime by the time we departed and after a while, I noticed we seemed to be wandering all about. I was looking around for landmarks when I suddenly realized we were over water.

I had not been paying attention to our navigation so I did not know whether we were lost over the Atlantic Ocean, the Gulf of Mexico, or some other large body of water. Out of the corner of my eye, I spotted some lights to the east of us and I motioned for Cliff to follow me. Heading east when you think you might be over the Atlantic Ocean tends to make one pause, but they were the only lights I could see.

Then to make matters worse, Cliff indicated to me that his engine was failing. Fortunately, as the lights slowly came into clearer view we identified a rotating beacon, which indicates an airport. So we landed at what turned out to be Dunnellon, Florida, which is located about 50 miles southwest of Gainesville and only about 20 miles inland from the Gulf of Mexico.

Once on the ground I asked Cliff why he was wandering all over the place and he said, "I lost the map." We spent the night in a hotel and

My 1929 Travel Air N648H, which I left in a passenger configuration and did not convert to duster duty. It is now on display at the Experimental Aircraft Association (EAA) museum in Oshkosh, Wisconsin.

returned to the field in the morning but Cliff refused to fly his Vultee because of the engine problems. So he flew back to Ft. Pierce with me.

Two or three days later, Cliff was talking to Jack Pallinger, another crop duster and mechanic, about leaving his airplane behind. Jack said, "I'll go ahead and get that airplane for you. I can fix that engine." So, I flew Jack back up to the airport and he ran the engine for a while and concluded that it was running fine.

We both took off and we didn't get more than eight miles from that airport when Jack's engine quit.

He made a successful emergency landing in a swamp, but his airplane turned over after landing and came to rest inverted. I circled the crash site and did not see Jack emerge. I was growing concerned and since I was wearing a parachute, I was just about to jump over the side to go down and save him when he finally crawled on top of the airplane.

He waved to me and I flew back to Dunnellon to notify the authorities. Monitoring the situation, after two days, Jack still had not been located by the search parties, so I flew back and successfully relocated him, directing the search parties to him. Jack had sat on top of that Vultee all that time awaiting rescue, puzzled by why no one was showing up. When he finally returned to us, he was one happy aviator and except for mosquito bites and hunger, he was fine.

It was never my intention to convert the Vultee into a duster and I flew it just for fun, eventually selling it for about $800. A few years after the sale, I received a call from the Sheriff's

Department in Greensboro, North Carolina stating that they were getting ready to auction it off for unpaid bills. I was told that if I wanted to keep this airplane, I had best get up there and pay all the invoices. I tried to explain to the deputy that I had sold the Vultee a long time ago but he replied that he didn't care. The previous owner had never registered it and the Vultee was still in my name.

I flew to Greensboro and to my amazement, the Vultee had been painted black with "Alaska Airlines" crudely drawn in silver paint down the fuselage in big letters. I paid about $50 in bills and took custody of the airplane. I flew it back to Florida and

soon thereafter, sold it again for $1,800. Truly a moneymaking airplane, considering I received $2,600 in return for my original $200 investment.

Move to Delray Beach

During these adventures, I continued to fly J.L.'s Piper Cub on various dusting contracts. But business started slowing down in Ft. Pierce at the end of the season so in November 1946, J.L. moved me to Delray Beach, Florida for dusting contracts there.

Unfortunately, business was not much better there and even worse for the holidays. I was also growing pretty tired of flying the Cub and in March

I am heading out to spray peaches in Spartanburg, South Carolina in this Stearman. The hopper system is clearly visible underneath the fuselage as well as the modified exhaust system for distribution of HETP. Note my nickname handwritten on the top of the photograph. I have been called worse.

The Stearman PT-17 I purchased in 1948 for $500 and converted into a duster.

1947, I started flying J.L.'s Stearman duster (side number NR49965) almost exclusively, frequently traveling north to Spartanburg, South Carolina for various contracts.

Southeastern Dusting Company

While flying from Spartanburg in 1947, I became close friends with Buck Moss, "Bub" Ginn, and Paul Brown, who were the owners of Fairforest Airport near Spartanburg. They were providing flight instruction using two Stearman biplanes (side numbers NR49964 and NR49965) flown by a former Army P-47 pilot by the name of Bill Hope.

These gentlemen noticed all the money that we were making crop dusting and wanted to get in the business. So with J.L.'s help, we formed the Southeastern Dusting Company and included R.B. Rocker as our contact man. Paul Brown converted

their two Stearmans into dusters while J.L. contributed some Cubs.

I flew for the Southeastern Dusting Company off and on until 1950 when they ran out of dusting contracts. We dissolved the company and we all amiably went our separate ways. In appreciation for my role, they gave me one of the Stearmans (NR49964).

One day Southeastern Dusting Company sent me to Winnsboro, South Carolina for some cotton dusting and I was working from a curved road adjacent to the Rockton-Ryan Railroad. As I made one landing, I felt my right brake grab so I got on the left brake and the airplane overturned.

I was now trapped upside down in the Stearman and then the engine caught fire. A passing motorist in a Model A truck came by and yelled, "Can I help you?"

I shouted back to him, "Do you have a fire extinguisher?"

He said "No, but I'll go get one." And then he left and never came back.

I managed to wiggle out on my own and somehow the fire went out on its own with no help from me. Paul Brown and his crew of mechanics came to Winnsboro and retrieved the airplane back to Spartanburg.

Spraying and Dusting

It was while working for the Southeastern Dusting Company in 1947 that I experienced my first use of fogging equipment for liquid chemicals. Liquid chemicals may be sprayed in pure form from liquid nozzles or mixed with exhaust to vaporize in a fogging effect.

The chemical we used was called hexaethyltetraphosphate or HETP for short. It was being used to control a curculio infestation on peaches. The curculio is a weevil that infests peaches in the same manner boll weevils attack cotton. The female curculio would puncture the peach to lay her eggs and the peach would eventually rot.

Southeastern had modified a Stearman's exhaust system where it was routed down to the right wheel to a small venturi. HETP was injected into that hot exhaust pipe and only a small amount of the poison would be dispensed. Corvis oil, which was used by skywriters, was also injected into the exhaust so we could see our swaths, as the spray was so small.

We were briefed that HETP was really bad stuff and we took all sorts of precautions while handling this highly toxic insecticide, including the use of protective suits and rubber gloves, which was nearly unbearable in the hot weather. However, it turned out that HETP was ineffective in controlling the pests and after we spilled some on ourselves without anyone getting ill, we discarded our protective gear.

The good news for me during this same time was that I was given the opportunity to return to flying a Travel Air (side number N346W).

This particular Travel Air was originally built as a passenger-carrying airplane and was purchased by J.L. from an owner in Kentucky. H.R. Carney, my fellow Cub pilot and one of the best in the business, was assigned to pick up the airplane, which had a tank engine in it. A tank engine was a water-cooled OX5 engine that had been converted to an air-cooled OX5 engine of 100 horsepower.

Carney told me that he had a hard time climbing through the Smokey Mountains during his trip due to the low horsepower. A Continental 220 horsepower engine from a PT-17 Stearman was installed and this helped its flying a whole bunch. Of interest, the aforementioned OX5 tank engine is of this writing in storage in Ocala, Florida.

The bad news for the Travel Air was that I was landing on a dirt strip when the left wheel fell into a small hole and the airplane nosed over. The left wheel was broken and the accident only damaged the propeller and a wing tip, all of which were quickly repaired.

Striking an imposing figure in front of my own Stearman in Ft. Pierce, Florida. I must have forgotten to wear my white scarf.

Going Independent

Seeking to add extra sources of income, I wanted to get some dusting contracts on my own outside of my work for J.L. So in January 1948, at Ft. Pierce I purchased a Stearman duster (side number NR62559) for $500. For the first time I worked independently and I handled my own dusting contracts.

Now the reader may wonder why I purchased a Stearman after all my disparaging remarks about its suitability for dusting. The answer is simple: they were cheap, low-time, and readily available.

J.L. remained a good friend and I continued to work for him either full or part-time throughout the 1950's, dusting cotton, peanuts, citrus, and peaches across Florida, Texas, South Carolina and Georgia. J.L. eventually retired to Delray Beach and closed his dusting business, selling off his assets individually rather than the company as a whole. We remained close and frequently visited each other until his death.

Broken Flight Cables

In 1948, I purchased Travel Air NR154V from Joe Basso and paid $300 for it. Of all the airplanes that I have owned over the years, I consider 154V to be my favorite.

On January 6, 1949, I was asked to dust the inside of the Markham Brothers tomato canning plant in Okeechobee, Florida, where I lived at the time. Apparently, the flies were really bad inside the plant and they wanted me to dust it with DDT.

So they opened the wide doors to the canning plant and I flew towards the building very low and very fast in my Travel Air. Just before reaching the building, I opened the hopper door and pulled up sharply, forcefully propelling the released dust right through the plant.

I repeated the maneuver several times and then my elevator cables snapped. It was a horrible experience.

I found that I had aileron control and I could push the stick forward and descend. But when I pulled the stick back, nothing happened. I immediately pushed the throttle forward to its stops and with the engine wide open and the elevator stabilizer set nose high I could actually climb about 75 feet a minute. I was leaning back in my seat forcing that airplane upward and if I had had anything bigger than a handkerchief on me, I would have jumped out.

I did not think there was any way that I was going to survive this extreme emergency. So I decided to write a note explaining to whoever found my body what had caused the accident.

It is interesting how an aviator's mind works in times of crisis. My primary concern when I resigned myself to the fact that I was going to crash and die was that I did not want any of my fellow crop dusters thinking the accident was caused by pilot error on my part.

As I started writing the note, I wondered exactly where the elevator cable had broken. So I looked down at the control stick and was astonished to see the broken elevator cable flapping where it had snapped off the rear of the stick. I discovered that I could reach down, grab the broken cable, and actually control the airplane.

I slowed the airplane down to a decent airspeed and I found that with the reduced air pressure I was able to pull the nose up. I set myself up for an approach to land at Okeechobee Airport. I made several passes at the airport and actually touched down once, but I was going so fast that I could not get the tail down. Securing the engine was not an option because I would surely nose over at such a high rate of speed.

It turned out that two people on the ground were watching all these wild maneuvers, a CAA inspector by the name of Buck McLain and a friend of mine named Joe Araldi. They thought I had gone crazy or was drunk.

Somehow, I managed to land the airplane and taxied back to the hangar near to where they were standing. I climbed out of the cockpit but I was shaking so bad that I could not stand up and fell to the ground. They walked over and McLain asked me "What have you been drinking? You're drunk."

I told them to look inside the cockpit and they were stunned when they saw the broken cables. McLain

An unknown farmer in Spartanburg, SC stands beside the Travel Air (side number N346W) I was using to dust at that time.

said, "I wouldn't have believed that you could have landed."

The reason the cable broke is that in the Travel Air the stick protrudes through the belly of the airplane where it makes connections with the control cables. We would put a sock around this point to keep the dust out of the cockpit. But dust and liquid had gotten in there and corroded the cables, which are under tension. When they broke, the cables snapped back into the fuselage under my seat.

Joe Bamberg

A review of my logbook during this era shows me dusting nearly every day in one of four airplanes: a Travel Air, Stearman, Cub, or N3N. For fun, I flew either my own Vultee or a borrowed Taylorcraft and Aeronca Sedan.

I was primarily operating on my own as an independent crop duster, no longer affiliated with any particular crop dusting company although I would sporadically help J.L. or other dusting companies as needed. I dusted crops in Okeechobee with occasional side trips to South Carolina or Georgia for additional dusting contracts.

Eventually I partnered up with my good friend Tag Eure and his brother and we obtained dusting contracts through a contact man by the name of Joe Bamberg. He was nothing if not a memorable character because he had only one eye.

After Joe secured a contract, he would hand draw a map to show us where to go. These maps were generally very crude but we knew the area so well that the fields were relatively easy to find and we were aware of all the hidden dangers that might pull us from the sky.

Occasionally, however, I would be asked to dust an unfamiliar field and I would be particularly attentive to any possible obstructions, despite what Joe might say about it being clear.

One early morning in Statesboro, Georgia, several crop dusters including myself and Tag Eure, along with mechanic Carl Hendrix, were gathered at the Nick Nack café for breakfast. While we were eating, one of the group outfitted one-eyed Joe's Kaiser automobile with small firecrackers attached to the spark plugs.

After we finished eating, we all went outside to watch old Joe crank up his car. The instant he hit the starter switch there was a loud explosion under the hood followed by clouds of smoke. I didn't realize that Joe could move so fast. He opened the door to his car, jumped out, and I don't think his feet hit the ground as he ran away at about 400 miles per hour. I will never forget the terrified look on his face.

We were all laughing and Joe joined in with us when he regained his wits. Other customers came running out to see what happened but we all left in a hurry as it was only 4:00 a.m. and we didn't want to be around when the police came. I still laugh to myself when I think of this practical joke.

Flying the Birds

One day while dusting in Okeechobee, I went to fly my Travel Air and as I was checking the oil, I found a bird's nest wedged between the oil tank and firewall. There were three eggs and I was going to throw them out when I thought to myself, "I really don't want to do that."

I put my oil rag on top of the eggs and went and flew for half of the day. When I landed, I took the rag off the nest and their mother flew over to sit on the unharmed eggs. She was a mockingbird and we repeated that routine every day until the eggs hatched.

Even after they hatched when I would check the oil, they would still be sitting there with their little mouths open. I would cover them, fly, land and return to uncover them where they would be greeted by their mother. One day they were gone, but they sure got a lot of instructional flying time before they flew on their own.

Birds of a Different Feather

While dusting peaches from Fairforest Airport in 1949, I encountered some CAA inspectors who were intent on clipping wings. I was loading my Travel Air 154V and as usual, I was by myself so early in the morning. Mother Nature called so I left the Travel Air at very slow idle for a few minutes. We always left engines running because they were hard to start alone. While attending to business, I heard the engine suddenly quit. This surprised me because it had never stopped before. When I returned after a few moments, I found two men standing by my airplane. As I walked up one asked me a rather stupid question, "Are you flying this airplane?"

My favorite airplane of all that I have owned or flown: my Travel Air 4000, side number 154V, converted to duster duty. It was burned in an accidental fire. The wreckage was abandoned but many years later I received a phone call asking if I would sell the airplane. I was still listed as the registered owner and the gentleman wanted to reuse the n-number.

Inasmuch as I was covered in dust with goggle tracks around my face, it should have been quite obvious what I was doing. They identified themselves as CAA inspectors from the Spartanburg office. They informed me that it was a violation to leave an airplane with the engine running.

I became a little hot under the collar with this intrusion and I told them that if they were the ones who shut the engine off, then they could jolly well just crank it up again for me. After some unkind words between us, they decided to help me start the engine, which they did. They mentioned that they had come out to Fairforest Airport to rent an airplane to go somewhere and upon their return, a violation would be forthcoming.

Anyway, as I was taxiing out with a load, they preceded me in an Aeronca Sedan and made a sharp climbing right hand turn out of a left hand traffic pattern, which is illegal. Needless to say, that afternoon I went to the CAA office and greeted them with the fact that I was filing a violation against them for reckless flying. After a heated discussion, we both agreed to drop the whole thing.

Losing My Travel Air 154V

While dusting in Spartanburg in June 1949, disaster struck. At Fairforest Airport, the usual group of motley aviators, including Bill Hope, Paul Brown, Slim Clayton, Buck Moss, and others were sitting in the office doing nothing in particular other than talking about airplanes. It was a very windy day so there was no crop dusting going on.

For the lack of something to do, Slim, a wealthy moonshiner who liked to fly, took some garbage outside, and of all things to do on a windy day, decided to burn the trash pile.

Unknown to us inside, some of the sparks and ashes were blown onto my Travel Air 154V and set it on fire. Suddenly someone noticed and we all rushed out of the office, someone grabbing a garden hose in a futile effort to put out the flames. All the fabric was burned off my airplane and some of the wood in the wings. I didn't have a fire extinguisher, but I did have a camera so I took a movie of my airplane burning.

The fire also consumed a Cessna UC78 owned by Fairforest Airport parked next to my Travel Air. I was heartbroken at losing my favorite airplane of all time. Despite his wealth, Slim never offered to pay me for the airplane and I did not have insurance, so I left the charred remains in place.

Many years later, I received a call from a fellow in Illinois who had found the remnants. He asked if he could buy them but I just gave them to him.

I never owned another Travel Air in the dusting configuration, although through the years, I have owned several others in a passenger configuration. One of these Travel Air's (side number N648H), is now on display in the Experimental Aircraft Association's (EAA) museum at Oshkosh, Wisconsin.

Pleasure Airplanes

For pleasure flights, in 1950, I purchased a Taylorcraft from Joe Marrs for $500 and in 1951, I purchased a 1941 Culver Cadet (NC32482). Make no mistake about it, I loved to fly and I took every opportunity to do so. My friends kidded me that I was like a postman who liked to go for walks on his days off.

In 1951, I purchased a Vultee BT-13, my first all-metal airplane. The first time I flew it to Spartanburg I was greeted by Bill Hope, a flight instructor at the airport with whom I had become close friends.

I jumped out of the airplane, walked out on the wing and hopped up and down shouting excitedly, "Hot damn, I finally got one with iron wings." Bill was a former P-47 pilot during World War II and to this day, he has never let me forget my exuberance.

Instrument Rating

Squeezed between all my crop dusting flights is an entry in my logbook on August 3, 1950, that simply reads "Link." In the comments section it states, "Airline training done by David Lee Smalley, Registrar." I was caught in bad weather too many times and I decided it was about time that I got my instrument rating.

For readers unfamiliar with pilot ratings, instrument training permits a pilot to fly solely by reference to instruments inside the airplane without the need to look outside. The training is intensive and a successful applicant must pass a written examination, an oral examination, and a flight test. Once completed, a pilot is then authorized to fly in instrument meteorological conditions, which is typically clouds and poor visibility.

In those years, a basic instrument flight simulator called the Link Trainer was used for ground instruction. Created by Edwin Link, it consisted of a single-seat, small wooden cockpit complete with flight instruments. The device was mounted on a base and connected to an instructor station. Covered by a solid canopy to simulate blind flying, the student pilot had no view

My BT-13 with all-metal wings sitting at the airport in Okeechobee, Florida.

of the outside and the trainer could be rotated through all three axes of flight: pitch, roll and yaw. It was also not air conditioned, so you can imagine how hot it was in that torture device during sweltering Florida summers as the flight instructor pushed the student through various maneuvers.

Later, I flew to Homestead to get my instrument rating with the Airline Training Incorporated company owned by Bill Conrad, who was really a nice guy.

However, I decided not to start the course when I found out that instrument training was very expensive. Years later, however, Bill gave me my type rating checkrides in the B-17G and DC-3.

A short time later, I was crop dusting in Fort Lauderdale in a Stearman with a fellow crop duster named Wayne "Pinky" North. We were contracted to spray cattle with DDT to control flies. We were based out of Ben Bradley's airport and I had brought my Vultee BT-13 with me so that I could fly home to my family in Okeechobee each evening.

Bradley also owned Broward Aviation Company, which also had an instrument school. One day he asked me if I had an instrument rating. I told him no and that I did not have any money to get one. Ben said, "I'll tell you what I'll do. I'll give you your training rating if you give me your BT-13. You can still use it to go back and forth every day and I'll furnish all the fuel until you get your rating."

I decided right then and there that I did not have any particular use for

that BT-13 and started taking lessons. I found myself back in the hated Link Trainer again. My instructor's name was Hardy Roundtree, a good guy who tried his best to teach me airspeed, needle, and ball, the core flight instruments of instrument flight.

He kept hammering these instruments into me and I told Hardy that when I got home at night, I ran around my house hollering "Airspeed, needle, and ball."

He told me, "Aw, you'll get it."

I replied, "Well, I am not getting it, I don't like it, and I would like to drop the course." Hardy was not one to let a discouraged student quit, so he reassured me and I stayed.

Anyway, the time eventually came when he said, "You're ready." I thought he was crazy as I didn't feel ready but he contacted a CAA flight inspector. My ride was scheduled for August 21, 1951 in my own BT-13, which we had used for the actual flight portion of the training.

The CAA inspector was a man by the name of Paul Revere. He climbed into the front seat and I sat in the back seat under the hood with most of the instruments covered up, except for the dreaded airspeed indicator, needle and ball.

The first part was recovery from unusual attitudes. He would put the airplane through all sorts of maneuvers to disorient me and then give the airplane back to me to return it to level flight only by reference to flight instruments. That went well.

The next part tested navigation by flight instruments and once again, he maneuvered the airplane until he had me thoroughly confused as to our position. Then he returned the airplane to me and said, "Take me to the Miami range station and then land at Miami Airport."

I tuned in the Miami station, followed my procedures to locate myself, and then commenced the approach. As we reached 400 feet he announced, "You don't see the runways, abort the landing," to test my missed approach procedures. He then had me make two more approaches using more complicated maneuvers until he said, "Let's proceed to your alternate airport."

Well, I had not considered this would happen and did not have a preplanned alternate so I blurted out, "Palm Beach" and turned the airplane toward what I thought was its general direction. After a long silence, he said, "I don't think you are going to get there on this heading. You don't have a chart, do you?"

I knew I had just failed. I said, "I don't have my chart, I don't know where I am, and I am pulling the hood up. I quit." He said, "Well, Ok, if that's what you want to do," and he took control of the airplane and landed us back at Fort Lauderdale.

After we climbed out, he told me "Well, you really didn't do so bad, you were all right. I am going to give you an instrument rating. I knew you didn't have a chart and I had to pull it on you."

Now I had an instrument rating and like my commercial pilot rating before, I had not paid a penny to get it.

I now had a total of 3,238 flight hours, of which 3,138 were flown during the day and only 100 at night. I had no actual instrument time, but I did have 41 hours logged under the hood.

Instructing Instruments

Ben Bradley then offered me a job teaching instruments in the Link as he had a contract with a nonscheduled airline named U.S. Airlines and needed an instrument instructor.

Since it was the end of the fall growing season and all my dusting contracts were fading off, I agreed. In October 1951, I began to instruct for Bradley at Fort Lauderdale in the Link Trainer.

I really didn't know what I was doing and one day one of the captains came out of the Link and said, "Who in the hell said you knew how to instruct instruments? I never saw an ILS work like that. I am going to tell Bradley that you are not qualified."

I told him, "That's all right because I am going to quit anyways."

Many years later when I was a Captain with National Airlines, this very same pilot was hired and he got his very first trip with me.

He knew what was up as he settled into the cockpit and he said, "This is be kind to your copilot week."

I replied "No, this is every dog has its day week."

He weakly mumbled, "Please don't."

I then told him rather curtly, "No problem, you can sit there and do the paperwork and turn your time in. I am not going to recommend you." Well, his face just fell and when we landed back in Miami, I told him, "I was just kidding, I hope you have a good career."

Teaching Aerobatics

My instrument instructor career over, Bradley put me to work instructing aerobatics in a Waco UPF-7, which I could also use to fly back and forth to Okeechobee and my family. I was heading home one evening over Lake Okeechobee feeling pretty good so I rolled the airplane over and was flying upside down when the parachute in the front seat fell out into the water. Bradley was not too happy about that when I told him.

I found myself in some of the darndest positions in that Waco trying to teach hay miners how to fly aerobatics. After three or four hours of aerobatic instruction, I would return with black and blue bruising from all the jostling.

Career Move

I was very content with my life as a crop duster and part-time aerobatics instructor. Crop dusting was a real art in the golden days and it was a type of flying I really enjoyed.

Then, like my good friends Bill Longino and Jimmy Crawford before me, I received an offer to fly for an airline.

I was not interested.

Chapter Eight
National Airlines

Standing in front of a 14-passenger Lockheed Lodestar, I am wearing the four stripes of a National Airlines captain. Some said that the only time that the Lodestar was safe was when it was in the hangar but I had a great time flying it.

ational Airlines was founded by George T. "Ted" Baker in St. Petersburg, Florida, in 1934 with an award by the U.S. Post Office of AM-31, a 142-mile airmail route between St. Petersburg and Daytona Beach with intermediate stops at Tampa, Lakeland and Orlando. Inexplicably, Eastern Air Lines, one of the four largest airlines in the United States at that time and the dominant airline along the entire east coast, failed to bid on this small route, an oversight that Eddie Rickenbacker, President of Eastern Air Lines, soon regretted.

Quickly realizing that this short route could never be profitable, Baker petitioned the Post Office for authority to extend his airmail routes throughout Florida. Rickenbacker, annoyed at this small carrier's audacity, fought these applications vigorously, quickly realizing that any expansion by National Airlines constituted a competitive threat to Eastern's Florida routes. Rickenbacker accused Baker of being a "pirate" and soon afterward, National Airlines coined the slogan, "The Buccaneer Route" for use on their Florida timetables.

Under Baker's astute leadership, National Airlines steadily expanded its route system and moved its headquarters to Miami. In 1937 AM-31 was expanded to Miami and in 1938 National Airlines was awarded a new airmail route, AM-39, which provided service between Jacksonville and New Orleans with intermediate stops at Tallahassee, Pensacola, Marianna, Panama City, Mobile, and Gulfport.

George T. Baker, founder and president of Florida-based National Airlines. I flew with him several times.

In 1944, the Civil Aeronautics Board authorized National Airlines to extend AM-31 south to Key West and north to New York City, with direct service between Miami and New York. In 1946, AM-31 was extended again to Havana, Cuba.

To service these routes in the early 1950's, National Airlines used the 14-passenger, twin-engine Lockheed Lodestar; the 72-passenger, four-engine Douglas DC-4; and the 78-passenger, four-engine Douglas DC-6.

And this is where I came in.

Airline Application

In December 1951 my fellow crop duster, Wayne North and I, were talking in Ben Bradley's office. He told me he knew some pilots at National Airlines and that he was going down to Miami to try and get a job flying for them. I was completely taken by surprise and asked him, "Why would you want to do that? Why would you want to fly for an airline with all their restrictions?"

"Because I can't make any money crop-dusting," was Wayne's simple reply.

I was not interested in airline type flying, but when Wayne asked me to drive down with him, I agreed. So we arrived at National Airlines' Miami offices, which I later found out were located in a formerly abandoned hotel, and we proceeded to the employment office. Wayne asked to speak to Dave Amos, the employment

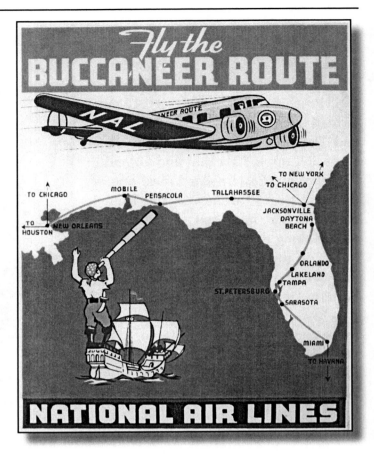

On January 26, 1952 I made my first line flight with National Airlines, a 4-day trip in a Lockheed Lodestar along "The Buccaneer Route" from Miami to New Orleans.

director, but his secretary, Peggy, told him that Amos was not available at that very minute. It was then that I realized that Wayne did not have an appointment but was simply cold calling the office.

We sat down to wait and Amos eventually stepped out. Wayne told him that he wanted to fly for National Airlines because he already knew some of their pilots, including Vic Fite and "Red" Beech, with whom he had instructed during the war. Amos had Wayne complete an application right in front of him to start immediately.

I heard Amos say to Wayne, "Well, I have to start a class next week and I need a few more pilots. Do you have any friends who might be interested in flying for an airline?" Wayne turned and pointed at me and said, "Mr. Brown, over there, flies."

I was taken aback and quickly shook my head and said, "I didn't come down here for a job."

Amos motioned me closer and said, "Why don't you want a job with the airlines?"

I told him, "I like crop dusting and to tell you the truth, I never thought about

My initial orientation to National Airlines consisted of posing for an identification badge, attending a four-day ground school, and then observing from a jump seat for 8 flights before flying the line as copilot.

I officially began my career with National Airlines on January 7, 1952 when I returned to Miami for my initial flight training in the Lockheed Lodestar. I was assigned an airline seniority number of 264, which was only a few numbers away from the bottom.

For those not familiar with this concept unique to the airline industry, this number would rule my life for my entire airline career. It determined my personal flying schedule, assignment to different airplanes, upgrades to captain, and even when I would be permitted to take vacation.

The way the seniority system works is that an airline pilot is given an overall seniority number based upon his or her date of hire and it is adjusted upward as pilots retire or leave the airline.

When I was first hired at National Airlines, George Baker, the founder and a qualified pilot, was senior on the list at number one. The top five was rounded out by E.J. Kershaw (hire date December 15, 1934) at number two; C.H. Ruby (hire date

215. Lowman, P. L.	12-3-51
216. Maynard, R. R.	1-7-52
217. Mennitto, F.	1-7-52
218. Lowe, H. H.	1-7-52
219. Brown, L. H.	1-7-52
220. McDaniel, J.R.Jr.	1-7-52
221. Howell, H.B.Jr.	12-15-52
222. Booze, G. L.	12-15-52
223. Spurlock, R. W.	12-15-52

I am number 219 on National Airline's pilot seniority list. I would rise to number 50 and I was on track for number 1 with Pan Am when I retired.

flying for the airlines." After asking me a few more questions about my flying time, Amos paused and then said "Why don't you come on in and try it, and if you don't like it you can quit. But this way you can help me fill my quota."

Wayne started egging me on, saying, "Go head, go ahead," so I finally relented and said, "Ok." Amos then had me fill out an application and he told us we were to return for ground school. At this point, I had more than 3,500 flight hours and little did I know what was in store for me as I had never been in any type of aviation school before.

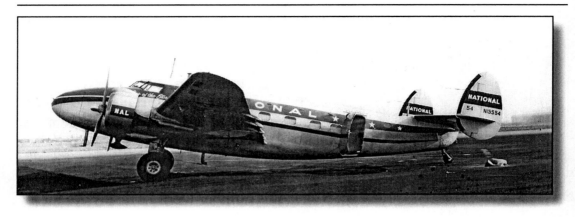

The Lockheed Lodestar's cockpit was freezing in the winter, stifling hot in the summer, leaked in rain, and was so noisy that the pilots had to communicate by hand signals. It was nicknamed the Lobster for its pot belly and I loved it.

January 16, 1935) at number three; J.M. Gilmour (hire date November 15, 1939) at number four, and H.H. Clark (hire date December 1, 1936) at number five.

In the airline industry, a pilot's monthly flying schedule is determined by bids for individual flights based upon seniority in your assigned airplane type. The process is simple. Those pilots with high seniority numbers get the schedule they bid for. Those with low seniority numbers do not. I didn't for a very long time.

Wayne and I started in the same class together with seven other classmates. Our orientation consisted of getting our picture taken for a security badge and then reporting to ground school. To my surprise, Wayne quit during the first week. I stayed for 29 years. Wayne later told me confidentially that he regretted that decision every day of his life, but there was no going back for him.

As will be seen, however, flying for National Airlines during the 1950's was not for the timid. During our first class, the chief pilot came in and welcomed us to the airline. He closed with the comment to move to Miami as we had a lifetime job. It turned out that he failed to mention that it might not be an uninterrupted lifetime job.

Service between Miami and New York was always highly seasonal, with northeasterners fleeing to Florida during the winter and scurrying back home during the summer. Florida was far from the tourist destination that it is now.

As a result, I would be subject to furlough when passenger loads disappeared during the off-season. To my surprise, I was furloughed five times during my first two years with the airline. But unlike other aviators, I always had crop dusting to fall back on. In fact, sometimes being a crop duster paid better than being an airline captain.

Lockheed's Twin-Tailed Celestials

The airplane I was being trained to fly was the second in a series of fast, economical airliners built by the Lockheed Aircraft Corporation that included the celestial names Electra, Lodestar and Constellation. The Lodestar, technically known as a Lockheed Model 18, carried 14 passengers and a crew of three, including a captain, copilot and a stewardess.

Baker, the President of National Airlines, selected the Lodestar because he felt the aircraft's speed advantage far outweighed other disadvantages. Eastern Air Lines, however, chose the DC-3 to replace their older aircraft. While the DC-3 could carry more passengers, 21 compared to the Lodestar's 14, the Lodestar purchase price was a great deal less and it was much faster than the DC-3 with a top speed of 276 miles per hour. Accordingly, whenever we were visually passing an Eastern DC-3 in flight, Baker's directions were that we notify passengers in our airplane of this fact and to make sure the passengers aboard the Eastern DC-3 also noticed us.

Lockheed Lodestar Training

My ground school training consisted of briefings on company procedures and the Lodestar's systems, none of which I understood. There were no manuals to study and, as it turns out, definitely no complicated systems on the Lodestar (which was nicknamed the Lobster). Before actual flight training I was assigned to take a Link Trainer class to learn airline instrument procedures. My instructor was Walt Mozo, a really nice guy, and somehow or another I managed to squeak through this little Link Trainer episode. When we finished, he walked over to me after I climbed out of that wooden torture device. He said, "I teach a lot of people Link, but undoubtedly you are the dumbest one I have ever had. You must have been a sheep herder."

I responded, "Well, when you are taught by a sharecropper, what do you expect?" He laughed and I headed to the flight line for my introduction to the Lodestar.

A day or so later, Captain Vic Fite, Wayne's friend and a Lockheed Lodestar check pilot, provided a familiarization flight. He was extremely disappointed when I told him about Wayne quitting.

We first walked around the airplane with Captain Fite showing me various things they looked at before each flight. We then climbed aboard this 14-passenger monster and as I settled into the copilot's seat, I thought to myself, "This is beyond me."

However, Captain Fite cranked it up, called ground control on the radio, of which there were many on the instrument panel, and the next thing I knew, he had me taxiing down to takeoff position. He kept reading and checking things contained in a checklist. Inasmuch as I had never heard of such a thing, I thought this guy was reading how to fly the airplane.

We were cleared to take off and he told me to open the throttles to 46 ½ inches of mercury as registered on the manifold pressure gauge. This was really something new to me, as I had never heard of such an instrument. So I opened the throttles to the darndest roar I have ever heard.

Of course, he was following through on the controls during my takeoff and the only way we could communicate was through an intercom system. As this machine leaped forward with the noise and acceleration, I thought to myself that I would never learn how to fly this beast.

However, after we got in the air with some altitude, he had me do turns, steep turns, and other things until I was more or less relaxed. We started our return to the Miami airport and I was still flying the airplane, my hands quite sweaty.

He really let me go too far with the landings as we bounced so hard I thought we were heading into orbit. I bet he wondered who had told this guy that he knew how to fly. But Fite was a very patient person and we did some more flying and landings and I began to catch on a bit. During some night training, I found out that the retractable landing lights on a Lodestar were about as bright as a flashlight with worn out batteries. I now had my three day and three night takeoff and landings in the Lodestar, so my training was considered complete.

We were told to buy our own uniforms and our official graduation ceremony consisted of someone walking into our classroom with a box of National Airlines pilot wings and passing them out, saying, "Here's yours, and here's yours, etc."

To show how short the training was, I reported to National Airlines on January 7, 1952 and I made my first flight in a jump seat on January 12, 1952.

Jump Seat Flights

Before we could be considered fully qualified to begin flying the line as copilots with passengers, we had to first ride in the cockpit jump seat as observers for about 15 or so hours.

My first jump seat flight was the Miami to Newark run in a four-engine DC-4. As I climbed aboard, I thought to myself my airline career would be short lived if I was assigned to this behemoth. I walked to the cockpit and the captain was Phil Wachtel. I introduced myself to him and he welcomed me aboard.

As I sat in the jump seat, I was overwhelmed by all the instruments, various radios, knobs, and switches and became convinced that perhaps my old Travel Air was the best way to go.

After the pilots went through a whole lot of motions, the engines were started and we started taxiing out towards the active runway.

I had on earphones to monitor the radio conversations and I could hear the copilot getting our air traffic control clearance to Newark, which consisted of the route we would fly and the altitude. I understood none of it and totally missed everything the controller said after, "Cleared to Newark via." I would later learn that when flying into major airports, you had to remain very alert as a common frequency on the radio was used by all airliners. They would call your flight number and issue various clearances, which at first were difficult to understand, especially by a "southern bean-picker." But I finally caught on to that and sometimes I knew what our clearance would be before I heard what they had to say.

As we approached the runway and took off, there was a lot of talk going on between Wachtel and the copilot about maximum power, V1, V2, rotate, gear up, flaps up, setting the propellers and Lord knows what else. I could fly my Travel Air duster with none of those shenanigans. I secretly hoped that this flight was going to turn out better than I thought it was.

We leveled off at our cruising altitude of 9,000 feet after much gibberish on the radio and turning here and there to stay on the airways. I had never been this high before and as a duster pilot I thought that if I got over 100 feet I might pass out due to lack of oxygen.

We continued toward what I guessed was the correct way to Newark and the pilots sat there as nonchalant as possible. Pretty soon, an attractive stewardess brought us coffee. The cockpit was much quieter than the Lodestar and I began to think that maybe this job wasn't too bad after all.

The pilots were continuously fooling with the radios and talking to various controllers. We were over the ocean much of the trip and they were using something called an ADF to try figuring out where they were. At least, that is what I thought.

As I listened on the earphones, I heard something about bad weather in Newark. Now I knew I was in the wrong job. We soon entered a cloud mass and it didn't seem to bother these guys at all as they kept right on going like nothing was wrong.

Then we got into some turbulence and the airplane shook in a motion I had never before felt and I was afraid it might come unglued. After about four hours of this, I heard the copilot talking to someone in Newark and after much conversation, we were cleared for the landing approach.

Now I knew we were in big trouble as we couldn't see a thing and I knew that what little instrument training I had would be useless in this stuff. We started down after having been cleared to land and I saw the altimeter get down to 400 feet. I braced for the crash that was coming because we still couldn't see anything out the cockpit windshield.

However, after much twisting, turning, descending, and a lot more gibberish on the radio I couldn't understand, we popped out of the clouds and the runway was straight ahead. I now knew this airline flying was not as easy as eating DDT in my crop duster and that perhaps my friend Wayne had made the right decision.

My next jump seat trips were to Idlewild, New York; Havana, Cuba, which was extremely exciting; and New Orleans, Louisiana. Things got better and I finished my training, deciding that this airline pilot stuff wasn't too bad after all. I was ready to fly the line on my own.

Standing tall and confident in front of a Lockheed Lodestar.

First Line Flight

My first National Airlines trip as copilot was on January 26, 1952. It was a four-day trip from Miami to New Orleans, departing Miami at night and stopping at Fort Myers, Sarasota, St. Petersburg, Tampa, Lakeland, Orlando, and Daytona before staying overnight at Jacksonville. The next morning we were scheduled to depart Jacksonville with stops in Valdosta, Tallahassee, Marianna, Panama City, Pensacola, Mobile and Gulfport before spending the night in New Orleans and then reversing the trip back to Miami.

As I walked through the terminal building, I was very self-conscious. I felt like everyone was looking at me and thinking that this guy must be brand new. I was sure they noticed that my airline uniform was pristine, my flight kit was gleaming, and that my suitcase was unscratched. But I made my way through to flight control where I met Captain John Hopper, my captain for this flight. I hoped he would take pity on me. After signing some papers, we walked out to our assigned Lodestar, walked around it, and then climbed aboard where we were greeted by a beautiful, blond stewardess named Norma Simon.

Quite naturally, this perked up my feelings, which were soon dashed as the flight progressed. After completing the checklists and making sure everything was in order, we took off in a noisy airplane with 14 passengers aboard. Hopper called for gear up and after much fumbling around on my part, I finally found the gear handle and retracted the gear. At the same time, he called for flaps up and there was more groping on my part before I got the job done. On the way to Ft. Myers, after a minimum of conversation between us, Hopper found out that this was my first line flight and I thought that it was probably going to be my last.

I can state unequivocally that I didn't know where I was or what I was doing that entire flight. Captain Hopper was essentially flying solo and if he had died during that flight, we would have all perished because I would have been of no help. It was definitely on the job training and I didn't feel like I was measuring up. I could tell that Captain Hopper was a little uneasy about having a first time idiot in the copilot's seat, but he never said a word.

In fact, I was so frustrated when we landed at Jacksonville that I was ready to quit. It was after midnight as I walked to our crew hotel with Norma and I told her that this was my first flight and that I didn't really like it. Norma told me that I was doing pretty well even though I had bounced the Lodestar on each landing that I made. She consoled me by telling me I should try it for at least another month and that I would find that after a while, I would like it. She was right.

On the subsequent leg of our journey, the next morning I also found out that even captains bounced the Lodestar on landing. After one prang, Hopper told me there were three ways to make a perfect landing

Another beautiful stewardess who flew for National Airlines, Marilyn Anne Johnson nee Talton, photographed on the boarding ladder of a DC-6.

in a Lodestar every time. The trouble was no one knew what they were. By the way, I was very thankful that the entire trip had been VFR.

Stewardesses

Norma was the first of many kind stewardesses to take me under their wing during my airline career. The Lodestar carried only one stewardess but as the number of passengers increased, as the airliners became larger, an appropriate number of stewardesses would be assigned.

When I first joined the airline, the stewardesses were required to be young, single, beautiful women with weight restrictions.

The stewardesses were subject to the same demanding training and in-flight performance checks as the pilots. Although the passengers thought that they were there only to make them

I took this 1954 photograph of stewardess Joan Chiles greeting passengers in Havana, Cuba. All National Airlines stewardesses were beautiful.

comfortable, they were highly trained for unforeseen emergencies and they were certainly capable of performing their duties. On rare occasions, they might call for help from the cockpit for an unruly passenger. I usually went back personally and I never had a problem after explaining to the offender that interfering with the duties of the flight crew was a federal offense and would be dealt with accordingly.

I must note that the stewardesses never failed to do nice things for the flight crew. They always kept us supplied with coffee or whatever else might be available on an all-night flight. And perhaps 30 minutes before our landing, they would bring hot towels up for us to refresh our face and hands. This was always welcome. I can truthfully say that we were a close knit group of people who shared love and respect for one another and I felt like this spilled over to our passengers, who were well cared for. After we all retired, it was always so nice to see them at reunions and many share a spot in my life to this day.

Next Leg

After arriving in Miami on our return journey, I had to turn in all the trip logs to flight control and check with crew scheduling about my next trip. They showed where it was all posted a month ahead of time and I discovered I had four days off and then I would make the same trip again. I went home to Okeechobee totally confused and totally worn out.

My next four-day trip was with Captain Willie Ropp, an older, very quiet gentleman who looked pretty gruff when I first met him. I was pretty sure that I wasn't going to like this.

After we were settled into the cockpit he turned to me and said, "Well, how long you been here?"

I told him that this was only my second trip. Time passed and he said, "Do you fly little airplanes?" I politely said, "Yes, Captain."

More time passed, and he said, "What was your favorite little airplane to fly?"

I told him that I was a crop duster but that my favorite airplane was the

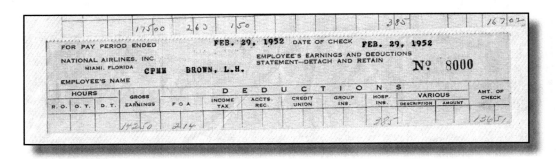

My first paycheck with National Airlines. I earned $142.50 for my first month. At the height of crop dusting season I could earn three times as much in just a few days.

C-3 Aeronca. Well, Captain Ropp's eyes just lit up and he exclaimed, "Oh, I just love C-3's!"

From that moment forward, we were best friends and he came off a hospital bed to attend my induction into the Florida Aviation Hall of Fame in 2009.

Shortly after this trip, one of our DC-6Bs crashed at Newark, killing many aboard. This accident was very unsettling to me as subsequent investigation found that the number three propeller had reversed in flight shortly after takeoff and at that low altitude and low airspeed, the crew lost control of the airplane. I knew my old Travel Air would never treat me in this manner.

Almost exactly a year later in February 1953, National Airlines lost another DC-6B when it disappeared over the Gulf of Mexico while flying from Tampa to New Orleans. The wreckage was eventually located 45 miles south of Mobile. In-flight failure of the airframe due to encountering a thunderstorm with extremely severe turbulence was found to be the probable cause of the accident. With this second crash, I thought seriously about saying goodbye to the airline industry and returning to the safety of crop dusting.

But I stayed and, lo and behold, I began to catch on. I thought I might actually like airline flying, even though the pay was in the poverty level. I could have made as much crop dusting in three days as I made in a month with National Airlines.

Flying the Lodestar

I have fond memories of flying the Lodestar. As a tail-dragger, the Lodestar required an inclined uphill walk to the cockpit. I cannot overstate how noisy the Lodestar cockpit was. We were forced to exchange hand signals for routine events such as lowering the landing gear.

The passenger cabin, though, was fairly quiet but required an awkward step over the plane's main wing spar that crossed the cabin, which provided the pilots an enjoyable view of the stewardess's legs as she crossed over. I could also tell when the stewardess was walking forward as the airplane had to be retrimmed to compensate for the additional forward weight. Pilots jokingly told the stewardesses that they could estimate their weight by the amount of trim that had to be applied.

During my trips I found that some of the captains were nice and some not so nice. All of them were tolerable though. Most would help you with your trouble spots, of which I had many. Some captains really seemed like they were unsure of what they were doing and really needed a good copilot to help them. All of the stewardesses were very nice to the flight crew.

Navigation along the Lodestar routes was mostly by pilotage and the various cities were located by tracking along the Old Spanish Highway or using low frequency radio ranges. These radio ranges worked wonderfully in good weather, but when needed most (in bad weather), performed poorly.

There were no instrument landing systems and if there was severe weather present at a scheduled stop, we might attempt a landing, but most times, we would simply pass over the airport to our next stop.

There was also no air traffic control and all radio communications were with National Airlines' own company radio who would relay messages to the various airports and facilities. When nearing an airport, we would report "in range" and the company radio would respond "CTF" which meant cleared to switch to tower frequency, if there was one. Most small airports did not have a tower. Communications with an airport tower would be the only contact with a governmental air traffic control agency during the entire flight.

When departing Jacksonville for points south, we would have fun with our main competitor, Eastern Air Lines. Our Lodestars cruised faster than Eastern's DC-3s and although Eastern had a flight leaving five minutes earlier than we did from Jacksonville, we would soon catch up with them near St. Augustine.

When we had them in sight, we would match their airspeed, lower the landing gear, and then slowly pass them only to accelerate with a sudden burst of power to show off our superior speed. We would then land at Daytona Beach ahead of them. Since both airliners were monitoring different company frequencies, it was not possible to talk to the other airline crew and we only exchanged hand gestures.

I found out some very unusual things occurred at the various stops along the way. At Tallahassee, three or four cats would run out and greet the Lodestar after we landed because they knew the stewardesses would give them some milk. I noticed later that these same cats did not go to any other airplane so at least they were happy to see us land in the Lodestar.

Flying the Lodestar in lousy weather was always a chore. If we were on a trip with a lot of rain and thunderstorms, we really earned our money making automatic direction finding (ADF) and low frequency range approaches without the assistance of a weather radar to guide us or autopilot to relieve hand-flying requirements. The ADF was unreliable in that the pointer would always point to lightning discharges, although this did help us avoid some of the worst area of the storms. Shooting low frequency range approaches where we had to listen on the earphones to fly the "beam" was very difficult because of interfering lightning static.

The Lodestar's engines also intensely disliked rain. They would both skip, bang, and backfire, generally acting up as if they were getting ready to quit. Engineers found that the reason this occurred was that heavy rain cooled the cylinder head temperature to the point where the valves started to stick.

The usual procedure when entering a heavy rain storm was to put the carburetor heat on, reduce the power to slow the airplane down a bit, turn the engines up to 2300 RPM, lower the landing gear, and then add enough power to keep the engines hot and maintain a good turbulence penetration airspeed. After a day of this, you were certainly worn out, but fortunately, this did not happen very often.

I also found out why all the captains carried a raincoat in their flight kit. The Lodestar's windshield leaked almost as much rain into the cockpit as was falling outside. So I purchased a rain coat that I put on my lap to stay somewhat dry.

In the wintertime, the cockpit was ice cold, and the captains usually had some of the passenger blankets brought to the cockpit to keep us warm. I also found that in icing conditions and snow, we had alcohol for the windshield on the outside to remove ice, but to remove ice from the inside of the windshield, the captains carried a putty knife. We would really have to watch for ice on the wings and we would turn the rubber deicing boots along the leading edge of the wing on and off periodically to remove any buildup. I did not like this kind of weather and stayed on the warmer, southern routes as much as possible.

Self-Loading Baggage

Sometimes things happened on the airline that are best kept quiet. Once I was on a Lodestar flight passing through St. Petersburg, Sarasota, and Ft. Myers, before arriving home at Miami. It was Christmas Eve and we had a full load of passengers. While we

With my mother in 1953 standing in front of a National Airlines Lodestar.

were still on the ground, two station agents from Miami approached me with a sad story. They had to be at work the following morning and, as this was the last flight for the evening, they asked me if I could help them get on the airplane.

I told them that I could not put paying passengers off, but I did have a wild idea if they were willing. The Lodestar had a rather huge baggage compartment in the nose of the airplane and it was empty. I told them that if they accidently climbed in there somehow without me seeing it, then I would not have to account for their being there.

They conspired successfully with the ramp agents in St. Petersburg and when I made the next scheduled stop in Sarasota, the ramp agents there who opened the baggage door quickly slammed the door shut when they saw

On the job for less than four months and I was furloughed in a routine reduction in forces.

what, or rather who, was in there. This happened again at Ft. Myers. How the station agents explained their arrival in Miami I do not know. Looking back, it was rather poor judgment on my part.

However, I didn't learn my lesson as many years later something similar in New York happened after all airlines were grounded for several days due to heavy snow. I was to be the first DC-10 to leave LaGuardia and quite naturally, the flight was oversold. There were four station agents from Miami who had been trying to get home and to work for three days. They requested my help getting on the airplane if possible.

Once again, I told them there was no way I could remove paying passengers. They begged and pleaded and I finally told them to go and get on the airplane, go to the cockpit, and shut the door and their mouth. I alerted the senior stewardess and she agreed with me. Of course, there was only one extra seat in the cockpit. Along with this, when we went to push back from the gate, the tug could not get enough traction on the ice to move the airplane away from the terminal building. I put the engines in reverse without adding a lot of power to generate just enough force to help the tug. We had a nice smooth flight to Miami and everyone was happy. Fortunately, no one ever spilled the beans.

First Furlough

On May 1, 1952, less than four months after I was hired, I was on a trip when I was handed a company teletype message at one of our stopovers. The message notified me that I had just been furloughed. I had no idea this was coming and I was not even paid for the remainder of the trip!

It turned out that this was a fairly routine reduction in flight schedules during the summer season. National Airlines was a seasonal airline and when they did not need the extra flight crews, they simply furloughed them. In fact, one time I was laid off when I was flying as a captain out of seniority with the rest of the low number copilots.

I simply returned to crop dusting and started working again with Tag Eure in Statesboro, Georgia, flying every day dusting peanuts.

Two months later, I received a telegram from National Airlines telling me to report for duty. I called and asked them for a 90-day extension so that I could finish my dusting contract. They agreed and in perfect timing, dusting season was just about over when I returned to the airline.

I was more fortunate than most furloughed airline pilots were in that I could always fall back on crop dusting. Most times, I made a lot more money than I was making as a junior captain.

Chapter Nine
From Two to Four

A National Airlines Douglas DC-4, which president George T. Baker dubbed the Buccaneer.

DC-4 "First with Four"

During World War II, all four-engine airliners were requisitioned by the military and it was not until the war drew to a close that they were made available to the airlines. As the airlines began to shift their focus to post-war air transportation needs, a requirement for four-engine aircraft for the longer transcontinental and transoceanic routes soon emerged.

At the end of World War II, National Airlines began looking for a four-engine replacement for the twin-engine Lockheed Lodestars currently used on their longer haul routes. When Eastern Air Lines and Trans World Airlines took all the early delivery positions for Lockheed's new four-engine Constellation, National Airlines president George Baker found himself without a four-engine airplane prospect. He met with the Douglas Aircraft Corporation and purchased war-surplus four-engine C-54 military transports that were modified to National Airline's standards into the commercial DC-4.

Branded by Baker as the "Buccaneer," this new airliner operated at one-third the seat mile cost of the Lockheed Lodestar with a much greater seating capacity. Staffed by two pilots and two stewardesses, the DC-4 could carry 72 passengers, 3½ tons of airfreight and airmail, and travel at 230 miles per hour. Baker also proudly announced that he would offer hot meal service aloft with the compliments of the airlines.

National Airlines took delivery of its first DC-4 on February 12, 1946, and launched the first non-stop, four-engine commercial service between Miami and New York. Locked in a fierce competitive battle with Eastern Air Lines on this route, one airline expert noted that the speed and capacity advantage of National Airlines' DC-4's over Eastern Air Line's slower and smaller DC-3's was almost monopolistic.

The DC-4 was an unpressurized aircraft and we were altitude limited to no more than 9,000 feet because of the rarified air above this altitude. It also did not have an autopilot and we routinely hand flew the DC-4 nonstop from Miami to New York.

Flying the DC-4

In November 1952 when I only had about six months service with National Airlines, I was told that I was going to be a copilot on the DC-4. This was nothing that I requested. As a junior copilot with a low seniority number, I was simply told to report to ground school for the appropriate training.

I was a little less than thrilled to be assigned to fly this airplane, especially after my jump seat ride from Miami to Newark. Once again, the nice simple systems of my favorite Travel Air duster flashed through my mind. However, I found out that the DC-4 training captain was going to be Captain Vic Fite, who had checked me out in the Lodestar. Vic and I got along great because he was a former crop duster pilot, besides being a real nice guy.

A National Airlines Douglas DC-6 over Miami.

I still had my concerns though. As I was walking through the Miami airport terminal to get to the airplane, somebody hollered at me. I turned around and sitting in a chair in the barbershop was none other than my old crop dusting friend, Bill Longino, now a Braniff Airlines captain. I stopped to speak with him and he wanted to know what I was doing.

I told him about the DC-4 and that I was anxious. He then said six words that I used for the rest of my flying career, "Don't worry, it's just another airplane." We talked for a few minutes about crop dusting and then I had to leave.

Captain Fite gave me a walk around on the outside of the airplane and then we climbed aboard this monster. We cranked up the engines, taxied out, and

took off. And guess what? Bill Longino was right. It was just another airplane although it had the advantage of having a training wheel up front instead of a tail wheel.

My first flight as an actual DC-4 copilot with passengers occurred on January 24, 1953. It didn't take me very long to fall in love with this four-engine wonder. It was a very nice flying airplane. However, I only got to fly it for a couple months before they were sold, so I only actually flew the DC-4 a little over 100 hours. Thank you, Vic Fite!

Douglas DC-6

The DC-6 was the first new post-war commercial airliner developed after the war. National Airlines took delivery of the first of these new aircraft on July 1, 1947. Replicating the earlier speed record, which he had set flying transcontinental in a Lockheed Lodestar, Baker piloted this aircraft from Santa Monica to Miami, setting a new southern transcontinental speed record. National Airlines pitted its DC-6's against Eastern Air Lines' Lockheed Constellations.

Between 1945 and 1953, the Douglas Aircraft Corporation introduced six different versions of this four-engine piston transport.

In December 1954, I was assigned to the DC-6, again not by my specific request. The training was simple: a short ground school, a little yakking about the plane, a couple of bounces, and then I was off to fly the line for some on the job training as copilot.

Flight Engineers

This was my first experience with a third cockpit member, the flight engineer. While the Lodestar and DC-4 had a two-pilot crew, I would fly with a flight engineer on the DC-6, DC-7, DC-8, and DC-10. As airliners increased in size and complexity, so too did the various electrical, hydraulic, engine, and fuel systems that made the airplane work. Experts concluded that the captain and copilot would be so busy concentrating on flight instruments that a third crewmember was needed in the cockpit who was trained in the technical operation of complicated airplane systems. Most times the flight engineer was a qualified engine mechanic who had received

specialized training on all the systems in the airplane as well as weight and balance, airplane performance, and fuel management. Other times, the flight engineer was a cross-trained pilot fully qualified as a flight engineer but who was simply biding his time until a copilot seat opened up.

I always thought flight engineers were valuable crewmembers and treated them as such. It was always good to have extra help in an emergency. Many a disaster was averted while the copilot and I concentrated on flying a wounded airplane while the flight engineer troubleshot the problem. I am sorry to say that new airliners have eliminated this position, which as far as I was concerned, was a great safety aid.

DC-6 Pets

The DC-6 airplane had a rather large cockpit and sometimes they would put dogs or cats in containers in the cockpit because the baggage compartments were not pressurized. Of course, this resulted in a considerable amount of barking and yapping and if we were in bad weather and needed full concentration on flying the airplane the dogs were a major distraction.

We soon found out that the only way to make the dogs quit barking was to get the CO_2 fire extinguisher bottle and discharge it at their fanny. They would mercifully stop barking because they were too busy licking the ice off their butt. Woe be unto us if their owners ever found out.

The DC-7 was billed as the world's fastest piston-powered commercial airliners with a top speed of 360 miles per hour.

Douglas DC-7

The last of Douglas' four-engine piston airliners was the DC-7 that first flew on May 18, 1953, and entered airline service six months later. With a top speed of 360 miles per hour, it was billed as the world's fastest piston-powered commercial airliner. This speed was actually a sales tool, since in regular cruise we usually traveled at about 350 miles per hour, which was still pretty fast in those days. It carried 87 passengers and its long range allowed the DC-7 to span the United States non-stop.

In 1953, National placed the DC-7 into service. It was the same set of circumstances for my upgrade to DC-7 copilot as it was for my upgrade to copilot on the DC-4 and DC-6. I received notice that I was to report for copilot training and shortly I was flying the line with passengers.

Convair-340

Seeking a replacement for his aging Lodestars that were still competing against Eastern Air Lines' faster DC-3's in the short haul market, in the late 1950s Baker purchased the twin-engine, pressurized Convair-340, followed shortly by the larger and more powerful Convair-440.

These aircraft were manufactured by the Consolidated Vultee Aircraft Corporation, known universally as Convair, and were originally designed to meet American Airlines' requirement for a fast, pressurized short and medium-haul airliner.

Convair's original design had 2 engines and 40 seats and hence was designated the Convair-240. It made its maiden flight on March 16, 1947, and it was the first twin-engine pressurized airliner to enter commercial airline service, the four-engine, pressurized Boeing 307 Stratoliner having entered commercial service in 1940.

The Convair-340, although based on the Convair-240, was essentially a new aircraft with larger wings and

National Airlines Convair-340.

Wanda and myself at the foot of a Convair 340.

a longer fuselage to accommodate 44 passengers. The first aircraft flew on October 5, 1951.

The Convair-440 Metropolitan was the final piston version of the Convairliner series with modifications that made it 5 miles per hour faster than the Convair-340 and much quieter due to added soundproofing in the cabin. Accommodation was provided for 44 to 52 passengers and the prototype first flew on 6 October 1955.

I was flying as a copilot on the Lodestar, DC-4, DC-6, and DC-7 and had never even been on board a Convair. One day I was in the crew schedule office when Captain Ed Ferguson, the chief pilot, walked in. Old Fergie used to be a crop duster so we had hit it off pretty well together. His nickname for me was "Okeechobee," referring to my Florida roots.

He pointed at me and said "Okeechobee, come along with me." I asked him where we were going and he told me that we were going to test fly a Convair.

I told him that I had never flown a Convair and he replied, "I didn't ask you if you had ever flown a Convair. I told you we were going to test hop an engine change." I said, "I hope you know what you are doing Fergie, because I don't know anything about Convair's."

We got out to the airplane and chitchatted about a few things and then I sat in the copilot's seat. Fergie said, "Get out of there. Go sit in the Captain's seat." I said, "Are you crazy, Fergie?" He replied, "Will you do what I tell you to do?"

He then showed me how to start the engines and I cranked them all up. We taxied out using nose wheel steering, which I had never used before. He showed me how to run up the engines and then he told me to take off.

I thought he was out of his mind but we launched and started flying around the local area, making steep turns and generally just testing out the airplane's feel.

After about 30 minutes I told him, "Man, I would really like to fly this airplane, Fergie" and he said, "Well, when are you going to start?" We continued our maneuvers, returned to land, and Fergie gave me a type rating on the spot.

Convair Passenger Complaint

One day I was flying a Convair-440 as Captain on my old Lodestar route from Jacksonville to New Orleans. We left Pensacola on a nice clear sunny day and had a nice smooth flight to Mobile. We made a normal approach into Mobile and proceeded on to New Orleans after a delightful flight. Completely uneventful.

However, the next day, after returning to Miami, I had a note in my mailbox to see the chief pilot. I went to his office to see what was up. He said he had received a phone call from a passenger saying that he was aboard my Convair flight and that during my approach into Mobile I made the last three turns below an altitude of 50 feet. The passenger said he knew exactly what I was doing because he had a sensitive altimeter with him and this reckless flying scared him rather badly. He thought that I should be reprimanded.

The chief pilot and I both laughed about this because the passenger had not realized that the airplane was pressurized and that the cabin pressure had been reduced to sea level, which would indicate 50 feet on his sensitive altimeter no matter what the altitude of the airplane. We both wondered why this passenger had not figured this out.

Air Transport Rating

It was now July 1955 and I was an instrument-rated commercial pilot with more than 7,000 flight hours. But I did not have an Air Transport Rating (ATR), which is a prerequisite for serving as a captain in scheduled airline operations. Now known as an Airline Transport Pilot rating, it is the highest level of pilot licenses issued by the Federal Aviation Administration (FAA). But since I was flying only as a copilot on the Convair-340 and DC-6, I was not required to have an ATR.

Lodestar Captaincy

However, an opening came up for a captain position in a Lodestar in New York. Despite my low seniority, I decided to bid for this position. I am glad that I applied because it turned out that I was the only copilot who did. In that one bid I jumped over 60 or 70 other copilots to become a captain. Normal progression to captain is usually five to six years but I had less than two years of actual service when my furloughs were added up.

I became one of the lowest seniority National Airlines Lodestar captains after I was selected to upgrade from copilot. There are not too many pictures of me wearing three stripes on my uniform.

As a newly minted National Airlines captain I was selected to fly for the executive charter branch based in New York. I flew one flight before they closed the service.

The vice-president of operations, Lou Dymond, called me and said, "You've won the captain vacancy on the Lodestar but being as you are low time with the company I want you to talk with Mr. Baker." I thought I might be in trouble because I bid for the position without ever thinking that I would get it.

So I made an appointment to meet with Baker and when I arrived at his office, he was smoking a huge cigar and was seated behind a large desk completely stacked with papers. The vice-president was present and he explained the situation to Baker and asked him whether I should be awarded the captaincy or not.

Baker, an experienced pilot himself, turned to me and said, "What've you been flying?" I explained to him that I was a crop duster pilot. He then asked me, "You ever fly any bigger airplanes?" I told him, "Well, I flew a tri-motor Stinson a few times." He then asked, "What are you flying now?" I told, "The Convair and the DC-6."

Baker then asked me, "Well, why do you want to fly the Lodestar?"

I said, "I would like to be Captain." By this time, he had me totally at ease and then he said, "If I let them check you out in that Lodestar, would you fly me down to South America?"

I immediately replied, "Yes." Well, Baker turned around to the vice-president and said, "Check that man out, I am going to fly with him."

But now I really did need the ATR if I was going to fly as captain. Applying for an ATR required the passing of a written examination, an oral examination, and a check ride. I had not even taken the written examination so out of my own pocket I paid $75 to attend Wilbur Sheffield's ground school in Miami. I passed the examination with a perfect score of 100. I now had ten days to complete my check ride.

The airline sent me to Jacksonville with a check pilot named Captain Jimmy Meyer. We were assigned a National Airlines Lodestar and Jimmy was told he had two days to train me to be a captain. I never worked so hard in my life. We flew four hours in the morning and four hours in the afternoon and I experienced everything that could possibly go wrong in the Lodestar, including engine failures, stalls, lost on the radio range, and single engine approaches.

On the third day, I flew with a CAA inspector for my check ride. The cockpit did not have a jump seat so the inspector simply stood in the doorway. I was as nervous as could be and Meyer made me do everything you could possibly do in an airplane except roll it inverted. Talk about pressure, sweat was dripping down my brow and the inspector finally looked at me and said, "Is it raining outside?" I replied, "Nope, you got me hot." He laughed and said, "Well, you've done all right. You've passed."

On that single flight, I got my multiengine rating, my ATR, a type rating in the Lodestar, and a captaincy.

Lodestar Captain in New York

I was immediately transferred to New York to fly as a reserve captain for National Airline's Lodestar executive charter service. The airline put me in a hotel at their expense and paid me my full salary but in three months, I was assigned only one trip. The rest of the time, I moonlighted at an airport on Long Island working as an aircraft welder to keep myself busy. I purchased a 1948 Buick convertible to travel back and forth.

The single trip I did make as a captain was absolutely horrible. I was assigned a brand new copilot on only his second flight who was even more clueless than I was on my first copilot flights. My charter was to deliver two rich people to their home in Portland, Maine.

It was snowing heavily and the weather was bad but flight control told me that they had checked with Northeast Airlines who told them that it was snowing in the Boston area but they were running their full schedule.

After we took off into thick clouds, we immediately started picking up some ice on the wings. Moisture also started freezing inside the cockpit's windshields and we had to use putty knives to clear off the ice.

We arrived in the vicinity of Boston and by this time the airplane had accumulated so much ice that it was beginning to lose airspeed. The Lodestar was equipped with deicing boots but when I reached to pull up the handle to activate them, I discovered that the copilot had already pulled them up prematurely and ice had accumulated on top of them, making them unusable.

There was no way I could continue to Portland so I diverted to Boston's airport and managed to land without incident, although it took quite a bit of power for me to maintain the approach.

As I taxied up to Northeast Airlines for service, I found only one person there. I shut down and he walked up to the cockpit and said, "What in the hell are you doing flying in this kind of weather?" I told him that flight control had told me they were operating a full schedule. He laughed and said, "We haven't had a plane here all day."

My passengers thought I had diverted for fuel, never realizing how close we had come to stalling due to the extra weight of the ice. I cancelled the rest of the flight and we spent the night in Boston before heading to Portland the next day.

I flew an uneventful flight back to New York without passengers, where I was about to meet the true love of my life.

Chapter Ten
Wanda's Story

I am sitting in front of my radio position in this 1956 photograph taken in National Airlines communications office.

I was born Wanda Gunderson in Southeastern Minnesota in 1936, the oldest of four children. I have one sister and two brothers. My parents were farmers and kept us all busy with the many tasks required to run a farm. We lived 10 miles from the nearest town, so there were not a lot of trips made unless it was absolutely necessary. Mother would rather bake bread on Saturday instead of running into town for it.

As I got older, I really liked farm life and all the different things we were required to do. I drove a tractor with a stick shift while cultivating corn, among many other things. We had cows to milk twice every day, hay to bale and bring in during the summer, and chickens, pigs, cows, and sheep to take care of. I also enjoyed riding horses, although I got a broken rib from one that threw me off. That was not a real good day.

One year when polio was very bad around the country, my brother and I contracted the dreaded disease. Our doctor came to our house and gave us "spinals" to see if that is what we had. We did, and our folks made a bed for us in the back of our car and we were soon on our way to the Sister Kenny Institute in Minneapolis, MN. They wrapped us in hot towels for hours every day.

My problem was my spine. I couldn't sit up when I arrived. Six weeks later, I could touch my nose to my knees, a requirement before I could go home. Both my brother and I got better with no after effects and I can still touch my nose to my knees.

I am standing next to my Dad. In front, left to right, is my brother, Dick, my sister, Anita, and my brother, Dennis.

I have always wanted to do something around airplanes. When a junior in high school, I signed up for some correspondence courses with Central Technical Institute in Kansas City, MO. After the courses were finished, I went to classes at Central for six weeks.

I graduated from high school and went to Hamline University in St. Paul, MN for a year, but I still wanted to do something around airplanes. I attended classes in Kansas City the summer of 1954 and enjoyed the communications, teletype and radio very much.

When school was over, I went home and soon received a telegram from National Airlines at Idlewild

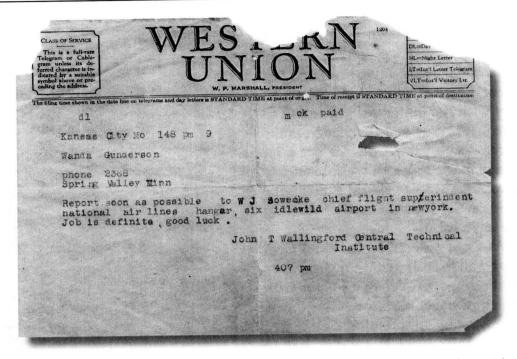

CLASS OF SERVICE

This is a full-rate Telegram or Cablegram unless its deferred character is indicated by a suitable symbol above or preceding the address.

WESTERN UNION

1204

W. P. MARSHALL, PRESIDENT

DL=Day
NL=Night Letter
LT=Int'l Letter Telegram
VLT=Int'l Victory Ltr.

The filing time shown in the date line on telegrams and day letters is STANDARD TIME at point of origin. Time of receipt is STANDARD TIME at point of destination

dl   m ck paid

Kansas City Mo 148 pm 9

Wanda Gunderson

phone 2368
Spring Valley Minn

Report soon as possible to W J Sowecke chief flight superintendent
national air lines hangar, six idlewild airport in newyork.
Job is definite, good luck.

                        John T Wallingford Central Technical
                                        Institute

                        407 pm

This telegram from my correspondence school teacher notified a Minnesota farm girl that she had a job waiting for her in New York with National Airlines.

Airport in New York City to report there for a job. I can still remember how excited I was. Here I was, a naïve farm girl on her way to a job in New York City.

I flew my first flight ever to New York City, not knowing enough to be scared. Guess the Lord was looking out for me because I sat next to a real gentleman on the flight. He found out I was traveling alone with no special place to stay when I got there. He insisted on taking me downtown New York and deposited me at an all-women's hotel. I contacted my new boss and it wasn't long before I found out I had a lot to learn, but I loved it, especially operating the radio.

In the 1950's, each company had their own radio frequencies. The flights kept in contact with their

I was soon an expert talking to pilots in aviation acronyms and abbreviations as I tracked their progress along their assigned routes.

company all the time until time to switch to the control tower. It was our job to contact air traffic control (ATC) to get all their clearances and relay them to the proper flight.

We kept up with each flight. If they had a problem, we were the first to get the information and then relay it to the proper person. Most of the time it was routine until there was bad weather. Then we had to get new clearances if they were low on fuel so they could go to another airport, plus many other things that would happen in bad weather.

It was also our job to send by teletype all their times off the ground to operations at their next stop and also where they were leaving from. Flight control needed this information and was very unhappy with us if we didn't know where each flight was.

In bad weather, the high frequencies had a lot of static and it was hard to hear and understand voices. Hopefully we could use VHF, the only problem being it had a short range. We learned a lot of short cuts and abbreviations. Everything said on air had to be typed and each call was a separate message.

One day when I was new, this poor pilot was trying to tell me his trumpet valve wasn't working and had to be fixed. I couldn't understand until, in desperation, he finally said that it was something you blew in. I finally understood, but was I embarrassed!

Sometime later, a couple of handsome pilots came into flight control where I worked. We were introduced to them and they asked a friend of mine and me out on a date. Trouble is, my friend was with LeRoy and I was with the other man. Before too much time had passed, I made a point of being with LeRoy and I have been with him ever since, celebrating 55 years of marriage in 2012.

He has been everything I could

I am standing in front of a Lockheed Lodestar during one of LeRoy's visits to New York. My office was directly on the flight line so it was easy for LeRoy to visit me.

want in a husband and father. He has been very dependable, full of fun, ready to do something on a moment's notice, and, of course, we both had our love of airplanes.

After we were married, I worked until our son was born. I then stayed home to raise our family. We also have two daughters. We always had an airplane of our own, so after our children got older, I had a chance to get my pilots license. What a thrill. I could hardly believe that I was actually doing this. I loved every minute of it.

My instructor did not tell me the day I was to have my first solo. I probably would have been up all night. On the big day, my instructor rode with me one time around the field and then had me stop and he got out. He said, "It is all yours. I want to see 3 takeoffs and landings."

Wow, what a feeling it was to be flying by myself. It is hard to say how good it felt that I had been able to do that. That little airplane almost jumped off the ground as I tried to remember everything I was told to do. All went well and I was heartily congratulated when I landed.

I continued my training and finally got my license. I flew a Cessna 150 for all of my training. Since then, I have accumulated time in a DC3, Mooney, Aero Commander 680S, Cherokee 140, Cessna 172, Butler Blackhawk (open cockpit bi-plane), PT-19, Aeronca Champ, Piper J-3 Cub and even a DC-10.

LeRoy was assigned as captain on a DC-10 being flown empty from

Photograph of myself and LeRoy when we were first dating.

Miami to San Francisco to get it in the right place for a flight. I went with him and he let me fly it part of the time. Here I was, a low time Cessna 150 pilot flying this big, beautiful DC-10 airliner going over 600 miles per hour and I was sitting in the first officer's seat.

I disconnected the autopilot but I soon found out that I could not maintain a steady altitude at 39,000 feet. By then, even ATC was

Getting ready to take LeRoy to the airport for his trip, in our 1939 Chevrolet. His father had given him this car.

LeRoy and myself in the cockpit of our DC-3.

with him. He flew this big 4-engine airplane by himself and I sat in the copilot's seat trying to imagine what it must have been like heading out on a bombing run. What were these young men thinking? If only this plane could talk. All these young men gave their lives so we could fly this B-17 with four engines running smoothly and be free and safe.

wondering what was wrong with our altitude. I kept thinking that if I were part of the younger generation, this is what I would have liked to do.

On our arrival back in Miami, LeRoy thought that he should tell the chief pilot that his wife had flown the DC-10 before someone complained about it. He walked into the chief pilot's office to find Skeeter Royal sitting at his desk engrossed in a ton of paperwork. He looked up with an inquisitive look and LeRoy said, "Skeeter, I let my wife fly that DC-10 yesterday to San Francisco." He looked LeRoy straight in the eye and said, "I wish you wouldn't come in here and tell me things like this. Now, get out of here." LeRoy never heard another word about it.

Before I had my license, my husband bought a B-17, which he used to fly cucumbers from Andros Island, Bahamas to Florida. I made many trips

While LeRoy worked for National Airlines, they had fly-ins at River Ranch, Florida for the airline employees. One time, not having anything else to fly but a 1929 Waco duster, we cleaned the dust out of the hopper, put a board in for a seat, and that is what I sat on as we flew to River Ranch. We had great fun and everyone was very impressed with our originality. We won a prize for oldest airplane and this was my introduction to open cockpit flying.

We made many trips to Minnesota where my family still lives. One year we flew our prize winning 1929 Butler Blackhawk biplane back home. You get back to old time flying with this.

We felt all the temperature changes at different altitudes and we were either too hot or too cold half the time. We smelled all the odors along the way,

*LeRoy is in the left seat and I am in the right as we fly our
B-17 to Andros Island to pick up a load of cucumbers.*

some good and some bad. Of course, we always flew in good weather; it was definitely a VFR airplane. You wonder as you fly along in this old time airplane how some of those pilots survived flying through bad weather with very few instruments.

We also flew our Culver Cadet to Minnesota. It was small, but pretty fast, and we were in a closed cockpit. We always said there was only room for the two of us and one toothbrush. We made many trips over the years in our airplanes, but as uncomfortable as it was at the time, I think we had the best times when we flew the Blackhawk.

Over the years, we always kept busy with new and different things.

For example, we both got our ham radio licenses. We also bought a Pearson Sailing Sloop and then proceeded to take a sailing class from the Coast Guard to learn how to sail. My husband, our two oldest children and I took the classes. The Coast Guard instructor was so impressed with the whole family taking the class that they put our picture in the local paper. We got our boating licenses the same day I got my pilot's license.

In 2012, as I write this, LeRoy has been retired 31 years and we still do most everything together. How lucky this naïve farm girl has been. I have so much to be thankful for.

Chapter Eleven
Flying the Line

I am standing in front of a DC-6 circa 1958. With all of the National Airlines airplanes I was type rated in as copilot, I used to joke that "I was never qualified on what I flew but I was legal."

As Wanda mentioned, the first time we met was in 1956 when I visited National Airlines' flight control office in New York. I immediately noticed this good looking, long legged, blonde pass me by but she didn't even look at me. But soon we were dating exclusively.

Return to Miami

My single flight as a captain complete, I was sent back to Miami when Lockheed Lodestar executive charter service was closed. I did not mind at all flying back and forth between Miami and Key West three times a day in a Lodestar while captains senior to me were flying the DC-6 from Miami to New York because they didn't want to go to Key West. I was flying in beautiful weather and I was home every night.

I continued to remain in contact with Wanda through National Airlines' radios. Once I landed in Key West, I would need a company clearance to return to Miami so I would call New York on my high frequency radio. Sometimes nearby Miami would break in on a VHF radio and tell me that they heard me loud and clear. I would disregard them saying, "Standby Miami, you are breaking up," so I could get my clearance from Wanda.

I would visit New York as often as I could. Occasionally, I would get a DC-6 round trip from Miami to New York in the morning as a copilot. Then I would turn around on the same

Boarding a Convair-340 in 1957.

round trip flight on the afternoon run just to spend a few hours with her.

Eventually, Wanda was based in Miami, but not until she convinced her boss, who did not like transfers, that she would leave National for Northeast Airlines, who had a Miami base. Additionally, company policy stated that you could not be married to another employee and still work for the airline. Nonetheless, we got married on February 14, 1957, in Tavares, Florida where my mother and step-father lived.

Boeing 247D

By late 1956, I was flying as a captain on Lodestar's and Convair-340's and -440's while doubling as a copilot on the DC-6 and DC-7. I was making fairly decent money, but I got wind of a serious pest about to ruin the Florida citrus industry. This pest was known as the Mediterranean fruit fly.

The Department of Agriculture was awarding massive contracts, via a competitive bidding process, for agriculture airplanes to spray all the groves in central and south Florida. As I was still registered as a former agriculture pilot, I was contacted to see if I was available. I found out that the pay would be two to three times as much as I was making on the airline, so I took a 90-day leave of absence

Wanda and I were married in 1957.

from National Airlines and went to work for Tatum Flying Service.

I was checked out by Tatum to ensure I was duly qualified and then assigned a Stearman PT-17 series with a 450-horsepower Pratt and Whitney engine. Shortly thereafter, Tatum acquired and assigned to me a former N3N-3 Navy trainer modified for crop dusting use and equipped with a 600-horsepower Pratt and Whitney engine. I really enjoyed flying this N3N. It was a little heavier on the aileron controls than the Stearman, but it could carry almost twice as much load as the Stearman could.

The insecticide we were spraying was to be dispensed at one gallon per acre and it was a mixture of malathion and steak sauce. The steak sauce was used as a carrier for the insecticide to attract the flies to eat it.

This mixture weighed almost ten pounds per gallon. All airplanes were calibrated by the agriculture department so that they indeed did spray one gallon per acre at their respective flying speed. We were to fly at 75 feet altitude so that the spray pattern would cover the maximum area.

To ensure compliance, Department of Agriculture representatives would occasionally check various spraying areas by putting empty oil cans on the ground to be sure that the insecticide that accumulated in the oil cans met their minimum requirements. If it did not, the area was to be sprayed over again at the bidder's expense. I never had to respray an area.

The groves were sprayed two or three times many days apart to

I am standing in front of the Boeing 247 former passenger airliner converted to crop spraying that I flew to combat the Mediterranean fruit fly infestation.

destroy newly hatched insect eggs. Sometimes, the grove would become reinfected and the procedure started all over again.

Tatum had contracts for several areas in central Florida that paid 30 cents an acre for the flying. Of this, the pilot was paid 10 cents an acre. Now that does not sound like very much per acre but I could cover a whole bunch of acres in nothing flat.

After I had completed about 30 days flying the N3N, the Department of Agriculture required Tatum to obtain a multi-engine airplane for operations over cities and highly populated areas. Tatum acquired a twin-engine Boeing 247D sprayer that was located in Miami and I was assigned to this airplane because of my combined airline multi-engine and agricultural flying experience.

Originally introduced in 1933, the twin-engine Boeing Model 247 was a revolutionary airplane for its time and is considered the first modern airliner. It featured all-metal construction, retractable landing gear, trim tabs, autopilot, gyros for instrument flight, and was able to fly on only one engine. Airlines flocked to order the 247, but when production was unable to keep up with demand, Douglas developed the DC-3 and the 247 was relegated to history. Boeing ended up building only 75 247's while Douglas built more than 10,000 DC-3's. The 247 remained in airline service until the 1940's when most were converted into freighters or personal transports.

The Boeing 247 I was flying was N75921 and it had already been converted to a sprayer. I had never really seen one before that I can remember until I picked up this airplane in Miami. This particular Boeing 247D was retrofitted with smaller engines to keep the airplane's weight below the 12,500 pound rule that required two pilots and a type rating.

So I flew it solo and it did not take me long to learn that the 247 was not really a very good crop dusting airplane. It did not fly as well as the N3N and I can only describe it as like driving a huge Mac truck without power steering around a racetrack.

It was really hard to make the steep turns required in spraying. However, I soon developed a turn method of my own. At the end of the swath, I would pull up with maximum power, get to a reasonable altitude of 200 feet, and reduce power on the inboard engine on the side of the turn. With an assist of full rudder, it would swap ends nicely. After the turn was completed, I would match throttles back to my desired cruising speed and mandated altitude of 75 feet. The 247 could carry up to 500 gallons of insecticide in a single load and it would take me about 22 minutes on average to spray 500 acres.

A lot of pilots and observers wanted to catch a ride with me when I was flying the 247, which

I always accommodated if possible. After experiencing my quick turn reversals and dives back into the field, however, they never seemed to want to ride with me again.

One time I had my wife Wanda with me as we were spraying St. Petersburg and she could see ladies running out of their homes trying to get their clothes off the line before I started spraying, and other people shaking their fists at me. I never saw any of this as I was too busy looking up at buildings and trying to avoid television towers. When Wanda told me about this, I really felt bad

Spray Planes Make Second Trip Over 8,000-Acre Infested Area

The second spraying for eradication of the Mediterranean fruit fly in this section of Pasco county began on schedule today when plans of the Tatum Flying service began the 8,000-acre task.

W. H. Williamson, assistant district supervisor, of New Port Richey, said today that there has been one find made since the first spraying. This was on September 7 when one male fly was found in a trap set in a sour orange grove a mile south of St. Leo, he reported.

Williamson said there are now 824 traps set in Pasco county, 188 of which are in the infested area, all being checked three times weekly by inspectors.

May Drop Some Areas

In an optimistic prediction, C. E. Harper, district supervisor of Brooksville, said that after the third application of malathion bait, some of the areas within the control district may be dropped from the spray program.

Williamson stated that children playing in school yards were not being purposely divebombed and that pilots were instructed to turn off the sprayer when going over school areas but that there was some possibility that wind drift might carry the spray into school areas whenever planes are spraying nearby.

Denies Spraying Children

LeRoy Brown, a pilot with the Tatum flying service denied reports that he purposely sprayed a group of children in Polk county earlier this week. Brown, who has been a commercial pilot for 15 years and is now on leave from National Air Lines, said that at no time did his plane spray nearer than 400 feet to a school.

The next spraying operations in this area are scheduled for Friday and Saturday, September 21-22.

While spraying against the Mediterranean fruit fly, I was falsely accused of deliberately spraying school children.

and I cried all the way to the bank to deposit my checks.

One thing that did seriously upset me was when I was falsely accused of spraying several schools and intentionally spraying the kids. This is totally untrue even though it was printed in the newspapers. I never sprayed a school intentionally or unintentionally.

One of our other National Airlines pilots, Kenny Pope, was flying a Stearman sprayer over the outskirts of Orlando when his engine quit. He ended up wrecking upside down in a schoolyard in Winter Park. Fortunately, Kenny was not hurt nor was anyone else on the ground. I used to own that particular Stearman and it was the same one in which I, too, ended up upside down in Winnsboro, South Carolina. That particular Stearman N49964 has had many accidents yet it is still flying today along with its sister ship N49965 that used to be owned by our Southeastern Dusting Company. These two Stearmans have certainly earned their keep having been crop dusters for more than 60 years.

One morning I was running a little late and as I sped through the city of Apopka at 4:00 a.m., I was stopped by a policeman for speeding. He asked me what my rush was and I told him that I was spraying the city of Apopka that morning. He turned me loose saying I had enough troubles.

I put a lot of hours on that Boeing 247 and I got to where I really liked that airplane. After the fruit fly program wound down, I contacted the Department of Agriculture to be put on

My Boeing 247D that I converted into a lobster hauler between the Bahamas and Florida parked on the West End, Bahamas.

their mailing list for future contracts. The Boeing 247D I was spraying with was returned to the owner.

I acquired another Boeing 247D (side number N7777B) for myself and proceeded to remove the interior and install a rather large fuel tank to provide extended range. It was quite a job to install a fiberglass tank that would meet FAA requirements, including dump valves to unload all the fuel in case of an engine failure. Inconveniently, as the spray tank was built inside the cabin, after it was installed, the only way to get in the pilot's compartment was through an overhead trap door.

I had purchased several Pratt and Whitney 600 horsepower engines and I retrofitted two of them to fit the Boeing. Altogether, it took almost four months before we got the airplane licensed and flying, including a lot of test hops for the FAA.

The results of one these test hops was never mentioned to the FAA. All the work was done at what was then called the North Wagon Wheel Airport located west of Hollywood, Florida. On the first test hop after its restoration, a qualified 247D pilot named Jess Bristow was in the captain's seat and I was riding co-pilot with him. The spray tank had not yet been installed and we had two passengers that wanted to go for a ride. I am quite sure they never begged for a ride again.

As Jess and I left the ground, at about 300 feet altitude, the left engine quit. As we were cleaning up the airplane to fly, the other engine quit. There was no place to go. Jess headed for a vacant street in a subdivision and we made a more or less safe landing. Jess and I soon discovered that the fuel tank selectors were hooked up wrong and we took off with only the fuel in the carburetors and fuel lines. We turned the selectors around to the full gas tanks and got both engines going once again. Our passengers decided to walk back to the airport. Without further ado, Jess and I took off from this vacant street and had no further problems. Believe me, only our dry cleaners knew how scared we were. This was not to be the first time I would have all two, three, or four engines on airplanes I was flying quit. This forced landing was not mentioned to the FAA and we were extremely fortunate that the subdivision was incomplete.

Hauling Lobsters

As there were no spraying contracts being let at this time, I looked for other means to utilize the Boeing 247D.

Someone suggested that perhaps I could use it as a freighter and transport live lobsters from the Bahamas to Miami. This sounded like a good idea, so I flew into the Bahamas to visit the Bahamas Transport Ministry to obtain a certificate of necessity, which was required to transport freight out of the Bahamas. I went to Nassau on a Saturday afternoon not knowing any better. Realizing that the offices were closed I went directly to the home of the transport minister, Mr. H.H. Thompson. I knocked on his door and when he answered, I told him what I wanted. He was rather upset that I would do such a thing on a Saturday afternoon, but I talked him into giving me a temporary certificate good for 30 days until the Transport Authority could issue a permanent one.

I was granted a permit to go from West End, Bahamas, to Florida. There were many other restrictions, including one that stated I could not buy the lobsters directly from the fishermen, but had to hire a Bahamian buyer. I found one named Brenda Neely.

My plan was for Brenda to buy the lobsters from the fishermen and then have them stored in underwater cages until there were enough to fly them to Florida. I was to pay Brenda for the lobsters, and she in turn would pay the fishermen. I had to pay her in Bahamian money and the cost of the lobsters in Bahamian currency was 7 pounds 10 for 100 lobsters regardless of their size. This came to about 21 cents apiece in US money.

We obtained several cages for the fishermen to keep the lobsters alive.

When I arrived to pick up my first load, they were packed in wet burlap sacks. After a certain period of time in the air, several dozen of the lobsters managed to escape from their burlap prison and fell over the sides of the tank to the bottom of the airplane. With no way of getting them out, the airplane soon developed a horrible stench from the rotting lobsters.

I usually brought back about 4,000 pounds of lobster at a time. I had many ready buyers in Miami for distribution to local fish markets, so during the lobster season, I carried many loads between the Bahamas and Miami.

One day I was bringing a load to Fort Lauderdale and after I landed, I noticed a large crowd on the west side of the airport sitting in front of a brand new Northeast Airlines DC-6. There was also a band present playing music for the crowd.

As the customs facility was located directly adjacent to their position, I asked ground control if customs could check me out at a different location so I would not disturb the crowd with my distinct odor.

Their answer was no. As the wind was gently blowing from the east and the congregation was to the west of the taxiway, I knew the entire crowd would soon smell this terrible odor. I was embarrassed at the thought of this but I had no choice but to obey customs' orders. As fortune would have it, though, I was taxiing directly in front of them when I blew out a tire and came to an immediate halt.

I looked out my left window and saw people in the crowd start to hold their nose and then the band stopped playing because the odor was so bad. I was too embarrassed to get out of the airplane. I hated to break up their gathering, but now that I look back on it, it was really kind of funny.

Several weeks later, I landed at Miami International. During rollout on runway 9 left, I had the misfortune of another tire blowing out and I could not move the airplane. I practically had Miami International Airport closed down until I got a tug to pull the airplane off the runway. I was cordially invited not to come back with that airplane.

Before long, it seemed to me that I was being shortchanged in the lobster deliveries, effectively paying for lobsters I was not getting. I spoke to Brenda about this and she agreed with me that something was not right. So unbeknownst to the fishermen, I stayed overnight during one trip to the West End to watch them. I found out that they were taking the lobsters out of our cages, putting them in their boats, and then drinking beer all day. They would then come back in the afternoon and sell Brenda the same lobsters that we had already paid for. Anyway, it was quite obvious that I had to stop the operation that day. Brenda was a mighty fine person and agreed with me.

By the way, the transport minister had a brother at West End and we soon became rather friendly. Consequently, I enjoyed the privilege of getting future permits without much trouble. Even though I didn't make much money, my wife and I did have many a fine lobster dinner.

A heart breaking sight for any aviator. One of my Boeing 247D's is cut up for scrap metal after I could not afford to retrieve them from storage.

Mexican Boeing 247's

I was so happy with my Boeing 247D that I eventually purchased from Jess Bristow three additional 247D's that were disassembled and in storage in Mexico City. I was content to let them sit there because at the time, I did not have the financing to retrieve them. Several months after my purchase, I received a letter from the storage facility in Mexico City saying we had to move the airplanes immediately as they needed this space for other things.

Not having the money to restore them and fly them to Florida, I had no choice but to cut them up with a blow torch and sell them as scrap metal. Needless to say, I was sick. I sent Jess to Mexico City where he sold what he could and destroyed the rest. It is too bad we couldn't restore them as there are very few Boeing 247's left. The same fate awaited N7777B. I really

enjoyed flying these old airliners and even though they weren't very fast, they were certainly very well built. I only wish I had one today.

U.S. Navy SNJ's

In the 1950s, surplus military airplanes were inexpensive and readily available, as evidenced by my purchases of the former U.S. Army Air Corps Vultee BT-13 and BT-15 training aircraft.

My leave of absence over, I returned to flying as an airline captain. In 1958 one of my fellow National Airlines pilots mentioned that surplus U.S. Navy SNJ pilot trainers were available in Pensacola. I immediately jumped at this opportunity because the SNJ was considered the cream of the crop of advanced military training airplanes.

The SNJ is the U.S. Navy variant of the single-engine, two-place T-6 Texan built by North American Aviation.

More than 15,000 T-6's were built to train military pilots during World War II and it is known by a variety of designations, depending upon which military service flew it. Models flown by the U.S. Army were known as the AT-6 while those operated overseas by our allies were called Harvard's. Loved for the throaty roar of their 600-horsepower Pratt & Whitney R1340 AN-1 radial piston engine, today these airplanes are very popular on the air show circuit and command prices of more than $150,000 each.

The model I could purchase was the SNJ-5, which was equipped with retractable gear, radios, and a tailhook for practicing aircraft carrier landings. These airplanes were physically located at Naval Air Auxiliary Station (NAAS) Bronson Field in Pensacola. As Pensacola was serviced by National Airlines I simply hitched a ride on a scheduled flight.

I took a taxi to the air station, which was in the process of being closed, and located the office of Queen City Salvage, Inc., which had purchased all of the airplanes from the Navy. They were asking $800 per aircraft. I bought 10.

After paying for the airplanes, I obtained a ferry permit from Pensacola to Miami from the Civil Aeronautics Administration and applied for registration numbers to turn the military serial numbers into civilian N-numbers.

For insurance reasons, the U.S. Navy would not let purchasers use the air station's runways. Instead, they cut a hole in the security fence and we taxied the airplanes out onto an adjacent dirt road and took off from there. I would land at Pensacola Municipal Airport to first refuel as most of the SNJ's had empty tanks. I would typically put in about 80 gallons of fuel at 36 cents a gallon.

From Pensacola I would fly nonstop to Tamiami Airport in Miami where I would be charged a monthly tie down fee of about $10. I flew all ten of my new airplanes to Miami one at a time and then eventually sold them at a handsome profit or traded them for other airplanes.

I made two group purchases, one in 1958 and another in 1959. While both ventures were very profitable, I would have made substantially more money if I had kept them in storage for a few decades.

Lockheed Constellation

The Lockheed Constellation is perhaps one of the world's best-loved airliners and is considered by many experts to be the most elegantly designed airliner ever built.

Built in response to a request by Howard Hughes for a pressurized 40-passenger transcontinental airliner with a 3,500-mile range for his Trans World Airlines, the prototype made its first flight on January 9, 1943. All production aircraft were diverted for military use and it was not until after the war that the first Constellations entered commercial service with Trans World Airlines.

Rickenbacker ordered his first Constellation, the L-749 improved model, in 1950. Not wishing to repeat his mistake of letting National Airlines gain an advantage over him when Baker became the first to use four-engine Douglas DC-4's on the New York to Miami route, Rickenbacker competed with his antagonist on even terms by pitting his Lockheed Constellations against National Airlines' Douglas DC-6's and DC-7's.

In 1957, National Airlines purchased four Lockheed 1049H Constellations. These airplanes came with wing tip tanks, which made them very beautiful airplanes. They could accommodate 107 passengers and flew at 320 miles per hour, much less than the DC-7B's 365 miles per hour.

In 1959, I was offered the opportunity to fly this airplane and I completed my training on June 4, 1959. I enjoyed flying the Constellation, even though it was not as spirited as the DC-7.

Items about the Constellation that did not impress me were the windshield being divided into so many sections, the hydraulic system, rubber boots on the wings, and the fact that the radar scope retracted into the floor between the pilots, which made it rather inconvenient. The cockpit was rather narrow compared to the Douglas airplanes and it only had one set of throttles for both pilots. The Constellation was very passenger friendly and was in an all-coach configuration.

I would have liked to have flown it for a longer period, but along came the Lockheed Electra and other jets that made all the other piston-driven propeller airplanes obsolete.

Violent End of Flight 2511

By January 1960 I was serving as a reserve captain for the Lockheed Lodestar, the Convair-340, and the Convair-440. I was also a qualified copilot on the DC-6B, the DC-7B, the Lockheed Super H Constellation, and the latest turboprop, the Lockheed Electra L188. My check rides on all these airplanes were current, which meant the airline could assign me to passenger trips on any one of them.

On January 5, 1960 I flew as copilot to Captain Sim Speer on a DC-6B trip from Miami to Idlewild. We were scheduled to ferry this same DC-6B back to Miami without passengers. As we were arriving at the gate in Idlewild, a National Airlines Boeing 707 crew taxiing out with a full load of passengers for Miami noticed that the copilot's windshield was cracked, rendering the 707 unairworthy. They returned to their gate and the Boeing 707 flight was cancelled.

Since it would take more than eight hours to replace the windshield, the National Airlines Flight Control department decided to load the Boeing 707 passengers on our DC-6B and a second available DC-6B commanded by Captain Dale Southard.

Captain Speer and I, however, were not legal to be rescheduled to fly passengers to Miami in the DC-6B because of FAA flight time restrictions. We had just flown 4 hours and 7 minutes from Miami to Idlewild. A flight of the same time returning to Miami would have put us over our legal FAA maximum of 8 flying hours in a 24 hour period.

Flight Control's solution was to reschedule Captain Speer and me to the faster Electra. The L-188 could make the trip in 3 hours and 30 minutes, thus keeping us within our legal limits. Captain Speer and I were both qualified and current on the Electra so this did not present a problem.

Given their choice of the turboprop-powered Electra or the piston-powered DC-6B, all the Boeing 707 passengers tried to squeeze aboard the faster Electra for the flight to Miami and it was soon filled to overcapacity. I recall that some of the "too many" people on the Electra did not want to get off but eventually the ramp agent advised us that all of the extra passengers had been resettled to Captain Southard's DC-6B.

We launched about 11:30 p.m. with 76 passengers, and Captain Southard departed right behind us with 29 passengers. Given our faster airspeed, we slowly left him behind and we arrived in Miami at 3:00 a.m. on the morning of January 6, 1961. Unbeknownst to us, Captain Southard was overdue at his next checkpoint after having radioed a routine progress report while passing Wilmington, North Carolina. Captain Speer and I debriefed with flight control before heading home for some well-deserved sleep.

I awoke to the shocking news that Captain Southard's DC-6B had mysteriously exploded in flight shortly after having completed his progress report and crashed in a field approximately 1 and a half miles northwest of Bolivia, North Carolina.

All of the 29 passengers and five crewmembers were killed.

An intense accident investigation by the Civil Aeronautics Board revealed that at about 2:33 a.m., dynamite had been detonated under the seat in row 7 occupied by a young lawyer by the name of Julian Frank. The timing of the explosion was such that the airplane should have been on the projected over-ocean 500 mile segment of the flight that ran from Wilmington to West Palm Beach, which would have hid the wreckage in the depths of the Atlantic Ocean. However, strong headwinds at altitude slowed the airplane's progress and passengers could not see below them due to a thick cloud layer. As a result, the explosion occurred over land and the wreckage of the doomed airliner was recovered for analysis.

While a tremendous amount of circumstantial evidence indicated that Frank had detonated the bomb, the Civil Aeronautics Board (CAB) refused to speculate on the person or persons responsible for the dynamite detonation. One alternative explanation was that Frank was murdered, as had happened less than two months before when National Airlines Flight 967, a DC-7B flying over the Gulf of Mexico, was brought down by a bomb explosion in a suspected life insurance scheme. Once its investigation was complete, however, the CAB referred the criminal aspects of Captain Southard's accident to the Department of Justice through its Federal Bureau of Investigation. The case remains open to this day.

I later found out that Frank was a passenger on the cancelled Boeing 707 flight. He was waiting to board my airplane just ahead of a couple that wanted to stay together. When only two of the last three passengers could be accommodated, Frank stepped aside, giving his seat to the couple, saying, "It doesn't matter to me which airplane I take."

It mattered to me.

Nearly two decades after the accident, I received a phone call from one of my former stewardesses, Susan Crawford Johnson. She told me that a lady had called her to see if she knew anything about that accident. Susan knew about my close call and she gave me a phone number to call the lady back, which I did.

Her name was Linda Silver Bufano and I told her I was the copilot on the surviving flight. She then told me that her parents were passengers on Dale Southard's flight and had perished. She told me she was 6-years old when the accident occurred and that she had never found out the true story of what happened. She thought that perhaps talking to me might bring her some closure.

I told her everything I knew about the accident and she was rather shaken up. She told me that she was going to the accident site in North Carolina to see exactly where her parents died. I asked her what day she was going and she told me. I told her I was sorry about her loss and we hung up.

I talked to my wife about this call and I told Wanda that this lady seemed very distraught and that she was going to be there on such and such a date. So Wanda and I decided to drive our motor home to North Carolina to meet her, which we did.

Linda was a very nice person and we had a nice long talk. The next day, we met her at the accident site and spoke with some of the neighbors who had heard the crash. We spent possibly an hour and a half at the site and she planted some flowers in memory of her parents. Wanda and I did the same for Dale Southard and his crew. We departed very good friends and we still communicate with her to this day.

I must say this is a poor way to meet someone, but it has developed into a warm friendship.

Chapter Twelve
Cucumber Bombers

"In the dark night I was cruising along trying to follow the coastline as best I could. I had no radios, I didn't have anything. I didn't even have any maps. I began to worry about what might happen."

My two B-17's sitting on the ramp at Fort Lauderdale International Airport. N3701G is in the background with N4710C in the foreground.

Having already disposed of the surplus U.S. Navy SNJs I purchased in 1958, I decided to purchase more in 1959. While I was signing for the last SNJ in Casco, Inc.'s Miami office, the salvage agent, Al Adams, mentioned that they had 2 B-17s for sale. They acquired them from the U.S. Coast Guard and the price was $40,000 for the pair.

With my big mouth, I said, "Shoot, I'll give you $20,000 for both of them."

The agent responded, "I'll take it."

I laughed, and then said, "I was just kidding."

The agent gave me a serious look and said, "We don't kid in here, you just bought them."

While I knew he was kidding, the opportunity to own an actual B-17 was too good to pass up. So, even though I had never seen a B-17 in person, I placed a $2,000 deposit for both of them. The B-17s were located on a dirt strip in Charlotte, North Carolina. I decided to take a look at them.

B-17G 44-85812 N4710C

Jack Kalemba, Tag Eure, Carl Hendrix, and I flew a Twin Beech to Charlotte, North Carolina where we rented a car and drove to the strip where the B-17s were located. I selected B17 N4710C, whose U.S. Army Air Corps serial number was 44-85812 and whose U.S. Coast Guard serial number was 77246, based upon its low engine times.

It was a PB-1G model that had been allocated to the U.S. Coast Guard for use in air/sea rescue in

DELTA LEASING CORPORATION
Post Office Box 9042
Charlotte, North Carolina

August 8, 1958

Gentlemen:

We offer for sale two very clean Boeing B17G Aircraft.

The B17G is a low wing land monoplane. It is an all metal airplane of semi-monocoque construction powered by four Wright Cyclone R1820-97 radial engines equipped with three bladed Hamilton Standard constant speed full feathering propellers. One B-2 or B-22 turbosupercharger per engine is used to boost power. The aircraft is designed long distance and high altitude operation. Engines operate on 100/130 grade fuel or 91/98 fuel can be used as an alternate. Maximum permissible airspeed is 305 miles per hour. Each engine has individual oil system with 37 gallon tanks. Aircraft is equipped with AC electric auto-pilot. Cruising range with 2780 gallons fuel (full wing tanks) at 55,000 to 65,000 lbs. gross weight is 2170 miles at 10,000 ft. altitude and 186 M.P.H. at power settings of 2050 R.P.M. and 30" manifold pressure. Basic weight of this aircraft is approximately 32,000 lbs. It is 74' 9" long, 19' high with a wing span of 103' 9". The landing gear, tail wheel, wing flaps and bomb bay doors are electrically operated. Brakes and cowl flaps are hydraulically operated. The aircraft is equipped with an auxiliary power unit. The fuel capacity is 2780 gallons without bomb bay tanks and 3600 gallons with bomb bay tanks. The B-17 stalls at 100 M.P.H. with 50,000 lbs. gross weight with flaps up, stalls at 96 M.P.H. with 150 flaps and 88 M.P.H. with full flaps at 50,000 lbs.

The R1820-97 engine horsepower is 1200 at 2500 R.P.M.

Maximum altitude is approximately 40,000 feet.

We are enclosing other data and photographs of the two aircraft we are offering for sale. They are ready to climb in and fly away. The price is $22,000 each or $40,000 for both. We welcome your inquiries and inspection of these ships.

Yours very truly,

DELTA LEASING CORPORATION

H. H. Tish

bh

Sales information sheet for the two B-17's offered for sale by the Delta Leasing Corporation.

When I arrived at Charlotte I found these two B-17's sitting at the airfield. They were for sale for $10,000 each and I decided to purchase the one on the left, which had been modified for use by the U.S. Coast Guard for air/sea rescue.

the North Atlantic. It was stripped of all the air/sea rescue equipment when I purchased it.

The two mechanics, Kalemba and Hendrix, looked over the B-17 to make sure everything was working, which included getting the birds' nests out of the engines.

The final sales price I agreed upon was $10,000. I actually did not have the money to pay for this B-17, so I borrowed it from Kalemba and the balance owed was then paid to Casco.

We called the local Civil Aeronautics Authority (CAA) office in Charlotte, North Carolina and requested a ferry permit, which would require an inspection of the airplane's airworthiness by a CAA inspector. The airplane looked absolutely beautiful inside and out.

The CAA inspector showed up and it turned out that I knew him, a gentleman by the name of Mr. Ravenstein. He asked me how much time I had in the B-17 and I told him, "None." Surprised, he replied, "I can't give you a ferry permit if you've never flown one."

At that time, I was flying four-engine DC-4's, DC-6's and DC-7's for National Airlines, so I was not intimidated by the B-17 at all. I said to him. "Look, I'm flying four-engine airplanes for the airlines and I am not going to have any trouble with that thing." At first he was pretty hesitant, but after I spoke with him a while, I talked him into signing the permit. After all, the B-17 had the same engines as the Lockheed Lodestar, so I knew all the basic power settings and all I had to do was keep the pointy end headed toward Orlando. I would get my official type rating later.

I asked Kalemba to fly co-pilot for me for two reasons. First, I might need

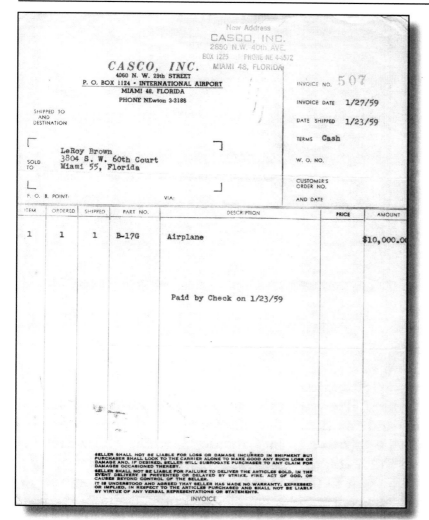

$10,000 was the going price in 1959 for a surplus B-17. Even in poor condition a B-17 today would sell for more than $3 million.

started. Kalemba, who had never flown more than a twin engine airplane, and I taxied to the runway, which was nothing more than a dirt strip located between a line of buildings and trees with not more than 100 feet of clearance on either wing.

I lined the B-17 up, poured on the coal to all four 1200-horsepower Wright R-1820-97 engines and that bomber just leaped into the air, Jack as white as a sheet beside me. Fortunately, there were no problems whatever. Flying the airplane held no surprises for me. In fact, I was quite comfortable with my new four-engine bomber. We flew to Orlando, the B-17 cruising comfortably at about 230 miles per hour, and I thought to myself, "Man, this thing is great." We landed in Orlando after a nice flight and I was amazed at the simplicity of the B-17.

a pair of extra hands in the cockpit, and second, if I had any trouble on the way to Orlando and had to land, as a mechanic he could help me fix any problem. Tag and Hendricks flew back home in the twin Beech. Entering the B-17, by the way, was done by performing a reverse chin up through a trap door located just below the cockpit on the bottom of the fuselage.

We managed to figure everything out and we soon got all four engines

Flying a B-17 Solo

Flying the B-17 solo was not as difficult as one would think. I rather enjoyed flying alone and I logged almost 300 solo hours in two different B17's and had absolutely no problem whatsoever.

Starting was simple and the aircraft systems were straightforward, so actually flying it solo was rather routine and it handled much like the DC-4's I was flying for National.

It doesn't get any better for an aviator: my own B-17 behind me and my hot Thunderbird in front of me.

My B-17 type rating checkride was given by Bill Conrad. He sat in the copilot's seat and worked me through all of the required maneuvers. I landed the B-17 for the final time and as we went to the office to sign the paper work, his only comment was, "Nice flight."

The gear and flap switches were readily available and within easy reach of the man in the left seat. I never had to leave the captain's seat to do anything required for safe flight, but I will admit, emergency landing gear extension was impossible due to the hand crank being located in the bomb bay. A gear up landing would have resulted in not much more than bending the propellers, because when the landing gear is in the retract position the wheels extend out of the wheel wells far enough to make a decent landing.

I purchased that B-17 just for pure fun, nothing more. We parked the airplane at Herndon Airport in Orlando, Florida. I flew several pleasure trips with Kalemba, Carl Hendrix, and Tag Eure. Hendrix put a couple of lounge chairs in the nose and we called it his "Florida Room." Gasoline was cheap in those days, running less than 30 cents a gallon and I flew that B-17 solo for about 20 hours, just enjoying myself.

One morning, I went to fly it and noticed the tail gunner's window had been knocked out. I found out from the field personnel a young teenager from nearby Apopka had started the B-17 up and taxied it into a ditch. Apparently, the boy had broken into the airplane, studied the manual for several nights, and then managed to figure out how to start the engines so he could go for a flight. I had to admire his spunk.

Sitting solo at the controls of one of two B-17's I owned. Flying the B-17 single piloted was actually quite easy. It resembled the DC-4 in which I had a lot of flight time and it handled like it.

Flying Cucumbers

Soon afterwards, I met a gentleman named M.E. Brown, a farmer from Bowling Green, Florida who had huge farms on Andros Island in the Bahamas. I don't remember exactly how all this transpired, but he wanted me to give him a price on hauling cucumbers from Andros Island to Ft.

My B-17 being loaded with cucumbers on Andros Island.

Lauderdale, Florida. The cucumbers were to be harvested in the spring and he needed them transported as quickly and safely as possible, lest they spoil. We soon reached an agreement and I hauled cucumbers for him for one four-month long season.

When I licensed the B-17, however, I had to acknowledge I could not fly it for hire. As a result, in order for me to legally haul the cucumbers I had to transfer ownership of the B-17 to Brown. Under the regulations, he was then permitted to haul his own crop in his own airplane with me as his employee. That is why you will find documentation online of me registering it in January 1959, converting it to civil use in July 1959, and then M.E. Brown Inc. assuming in January 1960. When the season was done, I had Brown sign the airplane back to me in more paper shuffling.

I told Carl Hendrix to strip the inside of the B-17 completely out, including the removal of all the bomb racks to increase my cargo capacity. I wanted nothing but a cargo floor in there, and Hendrix complied. He also made a small door where the waist gunners used to peek out, and the cucumbers were loaded through there. When Hendrix completed his modifications, we calculated my B-17 could haul 22,000 pounds of cucumbers, which were packed in 60-pound burlap bags. After receiving the appropriate permissions to fly freight in the B-17 between the Bahamas and Fort Lauderdale, I was ready to begin.

My first flight in the newly stripped B-17 was from Fort

Lauderdale to Andros Island, which involved about a 200-mile trip over the open ocean. After we were airborne and heading on our way I told Hendricks, "This airplane is not flying like it used to. It feels kind of limber." But I proceeded anyway.

There was no tower, and after landing on the 3500-foot long dirt, rock and shell runway, a Bahamian customs man was waiting for me. After clearing customs, we picked up a very light load of about 10,000 pounds of cucumbers.

On our return trip, the airplane just didn't seem to fly right and small, subtle things bothered me. For example, when I turned the ailerons it seemed the wings tilted but the fuselage wouldn't move. I flew several loads between the U.S. and the Bahamas and just couldn't figure out what was different.

Days later, I was talking with a fellow National Airlines pilot named Mike Miller who used to instruct in B-17s. He mentioned he still had a manual and asked if I would like to borrow it. I said, "Sure," and so one day when I was on Andros Island and waiting for the airplane to be loaded with a full load of cucumbers, 22,000 pounds, I glanced through the manual. To my shock, in the center page outlined in red was a warning: "Do not fly this airplane with the bomb racks removed. They are part of the primary structure." I nearly had a heart attack. Basically, there was nothing holding the airplane together other than the rivets. I was then notified the B-17 was fully loaded so I

gritted my teeth and made the return trip to Fort Lauderdale, expecting the worst at any moment.

After I landed safely and disposed of the cucumbers, I immediately called Carl and asked what he had done with the bomb racks. He told me he took them to the dump, so we scurried down there and miraculously, they were still there, intact and just covered in trash. We retrieved the racks, reinstalled them, and the airplane flew nicely again.

In this March 1960 photograph on Andros Island in the Bahamas, I am loosely supervising the loading of 60-pound sacks of cucumbers aboard my B-17. I didn't bring a lunch on these trips and just ate cucumbers and other vegetables.

I didn't always fly solo: Wanda often accompanied me on my cucumber hauling trips to Andros Island.

Truck Accident

An incident I remember on Andros Island was when I was waiting for the normal load of cucumbers to arrive so they could load them on the airplane. I heard a truck coming down the road with several field hands in the back of it. As the truck turned the corner, the driver lost control. The truck rolled over and all the field hands were thrown out. There were about 10 or 12 field hands and some were injured rather severely and needed hospitalization.

There were no medical facilities on Andros Island I was asked if I would fly them to a Nassau hospital. I readily agreed so they were carefully loaded aboard the B-17. They were laid on blankets on the floor. We took off and headed for Nassau, which was just a short flight. I called the control tower and requested ambulances to meet me. The tower was quite skeptical about a B-17 with injured people on board, but they complied.

After the ambulances left and I got ready to leave to go back to Andros Island, I was approached by members of the Air Transport Ministry about who gave me permission to fly a bomber into Nassau. After a lot of talking, they found out why and let me go. When I returned to Andros, I found that the natives had totally destroyed the truck with hammers, rocks, and whatever else they could get their hands on. They were destroying the evil spirits in the truck and I was hoping the evil spirits did not get into my airplane.

B-17G 44-8543 – N3701G

In February 1961, I decided I needed a second B-17 cucumber hauler. The one I currently owned was

Looking into the cockpit of my B-17 bomber.

My wife Wanda standing beside the cargo door where the cucumbers were loaded.

flying fine, but my cucumber hauling business was expanding rapidly. Since it was only a 70-minute flight from Fort Lauderdale to Andros Island, it occurred to me that the operation would be more efficient if I flew the first B-17 in and then while that aircraft was being unloaded retrieved the second B-17 and repeated the process. I would keep a small ferry airplane on Andros Island for this purpose and fly it back and forth between B-17 flights.

This sent me on the hunt for a new B-17. In 1961, I contacted a company called AeroAmerican in Tucson, Arizona who had advertised that they had several B-17's for sale. Their asking price was $10,000.

After speaking to their representative, an Australian by the name of Greg Board, I flew to Tucson. I closely inspected several B-17s, finding most were in poor shape. I finally selected one that had been used by a U.S. Army general for personal

transportation. At one time, it had been elaborately fixed up, as much as a B-17 can be remodeled for comfort, as it had desks and chairs installed. I paid them a deposit, an important point that will come into play later.

I found out later this particular B-17 had "Tokyo tanks," which were additional internally mounted fuel tanks installed in the outer wing panels to increase the airplane's range. Researchers have been unable to locate the early military records of this bomber, but it is likely it saw combat in Europe after it was first built. While I am not listed by name, I am the airline captain that put N3701G to work hauling vegetables mentioned in the book, *Final Cut*, which documented the histories of surviving B-17s.

Part of my deal with AeroAmerican was that they would install a cargo floor and remove all of the extras in

Even my father got in on the action, flying with Wanda and I to Andros Island in my B-17.

the airplane that I didn't need, to reduce the B-17's gross weight and increase its load capacity. I also asked for the installation of a wide cargo door at the rear to make loading the airplane easier.

The airplane was promised to be ready for delivery in just a few weeks. Full payment was to occur when all work was complete and the aircraft was ready for ferry.

After a week passed, Board called and told me that he couldn't get the work done in Tucson and asked if he could move the airplane to Brownsville, Texas to complete the work there. I had no objection to that, as it would not cost me any additional money.

In early February, 1961 I received a call informing me that the work had been completed and the airplane was ready for pickup. I purchased an airline ticket for a flight aboard Braniff Airlines and flew into Brownsville International Airport, which was located about four miles from the city and where the B-17 was located.

My intention was to accept the aircraft and fly out that same day, landing in Fort Lauderdale before nightfall since I had accidently left my navigation charts behind. Things did not go as planned.

I had made arrangements that once I accepted the airplane, my bank would wire AeroAmerican's bank their money in exchange for a clean bill of sale. I inspected the B-17 and found all the work to be satisfactory. I then made arrangements for the main fuel tanks to be fueled with

just enough gas for me to fly to Fort Lauderdale with a slight reserve.

I then called my bank and instructed them to wire the balance of the final payment to AeroAmerican's account. When all of the bank fund transactions were complete, my bank was given the bill of sale, perhaps one of the most valuable documents I have ever received in my life.

I preflighted the B-17 and started all four engines in preparation for takeoff. Suddenly four men from the Intercontinental Engine Service boarded the airplane and made me shut down.

They informed me that AeroAmerican owed them money for some work they had done on a C-46 and they were holding both airplanes until it was paid. I explained to them that this airplane was legally mine as of an hour ago. I owned it free and clear and they had no right to stop me. They ignored me.

So I disembarked and went into the company office and met with the vice-president of Intercontinental. He confirmed that the money owed them was actually for work completed on a different aircraft, a C-46, but he was nonetheless holding both airplanes until all bills were paid. I pleaded my case to him to no avail and then he directed me to leave the premises.

It was now late at night so I called a taxi and spent the night in a hotel in Brownsville. The next morning I found an attorney and explained the situation to him. He politely informed me it would probably take three to four weeks of courtroom wrangling to get the plane released to me, even though legally the airplane was mine. He said in Texas possession is 90 percent of the law and since Intercontinental was holding the airplane, there was nothing I could do until I went to court.

I returned to the airport and tried to reason with the Intercontinental people again, repeating the same unsuccessful attempts for two days. Meanwhile, the B-17 was just sitting there and I finally accepted that I was wasting my time. On my last visit, I told the people that I was returning to Miami and asked them to call me a taxi so I could get to Brownsville for my flight home.

The taxi arrived about 3:00 p.m. and we drove towards Brownsville. I asked the driver to stop the cab about a mile and a half from the airport, paid him the entire fare, and told him to continue ahead to Brownsville without me.

I then walked back to the airport, which was located in a heavily forested area, and hid in the woods where I could see the hangar in front of which my airplane sat. I waited patiently until about 5:00 P.M. when I was sure that everyone had left for the day and then I walked over to my B-17.

There was a padlock on the new cargo door but I had a copy of the key and walked up to the cockpit. They had tied a rope between the two control wheels and the throttles and attached was a sign that said, "Do not fly this airplane as it has been disabled."

I didn't think they could have done much to disable the B-17 in such a short period of time. So I took the rope off, threw it out the window, and sat down in the pilot seat with the full intention of cranking it up and leaving. But when I turned the master switch on, there was no electricity. I suspected that they had removed the airplane's battery.

The battery on a B-17 is located in the wing, so I climbed up, unlatched the access port, and found that it was indeed missing. I walked back to the hangar, looked in the window, and saw my battery sitting there with my name on it. A worker working overtime in the hangar saw me. I originally told everyone that I had thrown a brick through the window to get the battery. But this was not true. I spoke with the worker and he knew that I had been wronged. I got my battery and a work stand and reinstalled it, careful to return the work stand to its proper place.

I then started all four engines and since the airplane was already fully fueled, I was ready to launch. I tried to use the radios to contact the tower but they did not work and I thought that perhaps they too had been disconnected from their antennas. I was not going to wait around for repairs, however, as it was getting close to dark and I needed to get airborne.

As I was taxiing out to the active runway at the airport, I looked up at the control tower and noticed they were flashing a red light at me, which meant to stop. I could not see any reason for this as there was no one flying in the immediate area. I continued taxiing very slowly toward the runway, watching carefully for other airplanes that might appear in the traffic pattern.

Suddenly, I spotted two police cars with flashing lights headed directly for me. At this point, it looked like I would be in a heap of trouble if I didn't get out of there immediately, so I opened the throttles and took off right from my spot on the taxiway. Once safely airborne I started shaking uncontrollably, but it wasn't because of the cold air. It was still quite warm in the airplane at that point.

As I headed up the coast toward Corpus Christi, I soon became concerned what action the police might be taking. My imagination ran wild and I thought that perhaps they had requested U.S. Navy fighters from nearby Naval Air Station Corpus Christi to shoot down this stolen B-17.

By the time I actually passed abeam Corpus Christi, it was a pitch black night and I could clearly see the city's lights. I climbed above the clouds to avoid being an easy target for the fighters, although I realized with the availability of radar this was a futile effort.

While the B-17's navigation lights worked, I should mention that the airspeed indicator was also inoperative, as it too, had probably been disconnected. Although I had now been airborne for more than an hour, I was still shaking from all the excitement and the realization of what I had done.

For the first time, I began to think that perhaps I should not have done what I did. I began to worry about what was going to happen to me once I landed back home in Fort Lauderdale. But it was too late to go back now.

Under the stars, I cruised along trying to follow the Gulf of Mexico coastline as best I could. Although I did not have any charts, as a National Airlines pilot I had flown along this same route for many years in my various airliners and I felt exceedingly comfortable with my navigation.

I was forced, however, to change altitude many times because of the frigid temperatures in the unheated and unpressurized B-17. I started out at a VFR altitude of 9500 feet where the temperature was rather cold. Soon, I descended to 3500 feet where the temperature was much warmer.

As I passed the Houston area, I was a little concerned about a possible collision with nearby airliners, but it was getting late and I knew commercial traffic would soon subside. At one point, I desperately had to use the bathroom, more commonly known as the bomb bay. With no autopilot, it was quite a feat.

The weather remained cooperative throughout my flight, although as I approached New Orleans about 10:00 to 11:00 p.m., a slight haze appeared. I considered flying across the Gulf of Mexico to shorten my flight but since I had plenty of gas and no navigation charts, I thought it best if I continued along the coast.

It was an awfully lonesome flight and I reflected upon a lot of things in my life as I flew along in the darkness. With the cold and fatigue slowly setting in, I would have paid a hundred dollars for a single cup of coffee.

In the vicinity of Panama City one of the radio receivers suddenly started working and I picked up a weather forecast calling for fog in the Fort Lauderdale and Miami area. I pressed on although I thought the trip would never end.

To avoid military restricted areas around Panama City, I stayed north of this area and then went direct to Tallahassee, which I could see in the distance. I then proceeded south to Cross City and then turned southeast towards Orlando, which soon came into view. Then, as the coastline became more or less visible, I proceeded direct to Fort Lauderdale International Airport. All through the flight, the

THE BEST NEWSPAPER UNDER THE SUN

Established In 1896   Miami, Fla., Thursday, February 9, 1961

Miami News Photo by Jay Spencer

Here's Flying Fortress LeRoy Brown Flew By Himself

Atomic Sub Spied On, Agent Says

He Grabs Airplane --And Charges Fly

By MILT SOSIN

LONDON (AP) — A witness testified today details of Britain's first nuclear submarine were among royal navy secrets stolen by five persons accused of spying for the Soviet Union.

The witness was Capt. George

A Miami pilot flew alone today from Brownsville, Tex., to Fort Lauderdale in a World War II Flying Fortress which the Texas Rangers accused him of stealing.

The 38-year-old flier, LeRoy Brown of 3804 SW 60th Ct., said

International Airport with fuel for six hours flying left in the tanks.

NO PAYMENT?

Sprague charged that Brown turned up in Brownsville three days ago and tried to take the plane without paying $1,750 owed to Intercontinental for repairs and

"He must have used some kind of auxiliary starter to get the engines going."

Brown, after consulting with attorney John H. Payne, refused to say how he started the engines. But he said the flight was normal in every respect.

It didn't take long for my trip to make the headlines. I also received several offers to appear on television and radio, which I declined.

engines ran perfectly. It was really a nice flight considering the fact that I was all alone in a four-engine bomber without any coffee.

Finally, at about 2:00 a.m., Fort Lauderdale's rotating beacon and then runway lights came into view. When I arrived at the airport, the tower was closed, although it would not have made any difference as my radios had failed again. I circled the field once and then landed on runway 9. I taxied to where my other B-17 was parked and shut the engines down. I had made it.

As I leaped to the ground through the cubbyhole where one exited from this fool thing, I was promptly greeted by four or five border patrolmen. They all knew me because I had previously worked with them on various projects. One of them chuckled and said, "LeRoy, we've been expecting you." I laughingly told them, "I'm sure glad I'm among friends, it's been a long night."

They informed me that there was an all-points bulletin out for the seizure of the stolen plane and the arrest of its bold pilot. They graciously pronounced they were not going to do anything about the whole affair. I called my wife and told her I was on the way home, she having no knowledge of what I had just done. Grateful, but totally exhausted, I thanked them and drove home.

Wanda greeted me at the door and said that agents for Dave Garroway from the Today show had been in contact with her. One of the original pioneers of the television talk show,

he wanted me to appear with him. I told Wanda that my answer was an absolute, "No," and we didn't answer the constantly ringing telephone for the rest of the night.

The following afternoon, I contacted my attorney friend in Fort Lauderdale, who had joined the business with me and I explained the flight to him. He suggested that the airplane be put in an inactive corporation he owned. I said I guessed that would be all right. I later regretted this decision as it resulted in a lot of paper shuffling about ownership.

No legal action was ever taken against me because I had not really done anything wrong. Although the Federal Aviation Administration (FAA) did send me a shopping list of civil air regulations they thought I had violated and requested an informal hearing with their attorney from the Atlanta office. My attorney and I met and discussed the events. He decided he would not file any violations and he would accept a civil penalty of $300 to settle the case. I told him no way. My attorney, now my partner, said he would pay it, as he could not afford to spend much more time on the case. I told him to go ahead but leave me out of it.

One of the charges was that I did not use a runway for takeoff. However, at the time there was no Federal aviation regulation that explicitly stated a runway must be used, or any prohibition against using a taxiway for takeoff.

I was accused of flying without lights when I departed Brownsville, but my lights were working as I could see the reflection of the rotating beacon on the backs of the propellers. Also, my takeoff was before official sunset and therefore lights were not required.

I was cited for not obeying the tower's red light. But I counterclaimed that there was no safety concern and that they were trying to interfere in a civil issue over which they had no jurisdiction.

The people who should have been sued and charged were the maintenance people who disabled my B-17 and made it non-airworthy after it had been paid for and licensed. They had even removed all the airworthiness certificates from the airplane but I eventually got them back.

Traveling across the country in the middle of the night alone in that monster was not a lot of fun, especially when I knew the police were chasing me. But I knew they couldn't catch an airplane. It was also not the fastest trip in the world. But if I had had some coffee and someone to talk to, it would have been a pleasant trip.

Several months after this incident, an FAA inspector did get after me again. Ramp checking my B-17 for compliance with various directives, he asked me where my water survival equipment was since I was flying over the open ocean. I told him, "Have you ever tried to sink a cucumber?"

B-17 Cucumber Operations

The next day I readied my new B-17 for cargo service and I stripped everything out of it that I could to reduce weight, remembering this time to keep the bomb bay's internal weapon racks.

And the cucumbers? I still had the contract and within weeks, I was executing perfectly my plan of flying one B-17 between Fort Lauderdale and Andros Island while they loaded or unloaded the other.

I soon discovered I would have to hire another pilot to fly one of the B-17s. I chose Howard Meyers and got Wayne North to fly copilot for him. This worked out very well and I also recruited two standby pilots.

Eventually, competitors appeared using former military Curtiss C-46 cargo transports and I was underbid on my contract. We folded our B-17 cucumber freight transportation operation at the end of the harvest season, which meant my operation ran from March 1960 to March 1961.

During this whole episode, I had very few problems with either of the B-17s. I noticed one difference between the military operation and mine. I had to land with a full load while they dumped theirs on the enemy. I also had the advantage of no one shooting at me. I did carry many passengers who were interested in flying in a B-17 back and forth between the Bahamas and Fort Lauderdale, including former B-17 pilots and their sons, customs agents and their sons, and the farmers.

Flying Dynamite

Shortly after the cucumber contract ended, I was approached by a gentleman at Fort Lauderdale

International Airport inquiring if I would haul a load of geladyne powder to West End, Grand Bahamas where it was needed to build a harbor at Freeport.

I had never heard of geladyne powder and asked him what it was. He told me, "It is a form of dynamite and it will not explode without the caps." I told him I would check with all the authorities before I could provide him an answer. After speaking with the FAA, Border Patrol, Customs, and the Airport Manager, I found no objections.

Four days later, my B-17 was loaded with geladyne powder and I asked my friend, Wayne North, to fly as copilot. Prior to takeoff, we called the tower requesting light signals to clear us for takeoff. Wayne and I were both a little nervous about accidently igniting the geladyne powder and

we told the tower we would not be making any radio transmissions for obvious reasons.

We made a successful overwater transit and landed in West End after an uneventful flight. As we tried to clear customs, we were told we could not unload until we had written permission from the Nassau police. I told them I was not going to fly to Nassau just for a signature. They said a phone call would not be acceptable.

Wayne and I waited and waited and I finally requested the authorities to call my local friend John Purpall to come and get us to drive us downtown, which they did. They asked me why I was going downtown. I said, "The airplane is sitting there in the hot sun and might possibly blow up and I don't want to

My former B-17 N3701G is currently flying using its original military serial number.

be around when that happens." Less than 45 minutes later, the airplane was completely unloaded.

After returning to Fort Lauderdale, I got a message from the FAA asking me why I was carrying dynamite in the B-17. I told them that is what the B-17 was made for - to carry explosives. Obviously, this was not the right answer.

They again mailed me a list of civil air regulations I had violated, but I proved to them I had received permission from all the authorities involved. Even the customs agents in Fort Lauderdale, with whom I had always had a good relationship with, went to bat for me. The matter was eventually resolved and no further enforcement actions were taken.

Final Disposition

I continued to fly my B-17's until 1962, when I sold them to the Dothan Aviation Corp., after Carl Hendrix converted them into crop dusters. If I had just taken one of those fine warbirds, placed it in a barn in Pompano, and closed the door for 40 years, I would be a rich man today, as they now sell for millions of dollars.

It is fitting that both my B-17's were used as crop dusters by Dothan. Sadly, in 1976, after making a forced landing due to an engine fire while dusting fire ants, B-17 N4710C was destroyed by fire in Georgia.

B-17 N3701G was also substantially damaged in a forced landing while dusting but it has since been restored to airworthy status for use in air shows. It is now located near Norfolk, VA in a museum and is still flying.

Chapter Thirteen
Jets

The Lockheed Electra was powered by a turbine engine that turned a propeller and was known as the "prop jet." Our joke was that with a piston engine the pilot hoped that it would never be on fire but with a jet he hoped that the fire would never go out.

The end of the piston-powered airliner was in sight as military jet technology began to enter the commercial airline market. In 1957, Lockheed introduced the turboprop L-188 Electra, the first propeller-driven transport powered by four jet engines in the United States. Known as a turboprop, the Electra used a gas turbine to power a propeller at speeds nearly 100 miles per hour faster than existing commercial aircraft and its airspeed approached the maximum speed limit physically achievable by propeller driver aircraft. Some airlines even painted "Prop-Jet" on the sides of their Electras to charm an American public mesmerized by the new jet technology into believing they were indeed flying aboard a jet, despite the presence of propellers.

The Electra's 1959 debut into commercial service was marred by the loss of three airplanes in 14 months. An extensive investigation organized by the Civil Aeronautics Board determined that two of the Electra crashes were caused by an in-flight structural failure of the wings due to wing flutter. Consequently, Lockheed resolved the issue by modifying all the Electra's at considerable expense. The damage to the Electra's reputation was done, however, and production ceased in 1961.

National Airlines purchased 14 Lockheed Super Electra IIs taking delivery between 1959 and 1961. With accommodations for 84 passengers, the Electra had a pressurized cabin for the passengers and onboard weather radar for the pilots.

Despite a cruise speed of 400 miles per hour, this turboprop transport was soon overshadowed by the pure jetliners that had reached the airline market.

Flying the Electra

I officially entered the jet age in 1965 when I received notice to begin transition training into the Electra, with engines rated at 4,000 horsepower each. Training consisted of a 3-week ground school course that lasted eight hours a day with an exam at the end of each day with a minimum passing grade of 80 points.

There were about 15 pilots in my class, which consisted of a lot of the older captains and a few copilots. The instructor was a very nice guy, but one of the older captains really irritated him by continually interrupting with irrelevant questions that were not particularly suited to that particular day's class.

On about the tenth day of this annoying behavior, the captain again interrupted the instructor and said, "I would like to ask a stupid ass question."

The instructor answered by saying, "I will be glad to answer your questions, but I am not interested in any personal evaluations." This broke up the class with laughter and put a stop to the annoying questions.

After ground school finished, I got to ride jump seat on a couple of trips. At the first takeoff, I uttered to myself, "Wow, this is going to be a great airplane to fly."

Soon my turn came to qualify as second in command and I was really thrilled at the performance of this airplane. It was easy to fly and with a cruise speed of 400 miles an hour, it would go as fast, or faster than any of the other, similar airliners. It also had a huge cockpit with a lot of nice windows. I was really impressed with this airplane and for the first time found an airliner that was almost as good as my Travel Air.

My time to check out as captain on the Electra came sooner than I expected. After more ground school and training, I was ready for my first flight as captain in October 1965. This airplane was almost overpowered. For instance, if the number 4 engine quit on takeoff you merely reduced the power on number 1 engine to help maintain directional control and continued to take off. I flew the Electra for several years and never lost an engine.

I might add that our Electras had no autopilots and we heard rumors that Mr. Baker said he was paying us to fly the airplane and not an expensive autopilot. As the airplane was so stable and easy to fly, we cared not.

In the winter with snow and ice on the runways, this airplane was rather easy to handle, as the reversible propellers made it possible to stop on the well-known dime. Bad weather and icing conditions were of little concern. Of course, we slowed down for turbulence.

Sometimes, however, bad weather was not a piece of cake. As I was making an instrument landing system (ILS) approach during particularly lousy weather into Pensacola, the tower advised us of rather heavy rain but the wind more or less right down the runway. They claimed the cloud ceiling was approximately 250 feet.

After passing the outer marker with everything in order, the airplane started going below the glide slope. I quickly added power and pulled the nose up 3 or 4 degrees, but we were still descending. Concerned, I decided it was time to leave, but even with full power and 8 degrees nose up attitude, I could not keep the airplane from its uncommanded descent.

It was really raining hard. At about 600 feet, the airplane finally started to climb and I proceeded toward Panama City. I called Pensacola tower to advise them of our problem but received no answer. As we pulled out of the weather, we called air traffic control (ATC) for a clearance to Panama City and ATC advised us that a small tornado had crossed over the field without anyone alerting us to that fact. We had apparently run into an extremely strong downdraft. Had I been alerted to this fact, I certainly would not have made an approach and would have gone to my alternate. Thanks to the great Electra with its powerful propellers, we avoided a serious accident. This was one time I was glad I was not in my Travel Air. Overall, I find I have very little to write about as far as my experiences on the Electra because we had so very little trouble with them.

I do recall one night when I was descending into Daytona Beach from New York before proceeding on to Tampa, the termination point of the flight. About five miles from Daytona, we slowed down to about 170 miles an hour and put the landing lights on. Suddenly a very large bird of some sort, which wasn't watching where he was going, flew into the nose of the airplane breaking the radome. The sound in the cockpit was horrendous but our landing was successful and uneventful. Unfortunately, the bird could not say the same.

We easily patched up the radome with some metal tape we kept on board for minor repairs. To be safe, we decided to fly to Tampa at a reduced airspeed. Somehow, an FAA inspector found out about this and upon landing, he accused me of flying a non-airworthy airplane. After much discussion with the inspector, I reminded him that the FAA had placed a speed restriction on the Electra of 250 knots until the problem of its wings tearing off could be solved. I told him I had flown at a reduced speed for safety reasons, just as they had advised. That comment terminated any further problems.

Hauling Canaries

I did not like flying freight but occasionally, I would get stuck with one of these annoying flights. In this case, I was assigned an Electra to fly from Idlewild, New York nonstop to Miami. We usually carried a load of New York Times newspapers and other various perishable articles. For this night trip, however, we were carrying a load of about 500 canaries, supposedly secured in their containers.

After we were airborne for a while, somehow, a couple of the boxes holding the birds broke and there were canaries flying all over the airplane. We finally closed the cockpit door to keep them out of our hair. As a joke, I told the copilot to call flight control in Miami and ask them how the canaries that were now flying around in our cabin instead of sitting in their cages were going to affect our landing weight. Of course, I got some rather silly remarks from them.

Games of Chance

As the airliners got larger, so too, did the number of flight crew members as extra stewardesses were added to accommodate the growing number of passengers.

Probably every flight crew who has ever flown large civilian or military transports has played this same game. If we had ten crewmembers, we would put ten slips of paper with numbers on them. Each crewmember would then pay a dollar for their private number. The flight engineer would take a piece of chalk and mark on a tire with the chalk and divide it into ten numbers.

After we parked at the terminal, the crewmember whose number matched the number on the ground won the pot.

Thrilling the Passengers

I recently spoke with Captain John Wentworth, one of my former Electra copilots, and he reminded me of one of our more memorable trips together. It was a beautiful fall afternoon when

I gave him and the passengers a most wonderful treat.

On the first leg of the trip, we encountered an absolutely flat layer of clouds extending as far to the east as we could see. Because there was no convection associated with the clouds, there was no turbulence. We continued the flight and landed at our first intermediate stop. I was at the controls for the next leg of our eastbound journey and we ascended into the cloud layer until reaching a level about a thousand feet below the top.

I leveled off and allowed the Electra to accelerate to its maximum allowable speed and then aggressively, but smoothly, pulled back on the control column and rotated us to an unusually nose-high attitude, rocketing us up through the top of the layer like a cannon shot. The result was both dramatic and spectacular. Only an insensitive clod could have failed to be impressed and excited. John recalled that I looked over at him with a mischievous grin and exclaimed, "Heh, heh, that'll give 'em a thrill!"

Pure Jetliners

The first American true all-jet commercial airliner was the four-engine Boeing 707, whose prototype flew in 1954. The Boeing 707 entered transatlantic commercial service with Pan American World Airways in 1958.

Surprisingly, Rickenbacker of Eastern Air Lines, National Airlines prime competitor, was reluctant to acquire pure jet transports. Enormously expensive, Rickenbacker felt that jets were a fad and would never be feasible commercially. Baker, of National Airlines, recognized the potential of a pure jetliner but was waiting to purchase the less expensive Douglas DC-8, which was then in development.

The Douglas Company developed the four-engine DC-8 to compete with the Boeing 707 and its first flight was in 1958. The DC-8 was scheduled to enter service with Delta Air Lines in 1959. In 1961, it would become the first commercial transport to break the sound barrier when it exceeded 660 miles per hour in a controlled dive. Both Baker and Rickenbacker ordered the DC-8, but delivery was not expected for several months due to order backlogs.

In an incredible marketing triumph over Rickenbacker, Baker, who was always looking for a way to top his nemesis, flew to New York to speak with Juan Trippe, president of Pan American World Airways. He offered to lease two of Pan Am's Boeing 707's during the peak of Florida's winter passenger service and during Pan Am's lowest traffic period. To the surprise of everyone, Trippe agreed.

Accordingly, in December 1958, National Airlines launched the first domestic jet service in the United States with flights between Miami and New York. The leased National Airlines jets shuttled back and forth between Florida and New York at near capacity to the aggravation of Rickenbacker. The jets were returned to Pan American in the spring, so I was never given the opportunity to fly them. I was biding my time waiting for the DC-8.

The Douglas DC-8 was the first pure-jet airliner I flew with National Airlines. I particularly enjoyed flying the stretched version.

Flying the DC-8

National Airlines received their first DC-8 in 1960 and used them almost exclusively on the lucrative Miami to New York route. In 1961, the Civil Aeronautics Board awarded National Airlines the Southern Transcontinental Route, which extended the airline's passenger service from the east coast to California. National Airlines used the DC-8, including a stretch DC-8, on this route.

While I hated to see the Electra retired, I was looking forward to flying my first pure jet, that great big huge DC-8. I was checked out in the DC-8 as copilot in October 1964 and as captain in June 1972. The training was routine and similar in style to my previous piston-powered and turbine-powered upgrades.

My transition to actually flying pure jets was relatively easy, but with the aircraft's increased size and speed, many of my old destinations disappeared. The Miami to New Orleans route I flew in the Lodestar with its many landings was shortened with stops only in Fort Myers, Sarasota, Tampa, Tallahassee, Panama City, and Pensacola. Most of the time, I flew from Miami to the West Coast.

I flew all of the various DC-8 series that National Airlines owned or rented, including the basic model series 10 through 50 and the Super 60 series, which consisted of the 61, 62 and 63 stretched variant.

To increase capacity, the DC-8 series 61 was a stretched version of the DC-8, which had the same wings, engines, and pylons as the previous model, but had a 240-inch plug in the forward fuselage and a 200-inch plug in the aft fuselage. This increased its overall length to 187 feet 4 inches giving the stretch DC-8 its distinctive long, lean appearance.

The initial DC-8 type rating I received covered all models, including the series 61 because most of the instrumentation was identical. This was a fortunate thing because for pilot schedules, the various types of DC-8 were all co-mingled. When you went out to take a flight, you more than likely did not know which model they assigned the flight. However, it really didn't matter for they were all basically the same airplane except for the series 61's length.

I was very happy flying the DC-8. To start with, I loved the safety of having four engines. I never did like the idea of crossing a 4-engine ocean in a 2-engine airplane, as we frequently did cutting across the Gulf of Mexico. I thought the DC-8 was easy to fly as it was very responsive on the controls and despite its size, the stretched DC-8 was also easy to handle on the ground. As an added benefit, it also had a very roomy cockpit. It handled very well in turbulent weather and although I was struck by lightning several times, we always came through unscathed.

Of course, like all airplanes the DC-8 had some shortcomings, the main one of which was rain removal from the windshield. They replaced the windshield wipers with an air tube that ran the length of the windshield. It used engine air to blow away the rain before it reached the windshield glass.

A stretched version of the DC-8. The fuselage was lengthened to accommodate more passengers on short distance, high capacity routes.

One of my favorite jet age stewardesses, Betty Jackson.

flight control. It was a night flight and I filed a flight plan for 37,000 feet to be above the weather, which was forecast for rain. The trip was uneventful until we arrived at Mexico City where it was, in fact, raining really hard. During our approach, a completely unexpected event required our immediate attention.

Approach control brought us in quite high above the glide slope, so I reduced all four throttles to flight idle to get on the glide slope as soon as possible. We were about eight miles from the airport. After settling nicely down to the glide slope, I applied power to maintain the descent at the proper speed, only to discover all four engines had flamed out. I couldn't believe it. It was the proverbial dark and stormy night and I had no engines.

I immediately turned on the ignition override switch and told the flight engineer, Mugovero (Muggs), that we better get at least two engines going or we were going to have a long, wet walk. I stayed busy flying the airplane while the engineer and copilot were scrambling frantically to restart two of the engines, which they successfully did.

It worked well in theory, however, when you closed the throttles to land the air diminished.

DC-8 Engine Failure in Mexico City

Recalling my most unusual trip in the DC-8 is easy. On April 25, 1975, I received a call from crew scheduling advising me of a charter flight to Mexico City. Since they could not find anyone else, they assigned me the trip.

The flight was in one of our stretch DC-8's, so I got dressed and went to

These two engines gave us plenty of power to make a safe, successful landing. As we touched down, let me say the excitement level in the cockpit was quite high as we realized how close we had come to having a very bad accident with a full load of passengers. But, that was not the end. More problems awaited us.

An airplane holding for takeoff watched our landing and advised us on the radio that the tires on our right main landing gear were on fire. Thankfully, as I slowed the DC-8 down, splashing water from the wet runway doused the fire.

We were able to taxi to the terminal building and discharge the passengers. Muggs went out to inspect the tires and reported that two were flat. He also advised there were two wheels and tires in one of our baggage bins. I instructed him to put them on the airplane so we could go back to Miami.

Muggs returned to the cockpit to report the tires were the wrong size for this airplane. I asked him if they were round and full of air and if they would fit the axles on the airplane. He replied affirmatively, so I instructed him to put them on the jet as we were flying back to Miami without passengers.

After we pushed back from the gate for our return flight, all four engines started normally. We taxied to the runway where we received takeoff clearance. I opened the throttles for takeoff, but we were still plagued by gremlins. Only two of the four engines would accelerate, so I aborted the takeoff.

Naturally, some of the flight attendants came up to the cockpit to see what was happening and listened silently to our discussions. The copilot, Muggs, and I worked out a plan to get the two reluctant engines to accelerate. We decided we would begin the takeoff on the two good engines that would accelerate, and then as we approached 90 knots Muggs would attempt to add power

to the idling engines. Everyone was in agreement this would work so we decided to give it a try.

Cleared for takeoff once again, as we approached the 90-knot mark, Muggs got a third engine to put out power and a few seconds later, the fourth engine also produced normal power. If these engines had not started producing power, we could have easily aborted the takeoff as we had plenty of room on the runway to slow down. We proceeded to Miami uneventfully and thankfully, with no more surprises.

I really did not get scared until I got home that night, as I could not get the events of the four-engine failure off my mind. My external performance in front of the flight crew when faced with the near catastrophe of a four-engine failure at night, in bad weather, while close to the ground, by no means reflects my inner personal feelings at that moment. The instant I realized all four engines had quit, I was gripped with fear and an empty, sick feeling. However, I quickly overcame my fright by a great rise in adrenalin that enabled me personally to fly the airplane while ordering the rest of the crew to do the things necessary to save our lives and those of the passengers. The flight crew performed their duties flawlessly. There was no time to declare an emergency, read a checklist, or alert the cabin crew to the problem. Had we been successful in getting only one engine running, I am certain we would have had a safe landing.

I still thank my lucky stars and the good Lord for giving this professional flight crew the ability to overcome their shock and to execute a flawless performance in the face of an almost certain tragedy. This four-engine failure was the one and only time something like this ever happened to me or anyone else that I know of.

DC-8 Surprise

The DC-8 still had other inflight emergencies in store for me, although not quite as exciting as the engine-out approach into Mexico City. This surprise occurred during a night flight in a DC-8 from San Francisco to Miami, with a scheduled stop at New Orleans.

We had a rather uncomfortable trip on the leg from San Francisco to New Orleans as turbulent, rainy weather abounded everywhere. The New Orleans weather was moderate rain, low ceilings, and very choppy turbulence. Tower cleared to land on the northerly runway and I knew the passengers were concerned, as it was quite rough. The landing was to be even rougher.

When we were only a short distance from touching down, the airplane suddenly tried to make a violent turn to the left. On instinct, I sensed something was wrong and I slammed the jet down rather hard on the runway. Despite this heavy impact, I believe the passengers probably breathed a sigh of relief to be safe on the ground. I logged it as a landing even though it was more like an arrival. I was not proud of that landing, inasmuch as it was me that did it and not a new copilot who I could cheerfully tease.

Ground control cleared us to the terminal building and we stopped at the gate to let the passengers off. One of the parking crew motioned for us to retract the flaps, which was confusing, as we had already completed that checklist item right after the landing.

As I stepped outside to inspect the jet, I discovered it was a good thing I elected not to abort the landing when the airplane had swerved on landing. One of the mechanics advised me the left flap had retracted by itself in the air due to a broken flap actuating arm. Asymmetrical flap deployment typically induces an uncontrollable roll, which had just started before I arrested it by slamming the DC-8 to the runway. Had I elected to open the throttles to abort the approach and climb to a safer altitude to determine what had gone wrong, I would not be writing this book.

DC-8 Crash in New Orleans

One time, however, another airline's DC-8 nearly did me in. It was 1967 and I was flying a Lockheed Electra from Miami to New Orleans, the termination point of the flight. It was a very short layover in New Orleans and the whole crew was set up to stay at the Hilton Inn Hotel just across the street from the airport. Our flight was totally uneventful.

We landed late in the afternoon and I had a nice dinner and returned to my room to watch some old World War II movie on television. I went to bed about 9:30 and was sound asleep only to be awakened by a huge explosion. I opened my eyes in time to see flaming debris shoot through the roof of my room and explode out a portion of my room wall. Some of the flaming debris landed on my bed and set it on fire.

It took me less than 10 seconds to put on my trousers and open my door to escape the burning room. I could tell that most of the hotel was on fire. There were two Trans-Texas Airways stewardesses in a room adjacent to mine who were screaming that their door was jammed. I helped them open it from the outside so they could get out.

In 1962 Lewis Maytag (left) assumed responsibility as president of National Airlines from George Baker (right). In its entire history, these two men were the only presidents of the airline.

I had no idea what had happened, but as we reached the courtyard, we could see a jet engine lying there. Obviously, an airliner had crashed into the hotel. It turned out to be a Delta Air Lines DC-8 on a training flight without passengers.

The crew was practicing a two-engine out simulated landing when, for unknown reasons, the airplane stalled and crashed, smashing into our hotel and demolishing nearby homes. Eighteen persons were killed, including nine high school girls in our hotel who were part of a large group of seniors on a spring outing.

The scene around the hotel was total pandemonium. I knew the news media would have this all over the country instantly, so I called my wife, Wanda, at about 4 a.m. to let her know my whole flight crew and I were safe.

Our return flight directly to Miami in the Electra was scheduled for an early departure before any stores opened. Consequently, I had to fly the flight in dirty civilian clothes in my stocking feet, as I lost everything else in the burning hotel room. This was one hectic nightmare. We arrived home safely in Miami on schedule and once again, we were thankful for the powers that be. The whole crew was strangely quiet throughout the whole trip, everyone in total disbelief about what had just happened.

To add to my aviation resume, for a short while I owned a fixed base operation at Herndon Airport, Orlando, which included a Mooney franchise.

Lewis B. Maytag

In 1962, Baker sold control of National Airlines to Lewis B. "Bud" Maytag, heir to the Maytag Appliance Company fortune and former president of Frontier Airlines. The transition was transparent to us line pilots. We knew that Maytag was a licensed pilot and owned a beautiful Staggerwing Beechcraft as well as a Jet Commander. He was a very quiet person, but a good president. Under his leadership, National Airlines continued to modernize its fleet and expanded its operations, including new flights to London, Paris, Amsterdam, and Frankfurt. Sadly, a year later Baker died of a heart attack while vacationing in Austria. In its 46-year history, National Airlines had only two presidents, Baker and Maytag.

Air Orlando

In the mid-1960's, my attorney and I acquired an interest in a fixed based operation at Herndon Airport in Orlando, FL after some friends

of mine ran into difficulty with the Internal Revenue Service. Living in Miami at the time, I moved our family to Orlando and we renamed the business Air Orlando. We had a flight school, a maintenance shop, and a charter service. We were busy as heck and one of our most lucrative charter contracts was with General Electric to carry their personnel around the country, with frequent trips to the Huntsville, Alabama, Space Center. General Electric was supporting NASA and these people were involved with the first moon shot. We owned a DC-3 and four twin Beeches, and we were the only school in the area to offer private pilot, commercial pilot, instrument, and multi-engine training. I was certified by the FAA to sign off on every rating. Unfortunately, I got cross-wired with my attorney-partner and I left the business without a cent after we came to be on not too friendly terms.

Astor

After we left Air Orlando in 1965, we moved to Astor, Florida to get away from all the headaches. Astor was partly in the Ocala National forest and boasted a 3000-foot public access grass runway. We built a brick home on the St. John's River and I kept my various personal airplanes at the strip.

Since Astor was about 300 miles from Miami where I was based with National Airlines, I commuted by flying my Mooney Super 21 or a Cessna 310B. I also owned a Waco YKS7, but I did not commute in this airplane due

My two B-17's sitting at Air Orlando, a fixed based operation that I owned.

to its slow speed. National Airlines graciously let me park my airplanes on their ramp, making it easy for me to access my "other ride."

Frequently, my return flights home after completing a National Airlines trip were at night, which meant I had to land on Astor's little, unlit airstrip located in the middle of a big, dark forest. As I got closer to home, I would call Wanda on the Unicom frequency to come to the airport.

There was only one light to guide me to the runway. It was on the top of a radio tower and I would begin my approach passing this red light at 2000 feet on a north heading. I would then start a standard rate descent to 900 feet, turn on an easterly heading, and in front of me the airstrip would appear, lit up by Wanda with her automobile

headlights. There was absolutely no problem with this procedure. Well, except for one evening.

After a routine approach, I landed and taxied up to where Wanda stood backlit by her automobile lights. All of a sudden, about ten soldiers armed with machine guns pointed directly at us surrounded us. One of them shouted, "Raise your hands, we finally got you."

Now that was scary.

I asked them what this was about and they told me that they had been looking for us and had finally caught us. I told them I did not know what they were talking about. I was still wearing my National Airlines uniform and I told them I was just coming home from work and my wife was picking me up.

It was only then they realized their mistake. They told us that they were a Green Beret unit conducting a training session and they had surrounded the wrong airplane. I do not think Wanda and I slept very well that night from the fright.

Move to Zellwood

Astor was a delightful place to live, but with our two children having to travel 20 miles to the nearest school, life became a little difficult and we were thinking of moving.

At this same time, my good friend Tag Eure, who owned a crop dusting business in Zellwood, Florida, died unexpectedly. He had left his business in a rather unstable position, so to assist his wife and brother, I volunteered to help them out by crop dusting in one of their 1929 Waco Straightwings on my days off from the airline.

We soon reorganized the business into a corporation called Eure Brothers,

My Mooney parked on the National Airlines ramp. I would commute to work in this airplane, as well as others I owned, and National would graciously let me park near my "other ride."

Inc. It was very successful, as we had a contract with one of the biggest farmers in the area. In fact, the farmer planted between 500 and 600 acres of corn each year, as well as celery and carrot crops.

In 1970, Wanda and I decided to move to Zellwood as a result of Tag's death and me being a new partner in Eure Brothers. In the summer, we traveled to Statesboro, Georgia to crop dust cotton, peanuts, sunflowers and tobacco. Business was very good and we had our own dusting strip in Zellwood where we kept the business' two 1929 Waco dusters and two Piper Pawnees. My favorite airplane was the Waco, as it flew almost as well as my old Travel Air. We later switched to Cessna AgWagons. I was doing all this cropdusting on my days off from the airline until I stopped in 1975. This was my last year in crop dusting. Wanda and I still live in Zellwood to this day.

Commuting to Work

I also moved all my personal airplanes to our 3500-foot grass cropdusting strip and I continued to commute by air to Miami for my airline job. Over the years, I flew several personal airplanes from this field, including a Cessna 411 previously owned by Frank Sinatra. This airplane's registration number was N114FS, with the FS standing for Frank Sinatra. I had so much trouble with the engines on this airplane that I concluded it was not Frank Sinatra who owned it, but rather Fred Sanford of television junkyard fame.

Our DC-3

In the mid 1970's, I saw an ad in Trade-A-Plane (an aircraft sales publication) offering a very nice DC-3 for sale in Beaumont, Texas for the amazingly low price of $15,000. I called immediately to get more information about the airplane and I found it was in excellent shape with many high-speed modifications. This led me to purchasing my second DC-3 sight unseen.

I flew to Beaumont the next day, checked it out, paid for it, refueled it, and then flew it back to Zellwood. The original reason I bought the airplane was to convert it into a sprayer and duster combination. However, after much thought, Wanda and I decided not to convert this nice airplane. It had an executive interior and enough speed modifications to satisfy most DC-3 pilots.

I started commuting to work in this airplane but eventually the Airport Authority in Miami found out I was flying solo and told me I could not fly back and forth anymore without a copilot.

I also offered charter service in the DC-3. In 1964, I was featured in some newspaper articles as I ferried Robert King High, mayor of Miami and a gubernatorial candidate, around Florida. I rented it to his campaign for $0.80 a mile.

One day, Wanda and I, and our children, decided to go to the Adirondack Mountains in New York on a camping trip. We also took our dog, Brandy, a full size poodle. We had onboard arrangements for the dog

This is my Air-Orlando DC-3. Note the swimming pool that was built for our company to help attract patrons.

to use as a bathroom. We flew nonstop from Orlando to Rome, New York and we had good weather all the way. When we landed and opened the door, the dog bolted out, headed for the first tree, and circled the tree five or six times before he could slow down and relieve himself. We only stayed a few days as it was very cold and we returned to Orlando where the weather was nice. We had a delightful trip.

My personal thoughts about the DC-3 are that it was nothing less than an absolutely great airplane to fly. The cockpit was very quiet and it handled very well in bad weather. I never had any serious problems with either of the DC-3's I owned.

You may wonder, however, how anyone could afford the fuel for a DC-3, as the airplane burned almost 100 gallons an hour. Remember that at this point in time, aviation gas was about 25 cents a gallon. Today, I couldn't afford even to crank it up with fuel costing almost $5.00 a gallon.

Zero-Zero Takeoffs

Commuting by my own private airplanes was a delightful way to go to work. The flight only took a little over an hour each direction. Occasionally, however, I did have some challenges to overcome.

One of the airline requirements was that I call flight control no later than 2 hours before flight departure time to let them know I was not sick or whatever and ready to fly the assigned trip. On early morning departures, I would call in for my flight about 2 hours and 45 minutes before I launched from Zellwood. Normal transit time would put me in Miami with just enough time to appear in flight control in person at least one hour before departure, another standard airline requirement.

On occasion, Zellwood would be covered with thick early morning fog. Zero-zero weather is aviation vernacular for zero visibility and zero cloud height. In order to prepare for takeoff from Zellwood in zero-zero weather conditions, I would drive my car down the center of the grass runway and return, which would leave tire tracks on the wet grass. It was then a rather simple matter to follow these tracks on the takeoff roll until safely airborne. It was probably not the smartest thing in the world to do, but I got by without any problems.

Australian Crop Dusting

As I was still deeply involved in crop dusting, I was always on the

The Transavia was an Australian-made crop duster that I sought unsuccessfully to bring to the United States. I was required to obtain an Australian pilot's license to test fly it.

lookout for better equipment, and I heard about a new crop dusting airplane made in Australia. We checked out all the information we could get and it looked like an airplane we could use and possibly import into the United States as a distributor.

I successfully applied for a courtesy pass on Pan American World Airways and I rode in the passenger compartment aboard a Boeing 707 to Sydney. During the flight across the Pacific, a stewardess noticed my Air Line Pilots Association wings on my coat and asked if I was a pilot. Up until then, the service had been rather poor, so I told her I flew for National Airlines and asked her if I could say hi to the captain.

I received permission, so I went up to the cockpit where the crew was busy having a conversation. They totally ignored me. So I returned to the cabin thinking that if this was the way that Pan Am crews acted, then I was very glad that I was working for National. Even the cabin crew acted very indifferent. This should have been a fair warning to me about what was going to happen in the future when Pan Am bought National out.

After my arrival in Sydney, I contacted the factory that manufactured the airplanes and they invited me out to meet with them. They were very nice people. I was impressed with the looks of the airplane and their production and I watched a demonstration by one of their test pilots.

They told me they would take me out in the country to another airport and let me fly the airplane. There was a hitch, however. It seems that I could not fly an Australian-built airplane without an Australian pilot's license.

We checked with the air ministry and found that all I had to do was take a written exam and then they would issue me a certificate. So here I was, a National Airlines captain with thousands of flight hours, forced to take a simple private pilot written examination.

I failed it. It was a fill-in-the-blank test and the inspector looked at the results incredulously and said, "How could you not know what VMC stands for?" Well, VMC to a multi-engine airline pilot is minimum controllable airspeed, which I wrote, but he wanted visual meteorological conditions. Other questions focused on local flying procedures, like what prevents you from flying between Sydney and Kookaburra or some other location (there was a restricted area). Once he understood my American English to Australian English translation problem I retook the examination, passed it, and received an Australian pilot's license.

Then we flew to the other airport in the Ag plane, which would carry three people. It was specially designed to carry two crewmembers plus the pilot. It was a 45-minute flight over the Australian countryside at low altitude, which I really enjoyed. Once there, I wanted to fly the Transavia. Since it was a single piloted airplane, they could not give me any dual flight instruction and about all they could do was show me where the engine starter button was.

I flew the airplane for about an hour to get comfortable with its flying characteristics and I really liked it. I came back in and got a load of water so I could practice spraying. There were many cameras there taking movies of me flying and the factory people said I was the first American ever to fly an Australian built airplane, but I find that hard to believe.

The airplane did a great job spraying and I was ready to take one home with me. I stayed two or three more days before returning to Zellwood. After checking with the FAA, we learned they would not license that airplane without exhaustive and expensive testing, so we had to drop the idea.

Boeing 727

The competition between the Boeing 707 and Douglas DC-8 for airline sales was fierce, but both aircraft were much too large for the majority of domestic markets. What we needed were smaller versions of these airplanes to better serve the secondary airports with their shorter runways and fewer passengers.

The smaller three-engine Boeing 727 was the answer and it first flew in February 1963. It entered domestic service in February 1964, with United Airlines. Both Eastern Air Lines and National Airlines purchased the Boeing 727 with National Airlines putting it into service in 1964.

The Boeing 727's most distinguishing feature is the placement of the third engine at the base of the vertical stabilizer. This tri-motor jet was a little larger than the first tri-motor I had ever piloted, a Stinson tri-motor in 1944. The Boeing 727 had a cockpit crew of three: captain, first officer and flight engineer. It was also very passenger friendly. It had two stairways, the normal front one and one in the rear called the ventral stairway.

A senior captain at this point, I never flew copilot on the Boeing 727. However, the training on this airplane was a lot more detailed than what I had been used to on previous airplanes.

The Boeing 727 had a number of new high-lift devices on the wing that permitted slower landing speeds. At different flap settings for landing, various wing devices such as inner wing hinged flaps, triple-slotted aft-moving flaps, and extendable leading edge slats all worked nicely in conjunction with each other to provide a slow speed configuration for landing or takeoff. With the flaps fully extended for landing, it looked like the wing had been disassembled.

As with most high speed jets, with the flaps fully retracted, the outboard ailerons were locked out and small inboard ailerons or spoilers on the top of the wing were activated to replace the ailerons for high-speed roll control. Once you learned the flap settings, the Boeing 727 was as easy to fly as any other airplane. I was expected to know how every one of these devices operated.

The FAA check ride, which included both a ground oral exam and a flight test, was one of the most challenging I have ever taken. The ground oral exam given by the FAA inspectors was rather difficult, as you had to know about all the flight devices and many other items that affected flight characteristics.

On the day of my ground oral exam, which was conducted on a Friday, I was a little uptight, as all the captains on the four previous days had failed. The exam was given in a hotel room with lots of photos of the cockpit stacked around.

The inspector walked in and he seemed to be a real nice guy. The first question he asked me was about something I had never heard of. All I could say was, "Would you mind if I went and got a drink of water?" He said, "No, that's alright." When I

The Boeing 727 was a wonderful airplane to fly and I soon found myself landing this pure jet at airports where I had landed my piston-powered, tail dragger Lodestar in the early 1950's.

came back, I asked him, "What's the next question?" Thank goodness, he never returned to that first question.

The rest of the oral exam went fairly well. It was rather lengthy (almost four hours) and I noticed he had already smoked two big cigars and was lighting up a third. I asked him how many cigars he usually smoked during an oral. He said sometimes as many as four.

He then said, "Why do you ask, are you getting tired?"

I answered with a firm, "Yes!"

He said, "Ok, then, you passed the oral exam." What a relief. Little did I know that for the rest of my career flying the big jets that all of my oral exams would be similar to this grueling ordeal. With the ground portion of the evaluation complete, it

was now time to complete the flight portion of the check ride, which would be conducted first in a flight simulator and then later in the real airplane.

Flying the airplane, even in the artificial environment of a flight simulator, was a cinch. The Boeing 727 flew like a dream and it was very quiet, very fast, and very responsive to pilot control inputs. The cockpit was rather roomy with good visibility. It did have one disturbing feature that occurred when taking off in a strong crosswind. You had to be very aware of crosswind effect on the center engine air induction intake. A crosswind would disturb the flow of air causing the engine to run improperly.

The FAA inspector and I spent more than four hours together in that flight simulator. It looked exactly like the real airplane's cockpit and it could simulate almost every in-flight emergency, which is what that FAA inspector proceeded to do to me.

When the session was over, the FAA inspector handed me a piece of paper documenting that I had passed the "pilot in command" simulator check ride.

After a little more training, I was ready to take another check ride in the actual airplane. I sat in the captain's seat and a National Airlines check pilot sat in the copilot's seat. He made me go through all the required flight maneuvers, with an FAA inspector sitting on the jump seat behind us watching every move I made.

After I successfully completed this check ride, I was allowed to fly with passengers, although National Airlines policy required a company flight check pilot fly copilot with me. After all of this was done and passed, I was now deemed ready to fly as a captain with any qualified copilot with paying passengers on scheduled flights. After six months had passed, however, I faced the requirement of undergoing the check once again, including the oral and the simulator exam.

This sequence of 6-month oral exams and check rides continues for your entire airline career. So if you flew for the airline for 30 years, you were checked at least 60 times, not counting non-scheduled line checks.

A line check occurs when an airline check pilot or FAA inspector boards your airplane at any time on any flight to evaluate not only how well you operate the airplane, but also to see how you

I am either the first person to board this airliner or I am giving the engine exhaust area a detailed preflight inspection.

handle the other crew members, listen to the air traffic control instructions over the earphones, answer company radio calls, keep the passengers informed, and so on.

As a result, no matter how much experience you had in the airplane, you always felt under a lot of pressure because if you failed one check ride, you were out of a job. I really liked flying passengers, though, so I went through the motions without complaint and did so without any check ride failures, accidents or FAA violations.

As an airline captain, you also had to pass an FAA doctor's examination every six months for your first class physical. This was normal procedure no matter what airplane you were flying. I did not have to go through all this nonsense when flying my Travel

Air duster, but I suffered through it in the airline industry for 29 years. A failed medical examination ended your airline career on the spot.

I checked out as captain on the Boeing 727 in March 1968, and I flew all the routes National Airlines had, including my original Lockheed Lodestar routes. I flew mostly the model known as Boeing 727-235. As for experiences, there were many.

Boeing 727 Panama City Approach

One night as we were landing at Panama City, Florida and the weather was absolutely lousy. It was not only dark and raining, but the air was rough and bumpy. The long approach to the runway was over water and it was going to be a difficult landing at best. Normally, I would not have even attempted a landing in these conditions and simply flown on to the next stop. Your judgment was never questioned by the company under these conditions.

However, as luck would have it, the company chief pilot was about 30 minutes behind me and he was also landing at Panama City. I was concerned that if I bypassed this airport and he came in and landed behind me, he might wonder about my piloting skills.

I thought I would make one approach to the airport and only land if I thought it was safe to do so. The approach was as bad as I expected, but we were able to land safely. Shortly afterwards, the chief pilot came in behind me and also landed.

We disembarked and he cornered me in the lobby and jokingly said, "I was hoping you would pass this place up so I wouldn't have to try and land." After exchanging a few barbs, we went on our merry way.

Boeing 727 Front Door Air Seal Rupture

One bright sunny afternoon, I departed Miami in a Boeing 727-235 with a full load of passengers bound for New Orleans. It was a day when the weather was extremely nice; in fact, it is what we would call "severe clear."

We left on schedule, but climbing to our assigned altitude of 28,000 feet, the tranquility of the flight was interrupted by a mild explosion in the cabin. The flight engineer opened the cockpit door, heard the air escaping from the front door, and determined the front door air seal had ruptured and the cabin was depressurizing.

We were climbing through 21,000 feet and I quickly declared an emergency and notified Departure Control that we were returning to Miami, while conducting a rapid descent to avoid hypoxia. The stewardesses also advised the passengers that we were returning to Miami to get another airplane. We landed without further incident.

As the passengers were deplaning, I walked out of the cockpit door and met a nice looking elderly black lady who said to me with a twinkle in her eyes, "Captain, that almost scared me white." We both kind of laughed and went on our ways. That made my day.

Sunny day and short-sleeve shirt indicates that life does not get any better for an airline captain waiting to load his airplane.

Boeing 727 Engine Explosion

As all airline pilots know, 98 to 99 percent of flights are, thankfully, dull and routine. Infrequently, however, things were different and it was during these emergencies that I truly earned my pay.

On one such occasion, I was leaving Palm Beach, Florida for New York. The weather in Palm Beach was blue skies. We had a full load of passengers and we taxied out to take off to the west because of wind direction. Normally, we would have been taking off to the east due to prevailing winds, which would have had us climbing out over the city. This day was my lucky day, if you want to call it that.

During the takeoff run, as we approached flying speed with the nose wheel barely off the ground, the center engine exploded and hurled parts across the runway. My heart almost stopped at the same time the engine did.

The acceleration rapidly decreased and it felt like the airplane did not want to fly any further. But as I had run out of runway, I could not stop the airplane so we had no choice but to go flying. Fortunately, what acceleration I did have was enough to propel us into the air.

I lowered the nose to gain airspeed and raised the landing gear to reduce drag. I made no attempt to climb and flew at treetop level to pick up airspeed and retracted the flaps and wing slats.

We picked up sufficient airspeed in about a mile or so and so I climbed to 1,000 feet to make our return to the airport. The flight engineer and copilot were quite uneasy to be flying at this low level. As an old crop duster, this was a high altitude for my trusty old Travel Air, so I felt quite comfortable in this environment. I much rather preferred higher airspeed at low altitude, than a lower airspeed climbing to a higher altitude in fear that a second engine might decide to quit. I knew I had sufficient speed at this altitude to return to the airport on one engine. We made an uneventful landing.

Had I been taking off on our normal departure to the east, I would have been flying directly at some tall buildings and I would have had no choice except to attempt a climb, which I probably could have done and still made a safe landing, but I was sure glad I did not have to face that challenge.

Once on the ground, I contacted the company on the radio and they said they would get me another Boeing 727 immediately. It was a quick turnaround and after we were safely airborne again, I told the stewardesses to give free drinks to all who wanted them as a good will gesture. If it was not illegal, I might have joined them myself to calm my nerves.

Boeing 727 Static Electricity

I was flying a Boeing 727 from New York to Miami with stops at Norfolk, Charleston, Jacksonville, and Miami. We left Kennedy in the early afternoon and proceeded to Norfolk in a light to moderate rain. As we approached Norfolk, ATC cleared us from our cruising altitude of 28,000 feet to 9,000 feet. Below 10,000 feet, I had to have the airplane slowed down to 250 knots.

We had seen a flash of lightning or two on the way down and the air was highly charged with static electricity. We leveled off at 9,000 feet with the autopilot on when all of a sudden, a giant ball of static electricity appeared between the copilot and me. It was bluish green in color and at least two feet across. The instant I looked at the ball, it exploded with a big bang. The fluorescent lights on the ceiling in the cockpit fell down and broke and I later found out from the stewardesses that it was felt throughout the cabin, with flame-like images appearing on the outside of the windows.

I thought for a moment that the airplane had exploded. Everything was still operating normally, however, except for the lights on the floor. This all happened within a matter of seconds. I will guarantee you the cockpit crew was pretty shaken up, as we really did not know what had happened.

I had to make an announcement to the passengers, who were totally terrified. I told them that we were all okay, the airplane was operating normally, and that I suspected that it was only a static electricity discharge.

I tried to calm them down as much as possible by reassuring them we would land in Norfolk without any more problems and that I was sorry this might have startled them. I did not lie. Everything was normal inside the cockpit. I couldn't believe it. We proceeded to Norfolk and landed without further incident.

As a joke, before we landed, I called the chief stewardess on our telephone and jokingly asked her to please bring a roll of toilet paper to the cockpit. I have been hit by lightning many times before and after this incident, but this is the only experience I ever had of it appearing on the inside of the airplane.

Luxury Accommodations

One night we left Miami for a flight to Idlewild more than two hours late due to mechanical problems with our Boeing 727. We arrived in Idlewild about 1a.m. and by the time we arrived at our hotel in downtown Manhattan it was a little after 2:00. At that time, we were staying at the Belmont Plaza where our rooms were normally reserved. The clerk advised he did not think we were going to be there so he had sold our rooms. There were no other rooms available.

Well, the whole crew was tired and we really did not feel like putting up with this. I had the clerk make a phone call to the Waldorf Astoria, which was located right across the street, to see if they had rooms available for us, which they did. So, I thanked the clerk saying, "This is the best luck that we have had all day."

We picked up our luggage and walked across the street to the Waldorf. The clerk at the front desk advised us that they only had luxury

The DC-10 was the final airplane acquired by National Airlines in its storied history. What a wonderful airplane for me to finish my airline career in.

rooms left. I thought to myself, "Well, that is not too bad," so I told the clerk that we would take five rooms for the five of us. Of all the layovers I ever had in New York, these were the finest rooms I had ever seen.

We all had breakfast the next morning at the Waldorf where they had a chef cooking for us, not the usual short order cook. The entire crew agreed this was the place to stay when in New York. Lord knows what it cost the company, but I never heard a word about it. I would not have minded running late after this if it always had the same outcome.

Bumps in the Night

I departed Idlewild late one night headed for Miami in a Boeing 727-235. It was raining hard, quite turbulent, and the airplane did not really seem to be performing, as it should. It had developed a peculiar vibration, which I expected to disappear as soon as we got above the weather. It did not and the airplane continued to vibrate and refused to accelerate.

As we sluggishly winged our way towards Miami, we tried to figure out why the airplane would not accelerate to its normal cruising speed. To make matters worse, it seemed that the faster we went, the more the vibration increased. There were no cockpit indications of anything wrong with any of the three engines.

We tried different throttle settings and soon isolated the problem to number 3 engine because when we reduced the power to this engine alone the vibration was greatly reduced. Not knowing what the problem was, I decided to declare an emergency and divert to Baltimore, where we made a normal landing.

We taxied to the terminal and after disembarking the passengers, the flight engineer and I went out to look at Number 3 engine. We found that the reversing system on the engine was broken and in the reverse mode resulting in vibration and lack of performance. As it was rather late, we cancelled the flight and spent the night in a hotel.

First Exclusive All-Jet Fleet

Throughout the 1950's and 1960's National Airlines focused on improving its fleet of aircraft. The Lodestar's were replaced by the Convairs, which in turn were exchanged for a series of four-engine Douglas piston airliners and the turboprop Lockheed Electra. On April 21, 1968, the company retired the last of the Lockheed Electra turboprops and National Airlines became the first airline in the United States with a pure-jet fleet comprised of DC-8s and Boeing 727s.

National Airlines acquired two Boeing 747s and inaugurated service between Miami and New York in October 1970. In June 1970, National Airlines initiated service between Miami and London using these jets. The airline sold the 747s in 1976 and I never had the opportunity to fly them.

Flying the DC-10 Jumbo Jet

The final airplane acquired by National Airlines in its storied history was the McDonnell Douglas DC-10.

The DC-10 is a three-engine, wide-body jet capable of carrying 320 passengers on long-haul flights. The DC-10 first flew in August 1970 entering service with American Airlines in 1971. National Airlines began DC-10 service in 1971 between Miami and New York and later between Miami and San Francisco.

It was hard for this old 'duster pilot to imagine flying this monster. The DC-10-10 model had a gross weight of nearly 500,000 pounds, and yet it handled with ease. The cockpit was huge and comfortable, accommodated the captain, a copilot, and a flight engineer, and had additional seating for two observers, who were typically FAA inspectors, airline check pilots, or deadheading pilots. The airplane was very fast and we normally cruised at Mach .85.

I began flying the DC-10 in July 1975 as a captain. I never flew it as a copilot. When I first started to get checked out in this airplane, I found it had General Electric engines and I knew from past experiences, that some General Electric light bulbs did not last very long. This was not the case with the DC-10's engines. Most of my training was done in a flight simulator followed by an FAA check ride that lasted approximately an hour and a half.

My first revenue flight was from Miami to Los Angeles with a National Airlines check pilot occupying the copilot's seat. It is amazing to think that I was flying captain on my first actual flight in the DC-10 with passengers aboard and a grand total time of less than two hours in the airplane. But, I was entirely comfortable flying this airplane.

Of course, I had an experienced check pilot flying copilot for me. The check pilot usually flew three or four trips with you and after that, you were assigned a regular copilot while the check pilot occupied the jump seat to be sure everything was okay before you were released for regular duty.

The airplane itself was huge inside. It had nine bathrooms, three elevators down to the galley, and three motion picture screens. The seating was nine across and we normally carried 10 to 15 flight attendants.

The DC-10 burned quite a lot of fuel, averaging about 40 gallons per minute. I typically flew from Miami to West Coast destinations, including San Diego, Los Angeles and San Francisco.

The takeoff performance on this airplane was remarkable. The initial rate of climb was almost 6,000 feet per minute and the DC-10 would keep a good rate of climb up to 41,000 feet.

If the weather was nice and smooth, I would usually climb to 39,000 or 41,000 feet, depending on the direction I was going. The outside air temperature at these altitudes was usually around 70 degrees below zero but I was warm and toasty in the cockpit.

My children Cheryl, Charles and Lori sitting in the intake of a DC-10 engine.

DC-10 Engine Shut Down

During the six years I flew this airplane I experienced very few inflight emergencies and only two engine shut downs. We were at 39,000 feet flying from Miami to Los Angeles and we had just passed El Paso when I received a fire warning on the number 3 engine. This was announced by a warning horn ringing and flashing red fire warning lights.

We followed the proper procedure. We shut the engine down and discharged the fire extinguisher located in the engine. This should have put the fire out, stopped the deafening warning horn, and extinguished the fire warning light. But this did not happen. Instead, we still had indications that the engine was on fire. We discharged the two remaining fire extinguisher bottles into the engine compartment. The warning horn and fire warning light stayed on.

We had no choice now other than to make an emergency diversion and descent into El Paso. This was probably a little scary to the passengers because I needed to dive the airplane to lose altitude. I alerted El Paso tower that we had an emergency and that we were inbound to their airport. I asked to have the fire trucks standing by and for them to give us immediate priority for landing, which they did.

We landed safely and the fire trucks came up to the engine to douse the fire if needed but there was no indication of an actual fire. This is the one and only time this happened to me in all my years of airline flying.

We were highly trained to make emergency descents because a fire in an airplane is nothing to fool with. I must say that during our descent, which was almost straight down, the adrenalin was really flowing and we were all glad to be safely on the ground.

We had to put our passengers on another airline, as our airplane had to be thoroughly inspected before it could fly again. We spent the night in El Paso while our flight engineer, Bob Murell, spent half the night troubleshooting the engine. He did a fine job and eventually confirmed it was just a false alarm. The following day we ferried the empty airplane to Los Angeles. I might add that the crew enjoyed a mighty fine Mexican dinner while we were in El Paso.

January 10, 1978
8200 Pasadena Blvd.
Pembroke Pines, Fla. 33024

Mr. L. B. Maytag
President
National Air Lines
P. O. Box 592055-AMF
Miami, Florida 33159

Dear Mr. Maytag,

Last week I reported to a new job with AT&T in New York after being transferred from Miami.

Even though the move involved a promotion, leaving the family behind (to sell the house) was a difficult occasion. After I boarded the plane (Flight 146), apparently the family looked quite down in the mouth, because the Captain came along and tried to cheer them up. He invited them aboard to say 'bye' to me again, and he let my five-year old son and 10-year old daughter into the cockpit for a look around. It, of course, "made" the kids' day, and it helped my wife, too.

You are fortunate to have a man like Captain Brown on the National team. We won't forget his fine gesture of friendship.

Sincerely,

David Seymour

P.S. His landing was so beautiful it drew a round of applause from several of the passengers.

One of the pleasures of being an airline captain was helping our passengers.

Love of a Father

On another occasion, I was flying the DC-10 to New York with a stop at Fort Lauderdale. We pulled into the gate, stopped, and I found we could look directly into the terminal building which was covered with many windows so that the passengers could see us.

It was a quick turnaround and I waited patiently as they loaded the Fort Lauderdale passengers who were bound for New York. I happened to notice a lady with two children staring at us from the terminal building. It looked like the children were crying and I waved to them with no response.

Then I got a call from the ground saying we were delayed for about ten minutes while waiting on mail. I got up out of my seat and walked into the terminal building to find out why the two children and their mother were crying. They explained that their Daddy was on the airplane and that they would not see him again for almost a year. I told them, "You will see him sooner."

I took the children's hands and we walked back on the airplane and found their father. They were happy to see their Daddy and kiss him again. Then I took the mother and the kids up in the cockpit and let the kids sit in my seat for a moment. I was notified it was time to go so I returned them to the terminal and told them we would take very good care of their Daddy. As we pushed back from the gate, they were once again at the window, only this time smiling and waving goodbye. This was one of the many nice things that could happen to a flight crew and it happened to me often during my career.

There were many, many other stories involving passengers but I do not have room in this book to tell them all. I have made unscheduled landings at various airports due to the passengers having heart attacks and I always had ambulances waiting for them. On one or two flights, I had to land to put off unruly passengers but these occurrences were very rare. I still remember when we had to divide the cabin between smokers and non-smokers. As the cockpit was tightly closed, I never allowed smoking in my cockpit. As far as the passenger cabin was concerned, I could never see any benefit, as you can smell cigarette smoke throughout the cabin. To me it was kind of like having a no-peeing section in a swimming pool.

Burning Tires and Overflowing Commodes

One time shortly after taking off from LaGuardia bound for Miami, I received an emergency call from the tower. They advised me the airplane waiting behind us to depart noticed that all the tires on our right main landing gear went flat during our takeoff roll and had deposited a substantial amount of rubber on the runway.

We did not feel anything in the airplane, so we did not know if it was true or not. I called the company radio and told them that we did not need tires to fly so I was proceeding to our intermediate stop in Fort Lauderdale. When we were in the vicinity of Cape May, the company radioed us to say they had scooped up the rubber left on the runway and the serial numbers they found matched the serial numbers of the tires that used to be on my airplane. I told them that I wished they had not called me up and told me scary things like that.

With this knowledge in hand, I decided to bypass Fort Lauderdale and land directly at Miami. I also knew that what was left of my tires on the right side would catch fire on landing due to the high speed of the landing. I contacted Miami and arranged for fire trucks to be placed where we would come to a stop on the runway. I intentionally landed on the left landing gear and then let the right gear down as gently as possible. We came to a halt directly in front of the fire trucks as planned. For whatever reason, the rubber remnants did not catch fire and since I still had one tire intact on that side, I taxied to the terminal building without any further problems.

My next mechanical problem with the DC-10 was much more unpleasant. And disgusting.

We had departed San Francisco in the DC-10 headed for Miami with a stop at Las Vegas. Before we departed Las Vegas, my flight engineer, Goldie Hanks, cornered me and told me that one of our nine bathrooms was plugged up. As he could not get any local help for over an hour, he asked if I would help him. I was to hold a flashlight while we both climbed into a tiny hole in the tail of the airplane where all these bathrooms were tied together. Since the flight was scheduled with a full load of passengers, it was paramount that all of the bathrooms were operating. I reluctantly agreed to help Goldie. What a mistake.

We were both crammed into the tail and right after Goldie unhooked the pipes to the bathroom to unplug the stoppage, a stewardess used one of the other bathrooms and flushed the commode. Almost immediately, both Goldie and I were covered with you know what.

I couldn't believe it. Here I am, the captain of the airplane, coated with stuff that I cannot fly, nor even appear in public, in. We just sat there in that tiny space and I told Goldie, "I'm going to kill you."

We finished putting the bathroom pipes back together with Goldie apologizing profusely for forgetting to pull the circuit breaker to prevent anyone from flushing the commodes. I told him that I would not accept his apology and that he was going to die when we got out of the tail.

We both crawled out of the hole and climbed down to the ramp. We both stood there looking at each other and we just had to laugh. What a pitiful sight we would have been if the passengers had seen us. We went into the operations building and took a shower, threw our clothes in the trash, and flew the remainder of our trip in civilian clothes. Of course, we were the butt of many jokes by the stewardesses (no pun intended) when they found out what had happened. I did all this and didn't even get plumbers' pay. Goldie is gone now but we remained solid friends.

Merger with Pan American Airways

By the late 1970's National Airlines had become an attractive takeover target with its cash liquidity and state-of-the-art airliners.

Pan American World Airways, strictly an international carrier, desperately needed a domestic feeder route system. Consequently, Pan Am purchased National Airlines to achieve that goal.

The merger from my perspective was fairly easy. Pan American did not own any DC-10s so they simply repainted National's in their colors and my life carried on as usual. They still called their airplanes Clippers after the tradition established by their founder, Juan Trippe. Instead of flying Barbara, Betty, and Eileen under

National Airlines "Fly Me" campaign, I found myself flying the Clipper Meteor, Clipper Morning Star, and the ultimate irony, Clipper George T. Baker, former president of National.

The airlines officially merged on January 1, 1980, but Pan Am, already mired in a deep financial crisis, bungled the integration of the two carriers' personnel and route structures. Pan Am eventually declared bankruptcy and ceased operations in 1991.

Nonetheless, I was given the opportunity to fly as a Pan American Airways Clipper Captain for more than a year, fulfilling the improbable daydream of a 14-year old boy who once stood on a seaplane ramp in 1935 marveling at the Pan Am seaplanes.

I enjoyed working under the Pan Am banner as it had a reputation of being a world-renowned organization. But it seemed to me during my short time as a Pan Am captain, that there remained unresolved friction between the orange, former National Airlines employees, and the blue, current Pan Am personnel. My personal thoughts were that Pan Am was more of a military type of operation with a rigid chain of command, while National employees had enjoyed a more relaxed, friendly relationship with their supervisors.

We all got along as far as our jobs were concerned, but the Pan Am people always gave us the impression they resented the National Airlines folks. In my opinion, Pan Am had too many chiefs and fiefdoms to restore it to the huge success it once enjoyed. They were also not very responsive to changing situations.

I will give you an example. I was operating a DC-10 flight from Los Angeles to Miami with intermediate stops at Houston and Tampa. Because of maintenance problems, our takeoff was delayed from Los Angeles for more than two hours. Arriving late in Houston we were forced to park at an international gate.

Even though we had never left the United States, a customs man came aboard and claimed we all had to go through customs because we were at his gate. I complained to no avail, so we all went through customs, which further delayed our outbound flight.

When we returned to the gate where our airplane was parked, I found Pan Am ground personnel had towed the airplane to our originally assigned gate without telling anyone on our crew. Now we had to take an underground train to the other terminal building.

As you can imagine, our passengers were very upset and I could not blame them – I was teed off also. We got to our regular gate, loaded everyone on the airplane, and were preparing for immediate departure. We were now three hours late for our takeoff from Houston.

I checked with the engineer for our fuel load and we discovered the airplane had not been refueled. I disembarked and went to flight operations to find out why. I was told that they could not do it right then because it was time for coffee break. I blew a fuse and demanded why, at 2a.m. with nothing else going on, they had to stop and have coffee. They just shrugged.

Now I was furious, so I got on the telephone and called the chief executive officer of Pan Am on the telephone and woke him up. He said I should have called the worldwide duty officer. I told him I had never heard of such a thing. He was mad because I woke him up and I guess I kind of chewed him out in return. I insinuated that perhaps he did not know how to run an airline. Needless to say, I should have kept my mouth shut.

We were finally refueled and flew out, running nearly four hours late when we arrived at Miami. The entire delay was unnecessary, as I could have made up all the lost time from our original departure in Los Angeles in Houston. I told the passengers I was sorry about what happened and assured them the flight crew had done all they could.

Later that day, I received a phone call to report to the chief pilot's office where there was a conference call with New York wanting me to explain my actions of waking the chief executive officer in the middle of the night. I was not fired and I understand the Houston station really caught a lot of flak. Needless to say, when I flew through Houston again, they were not exactly enthused to see me.

There were more unfortunate instances of this kind in the days ahead for me. I learned that some, but not all, of the Pan American blue captains looked down their nose at us orange, National Airlines guys. My friends overheard comments from Pan Am captains stating that it looked like National Airlines hired just about anyone to fly their airplanes, that we were nothing but a bunch of ex-crop dusters, and that we were not as professionally oriented as they were.

This divisive attitude never changed and I consider this to be a key reason for Pan American's eventual downfall. I never looked down at any other pilot, whether they were military, civilian, or anything else. We all had to pass the same rigorous FAA check rides and we were all very successful professionals. In spite of this, I am still proud to say that I flew as captain for Pan American World Airways.

One of the few photographs of me at the controls of an airliner. It was taken aboard a DC-10 by a TWA pilot who visited the cockpit. He asked if he could take a picture of me at work and had me put my hat on, which we never do in the cockpit. This was in 1979 while enroute from Los Angeles to Miami at 41,000 feet approximately 45 miles west of El Paso.

Chapter Fourteen

Retirement

On February 20, 1981 the FAA's mandatory airline pilot retirement age regulation caught up with me. I flew my final airline flight as a captain on a DC-10 traveling from Miami to San Francisco. The stewardesses asked the passengers to write me a congratulation note on any scrap of paper at hand, including airsickness bags, and this is one of my favorites.

While the travel was always fabulous, the pay fantastic, and the prestige unmatched, I was always unimpressed with the life of an airline pilot. I have forever been a self-reliant crop duster at heart. After nearly 30 years with the airlines, I soon found myself growing more and more aggravated with the endless government interference, constant airline management oversight, annoying annual check rides, and never-ending Class 1 flight physicals necessary to maintain my captain qualification. It was becoming a hard way to make an easy living.

Mandatory Retirement

However, what innate stubbornness could not force me to do, my birthday did. According to the Federal Aviation Regulations, I had to retire the day before my 60th birthday. Literally. On the day of my 60th birthday, I could no longer fly as captain for a U.S. commercial airliner. I did not agree with this regulation. I saw no reason why, as long as we passed our physical exams, that we should be disqualified as unfit to fly. I personally lost five years of income for my family and the airlines lost years of experience that could not be duplicated. I will resent this to the day that I die. The FAA has since modified this regulation to allow airline pilots to fly until their 65th birthday.

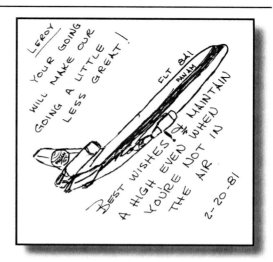

Another souvenir from my last flight drawn on a napkin.

My Final Airline Trip

The day of my final flight arrived much too soon. On February 20, 1981 I flew my last flight as an airline pilot, serving as captain on a scheduled non-stop DC-10 flight from Miami to San Francisco.

The company had a gracious policy that on your final flight your family could ride with you in the first class section. Some pilots thought that it was ill advised to take your family on your last flight because sometimes that is when bad things happened. While I am a firm believer in fate, I did not hesitate to take my family.

The weather was forecast to be excellent all the way, so after takeoff we climbed to our requested altitude of 39,000 feet. Somehow, the airway traffic controllers found out it was my last flight and they all wished me well as air traffic control tracked our progress across the country. I was down to the last 5 hours of a 29-year career and as I sat there peacefully cruising along, it was hard to realize this was the end.

Everyone was treating me wonderfully and the stewardesses evidently told the passengers about this being my last flight, so I thought that I had better say something to them. So I made an announcement as we passed Las Vegas thanking them for being with us.

I also told them that to make this flight as memorable to them as it was for me, we were going to do something in this DC-10 that had never been done before. Then I did not say anything for four or five minutes until that sunk in.

A stewardess came in and asked me what I was going to do. I told her I would make another announcement. I finally said, "Ladies and Gentlemen, I know you are wondering what we are going to do that has not been done before. We are going to be the first DC-10 to fly under the Golden Gate Bridge."

The stewardess rushed back into the cockpit and asked if I was really going to do that. My answer was "Yes, I measured it last trip and it will just barely fit." She said "Oh, no!" and left the cockpit.

In the meantime, the stewardesses asked the passengers to write me a farewell note on any piece of paper they could find, even an airsickness bag. One passenger drew a nice picture of the Golden Gate Bridge with a DC-10 under it, one of my most treasured mementos of this final trip.

I reassured the passengers that I really was not going to fly under the Golden Gate Bridge, although I must admit that I had really thought about doing it. San Francisco Airport soon came into view, along with the final landing. We taxied to the gate and everyone deplaned and I just sat there dumbfounded that I could never do this again. It was very difficult to undo my seatbelt and leave the cockpit.

After good wishes from my crew, we departed the airport and my family and I stayed in San Francisco for a few days on vacation before returning to Zellwood.

As I sit here remembering this flight, I have tears in my eyes. It seems like only yesterday that I learned to fly. Someone stole all of my time. But, I must admit, I was one of the lucky ones who knew when my last flight was coming. Some of my good friends left home without realizing that that day would be their last flight. May the good Lord bless and keep them.

My official retirement date from the airlines was March 5, 1981. For the last year and a half of my career, I was a Pan American World Airways Clipper Skipper, fulfilling a dream wished by a small boy on Pan Am's seaplane ramp in 1935.

Post-Retirement

Now age has nothing to do with flying private airplanes and by my own account, I have owned more than 150 airplanes. When interviewed by a reporter at Sun 'n Fun about my hobby flying small airplanes, I jokingly told her, "As a retired airline pilot I'm over the hill. What else can I do? My wife won't let me chase girls." After my retirement, Wanda and I focused on flying antique airplanes.

Butler Blackhawk

One of the first projects I completed in my retirement was the restoration of a wonderfully historic biplane. In fact, of all the airplanes I have owned and restored I am most proud of my beautiful, award-winning 1929 Butler Blackhawk Sport.

The Butler Aircraft Corporation, a subsidiary of the Butler Manufacturing Company, built Butler Blackhawk airplanes, which was a leading manufacturer of building systems located in Kansas City, Missouri. Butler decided to get into the airplane manufacturing business after a wave of aviation enthusiasm swept the country following Charles Lindbergh's famous flight to Paris in 1927.

The Butler Blackhawk was developed by Waverly Stearman, a well-known airplane designer and the younger brother of Lloyd Stearman, head of the Stearman Aircraft Corporation located in Wichita, Kansas.

The Blackhawk was a rugged 3-place biplane featuring robust speed, an exceptional payload including room for two passengers in the front cockpit, and a long fuel range for cross-country travel. They were priced at $7,995 each. Unfortunately, the crash

My Butler Blackhawk Sport undergoing restoration in 1978.

The Blackhawk completely restored. I invested about $30,000 in returning it to new condition.

of the stock market and the ensuing Great Depression depressed sales. The company produced only 11 airplanes before manufacturing ceased.

The very last biplane Butler built was a unique Sport version assembled in 1930 and assigned manufacturer's serial number 111. As it was a smaller, different version of the original Blackhawk design, the Aeronautics Branch of the Department of Commerce assigned an experimental registration number X-299N to the biplane until the company could submit technical data to comply with current airworthiness requirements. Unfortunately, the Butler Aircraft Corporation went out of business before the required engineering data, stress analysis, and flights tests were completed. As a result, the lack of a type certificate would haunt future owners of the

airplane when they tried to register it for crop dusting work. When my own restoration was complete, however, I had no problems registering it.

The original purchase of my Blackhawk occurred in 1935 by George King and Robert Leuthart of Louisburg, Kansas. After I restored the Blackhawk, Robert Leuthart's wife, Anna, noticed an article about it. She asked her son Laurence to contact me, and he passed to me several stories relayed by his mother on the pleasant memories they have of flying the airplane. Perhaps the most interesting story was that during inclement weather, water separated around her in the front cockpit and entered the rear cockpit to drench her husband.

The Leuthart's flew the airplane for two years before selling it in 1937 to Claude Timmons in Pampa, Texas.

Preparing for the very first flight of my restored Butler Blackhawk.

by old rugs and was all in pieces. Surprisingly, all the individual components appeared to be in good shape. I agreed to pay Knowlton $450 for the airplane, which he told me was a Butler Blackhawk.

I had never heard of that model but when I researched it further, I realized I had a rare airplane on my hands, as I could not find any other Blackhawks flying. A title search from FAA records indicated that Tankersley was the last registered owner so even though I had paid Knowlton for the airplane, to close the deal cleanly, I located Tankersley and asked him to provide me a bill of sale, which he graciously did.

I delivered the parts to Bob Lee and Charles Caswell, who were expert airplane restorers and lived not far from me in Deland, Florida. I didn't want to invest a lot of money in the restoration, so I told them to

The airplane then passed through several more owners until acquired by J.C. Tankersley, Jr. where it fell into serious disrepair. Here is where I entered the story.

Along with the FBO called Air Orlando, I had my cropdusters parked at Herndon Airport. My barber, a gentleman by the name of Duffy Knowlton, also kept his airplane at the airport. Every time I got a haircut, he asked me if I was interested in buying the pieces of an old biplane that he had stored in his garage. And every time he asked, I turned him down.

Finally, in 1962 I went to look at the wreck. It was largely covered

The original Blackhawk Company logo that I had painted on my biplane.

Wanda and I flying our 1929 Butler Blackhawk Sport. This airplane is now on display in a Kansas City museum.

work on it only on a time available basis. As a result, little work was done on the airplane for the next 18 years.

Caswell passed away in 1979 and Lee was not interested in continuing, so I passed the parts to Bob White who lived near my home in Zellwood. White specializes in the restoration of antique airplanes and he had previously completed award-winning restorations of several other vintage airplanes.

I asked him to complete the project with the help of his two mechanics, Jim Kimball and Ralph Braswell, and to keep the airplane as original as possible. Fortunately, they found that nearly all the pieces to the airplane were there and what was missing was easily reconstructed based on airplane blueprints provided by the Butler Aircraft Corporation.

A search of the records of the Butler Aircraft Corporation turned up a picture of my Sport just after it was originally finished in 1929. Therefore, I was able to duplicate the original markings.

The engine installed was the original slightly modified 235 horsepower Wright Whirlwind J-6-7. This engine was rebuilt and was capable of propelling the Blackhawk to a top speed of 130 miles per hour, which is pretty fast for a 1930 airplane.

After nearly 20 years of off-again, on-again restoration, my Butler Blackhawk Sport was finally completed in July 1980. I made the first flight from our grass airstrip in Zellwood in front of a large crowd that had gathered to watch the inaugural flight. The Blackhawk Sport flew beautifully. In fact, the airplane was so stable that upon my return I made a low pass down the runway and lifted both my hands in the air as I passed them. When back on the ground, I told my friends, "She flies like a lady."

My wife made the second flight and then because it flew so well, I let my friends, Jim Kimball and Bob White, who had rebuilt the Blackhawk, fly next.

I probably invested more than $30,000 restoring the Blackhawk but it was worth every penny. Wanda and I flew it to many air shows and fly-ins around the country. One of our longest trips was a cross-country flight to the annual Antique Airplane Invitational Fly-In at Blakesburg, Iowa, sponsored by the Antique Airplane Association. I am a lifetime member of the Antique Airplane Association and I am privileged to have my portrait on display on their Wall of Memories in the Air Power Museum.

We also flew the Blackhawk to Oshkosh, Wisconsin, home of the Experimental Aircraft Association and their annual summer fly-in,

AirVenture, which is billed as the world's greatest aviation celebration. We received one of their highest awards for antique aircraft.

Living in Florida near Sun n' Fun of Lakeland, we made many flights to their annual fly-in too, receiving many awards for our Blackhawk.

I would like to say that if you have never flown an open cockpit biplane across the country on a trip of a thousand miles or more then you have missed some of the greatest flight experiences any aviator could have. We did have our sporting adventures, particularly on our trip flying the Blackhawk to Blakesburg, Iowa.

We were caught in low visibility

From The Past
These two airplanes landed at the Humphreys County airport last week. Both are owned by a Florida man who landed here when one of the planes developed engine trouble on its way to an air show in Iowa. Both planes have been restored and are very rare. (see story).

This photograph shows my two airplanes, a Butler Blackhawk (left) and Boeing 4E Stearman sitting at Humphreys County Airport after an engine failure in the Stearman forced me to make an emergency dead stick landing there.

in some mountains near Talladega, Alabama. This was not an instrument airplane but I did have airspeed, needle, and ball. This was the only time that Wanda and I flew together that I genuinely feared for our safety. I thought for sure that we would collide with a mountaintop when suddenly a little bit of light broke out of the clouds and I headed right for it, escaping into clearer weather.

Another incident occurred in August 1983, when Wanda, our daughter Lori, and I were flying our Boeing 4E Stearman, a large biplane with a 450 horsepower engine, to another air show in Blakesburg.

The Stearman was owned by a crop duster from Iowa who came to Zellwood to fly the airplane but was selling it because he said he was not making any money. So I bought it from him. The Stearman really flew well although it was big and heavy. I researched the history of the biplane and found out that it was originally built for Western Air Express in the 1930's for use as a mail plane. It had been restored to the passenger configuration and could carry two people in the front cockpit, although usually my wife Wanda occupied the front seats solo.

On this trip to Blakesburg, I was flying the Stearman accompanied by my own Blackhawk, flown by Jim and Jane Kimball in loose formation with us. Jim and I were talking on the radio about where we were and that there was an unknown airport right below us. As soon as we finished our conversation, the engine on my

airplane quit. My wife turned and looked at me inquisitively while our daughter knowledgably very quickly tightened up her seat belt. At the same time, I radioed Jim that I had an engine failure.

The big Stearman did not glide very well. But being directly over the airport was extremely fortunate and I commenced a rather steep descent to the airport and a successful dead stick landing. The engine was covered with oil and upon investigation, we found that the supercharger oil seal had failed. Jim landed behind me and we spent the night in Waverly, Tennessee. The next day my family and I proceeded to Blakesburg in a rented Piper airplane.

This was the last forced landing in my aviation career. Later in the month, the engine was repaired and I flew the Stearman back home to Zellwood.

Wanda and I were featured in a 1980 article when we brought our restored 1929 Butler Blackhawk Sport to the original Butler Aircraft Corporation factory in Kansas City, Missouri.

Returning to the Butler Aircraft Factory

Due to the efforts of Al Waas, a former employee of the Butler Aircraft Corporation, arrangements were made for Wanda and me to fly the Blackhawk back to its home in Kansas City, Missouri in 1980. So Wanda and I gathered up the necessary maps and had a nice flight to Kansas City. Little did we know what was in store for us after we landed.

We called ahead, so they knew our approximate arrival time, and when we landed and taxied to the FBO, to our surprise, Butler had released all of their workers from their jobs to see the airplane they had built. What a crowd. We had a very warm welcome and talked to some of the people who had actually built this airplane.

To add to our astonishment, the local television station was on hand to record the event for a newscast that evening. All the employees of the Butler Aircraft Corporation were as proud of the airplane as we were.

The original treasurer of the Butler Aircraft Corporation, 88-year-old Oscar Nelson, was there in his wheelchair. We took a picture of him in front of the Blackhawk and when it was completed, he motioned for me to come over to him. With a tear or two in his eye he said, "I wish today would never end." I agreed with him 100 percent.

After the airport welcome, we were taken to the factory, where in a special room they had all the company's aircraft records spread out on a table for us to examine. When done, we were escorted to the company's in-house restaurant where we were treated to a great meal and where various officials gave many talks. I still believe it was one of the most noteworthy events that Wanda and I have ever experienced. We shall never forget their hospitality.

By the way, three famous people owned some of the first production Blackhawks that were built. These were Art Goebel, a WW1 ace who liked the airplane so much he bought one; Hoot Gibson, a famous movie star; and last but certainly not least in my heart, George T. Baker, founder and president of National Airlines.

Back in Miami, as soon as National Airlines executives found out that we had a flyable Butler Blackhawk, several executives contacted us. One was Dave Amos who contacted me one day and said he certainly would like to have a ride in a Butler Blackhawk once again. I took Dave for a nice long ride and I was proud to be able to do so. This was the same Dave Amos who was director of the employment office when I first walked into National Airlines headquarters with Wayne North in 1952 and who talked me into flying for National Airlines despite my objections.

Wanda and I flew the Blackhawk steadily until we sold it back to the Butler Aircraft Corporation. Jokingly I told the Butler people that I was only bringing it back for warranty work. Jim Kimball's brother, Al, flew it back to Kansas City and Wanda and I drove our motor home to meet him there. It

Logo of the wooden propeller manufacturing business I owned in the late 1980's.

is now on display in Union Station in Kansas City, Missouri, home of its birth.

This airplane served us very well for many years with no engine problems whatsoever. This closely resembled the good times I had flying my old trusty Travel Air. Now don't misunderstand me, flying an airliner at 41,000 feet with a full load of trusting passengers had its satisfying moments, too. But nothing beats flying an open cockpit biplane in tranquil air over fragrant America.

Falcon Manufacturing Company

One day in 1986, I was reading Trade-A-Plane and saw a wooden propeller manufacturing business named Eagle Air, Inc. for sale. I called the listed number and found out that the owner was in debt to the SBA and needed to bail out.

I became very interested and flew out to Colorado to see his manufacturing facilities. The shop was a complete wreck and the owner blamed this sad state of affairs on his wife. I overlooked this unnecessary

piece of information and bought the business anyways.

He had purchased the company from the original owner, Ole Fahlin, who built certified wooden propellers for almost all of the light airplanes of the 1920's, 1930's, and 1940's. In total, Fahlin owned 87 FAA propeller type certificates and his propellers were world renowned for their quality, performance, and craftsmanship.

The owner possessed all of the necessary production tools and equipment, including drill presses, band saws, table saws, glue presses, sanders, welding tables, lathes, and various tipping and balancing stands. He also agreed to build for me a duplicating lathe designed to operate within a tolerance of one 20,000 of an inch to duplicate propeller patterns, similar to the way a duplicating key machine works, except much bigger.

The sale included all of the FAA type certificates and associated designs, drawings, engineering data, and manufacturing rights for the production of Fahlin propellers. These 87 FAA-approved type certificates alone were valued at more than $5,000 apiece. Since all of the engineering requirements and FAA certificates were already issued, no further costly research or development tasks were required to operate the business.

I had all of the assets of the company loaded on a semi-trailer truck and moved to my home in Zellwood. I built an addition to an existing building on my property and proceeded to manufacture the propellers. He also owned a Rearwin Sportster and I bought that too and he flew it to Zellwood for me.

As part of the sales agreement, he also consented to work for me so I could learn the business. During this period, as the former owner, he would moreover act as liaison between me and the FAA to get FAA approval for my new business. This took quite some time.

I contacted Ole Fahlin to receive permission to name my company Fahlin propellers but he refused, in case he wanted to start manufacturing propellers on his own again. Fahlin was from Sweden and I was told that the word, "fahlin" in Swedish, meant a bird similar to a falcon. So I named my new company the Falcon Manufacturing Corporation.

Making a wood propeller from scratch is not as easy as one might think. During one of the many FAA inspections, I was asked by an examiner to prove that the wood I was using was birch, select number 2 or better. I told him we purchased all of the lumber from an authorized lumber company. He replied that the FAA did not recognize lumber companies individually and that I had to prove that I knew what wood I was using. With the help of the US Department of Agriculture, he was finally convinced that I knew birch wood when I saw it.

As a joke, a friend of mine returning from a Maine vacation brought me a

The last Travel Air I owned, a 4000, sitting in front of my fixed based operation in Orlando. It is now on display in the Experimental Aircraft Association museum in Oshkosh, Wisconsin.

large branch off a birch tree. For the FAA's benefit, I mounted this branch on the wall in my garage with a sign under it saying, "This is part of a birch tree." I then broke a small branch off and mounted it on another plaque and it read, "This is a son of a birch". I don't think the FAA examiner thought this was very funny.

I made about one hundred propellers for light planes with the help of the previous owner and he was very knowledgeable, as he had made many propellers prior to my purchase of his business. He worked for me for a few months and unfortunately, I found out that we usually didn't see eye to eye on various matters. So he left in the middle of the night and I have never seen him since. I hired other people to help to make propellers.

Typical materials for a single wooden propeller were about 37 board feet of clear birch, epoxy glue, solder, a brass tip and associated rivets, epoxy varnish, and a slick decal for a total cost of about $80, not including labor, which was extensive. In turn, I could sell a type-certificated propeller for anywhere from $400 to $800.

But I soon got tired of breathing saw dust, sanding propellers, putting brass leading edges on them, etc., so I sold the entire business to Jim Kimball including the type certificates. Jim operated the business for quite some time in conjunction with his antique airplane rebuilding business. He later sold the business to someone else out west. When all was said and done, I did not make any profit out of this adventure, but I sure got a lot of experience. If you

ever come across a Falcon propeller then you know who made it.

Airplanes Owned and Flown

In my more than 50 years of active flying, I estimate that I have personally owned more than 150 airplanes. The first airplane I ever purchased was an Aeronca KCA in 1942 while the very last airplane I owned was a Culver Cadet that I sold in the early 1990's. Documenting all the models in between is what presents a challenge.

Surprisingly, the earliest airplanes I owned are the easiest to record because they were relatively few and far between and I documented each airplane in my logbook. As my salary increased as a National Airlines captain so did my purchases. Oftentimes I would purchase an airplane just because I wanted to see how it would fly. As an experienced mechanic, airworthy inspections were relatively easy and I rarely got burned with a bad performing airplane.

The problem is cataloging the more recent airplanes that I owned. As an airline captain, all of my flight time was documented in trip logs so I saw no point in keeping a civilian logbook. As a result, most of the airplanes I owned from 1952 on can only be documented from photographs, old registration paperwork, or memory.

Former commercial airliners I have owned were a Stinson SM6000B Trimotor, two Douglas DC-3s, and two Boeing 247Ds.

Former military planes I have owned were the two U.S. Army

I liked Mooney's so much that I owned seven and I also owned a Mooney dealership.

Preparing to fly my Waco BSO. I never converted this one to duster duty, preferring to fly it in the passenger configuration.

I have also owned all types of agricultural airplanes, including this Cessna AgWagon.

The last classic J-3 I owned.

Another one of my Waco's, a CTO model.

I owned two Aero Commanders, to commute to my day job with National in speed and style.

The big ticket: an Air Transport Rating with my various commercial airliner type ratings. Also included is a type rating for the B-17 which authorized me to fly the civilian Boeing airline model 307 Stratocruiser.

Air Force B-17's, two U.S. Navy N3N's, four U.S. Army Air Force Boeing Stearmans, more than 10 U.S. Navy SNJ's, a U.S. Army Air Service PT-19, a Canadian Air Force PT-26, two U.S. Army Air Force Vultee BT-13's and a Vultee BT-15.

Former airmail planes I have owned were a Pitcairn PA-5 Mailwing and a Stearman 4E Speedmail.

Antique biplanes I have owned included a Butler Blackhawk Sport, nine Travel Air's, and eight Waco's.

General aviation airplanes I have owned include an assortment of more than 100 Aero Commanders, Beechcrafts, Cessna's, Culver Cadets, Fairchilds, Mooneys, Piper Cubs, Taylorcrafts, and other one of a kind airplanes.

National Airlines Airliners Flown

In comparison, identifying which commercial airliners I flew is easy. They are all recorded in my National Airlines trip logs. I was qualified as captain on the:

Boeing 727-35
Boeing 727-235
Convair-240
Convair-340
Convair-440
Douglas DC-4
Douglas DC-6
Douglas DC-6B
Douglas DC-7
Douglas DC-7B
Douglas DC-8-21
Douglas DC-8-31
Douglas DC-8-32
Douglas DC-8-51
Douglas DC-8-54F
Douglas DC-8-61 (Stretch 8)
Douglas DC-10-10
Douglas DC-10-30
Lockheed L-18 Lodestar
Lockheed L-188 Electra
Lockheed 1049H Constellation

As you have probably guessed by its frequent mention throughout this narrative, my favorite airplane out of all these wonderful steeds was my Travel Air B4000 154V.

Vision

Of all the physical characteristics needed to be a successful aviator, visual acuity, with or without eyeglasses, certainly stands out as one of the most important.

Fate dealt this old crop duster a cruel hand when I reached my 70's. I was diagnosed with age-related macular degeneration (AMD), an eye disorder that slowly damages one's central vision. Doctors do not know what causes macular degeneration and there is no cure for severe dry AMD, which I have.

My symptoms began as slightly blurred vision but I am now at the point where I am legally blind although I do have some peripheral vision. This impairment has not slowed me down in the slightest and with the help of my loving wife Wanda, I am still able to travel, dance, take music lessons, and talk flying with friends and guests, although I do find myself using my hands a lot more than usual when I explain complicated flight maneuvers. I still fly occasionally with a flight instructor in a Cessna 172.

Awards and Honors

What the good Lord taketh away he often returns in other glorious ways. In 2009, I was selected to be included in the Florida Aviation Historical Society's Hall of Fame. I was flabbergasted when I learned that I had been selected, convinced that they had made a mistake. While I may have quoted Shakespeare's

"much ado about nothing" to a local newspaper reporter when asked how I felt, I was deeply moved.

The ceremony was held during a special luncheon at the Florida Air Museum in Lakeland, Florida. I was inducted into the Hall of Fame with esteemed company, including Amelia Earhart, the world-famous aviatrix who disappeared in 1937 during an attempt to circumnavigate the globe; and David McCampbell, a decorated World War II Navy ace.

Brochure from my induction ceremony into the Florida Aviation Hall of Fame.

In 2012, I was again deeply honored when I received the Federal Aviation Administration's highest honor, The Wright Brothers Master Pilot Award at a special ceremony. The Master Pilot Award is given to those pilots who have demonstrated professionalism, skill and aviation expertise by maintaining safe operations for 50 or more years. I was awarded a beautiful signed plaque and my name is now listed in the Wright Brothers Master Pilot Award Roll of Honor located online.

My Wright Brothers Master Pilot Award from the Federal Aviation Administration.

Leroy Brown, 91, (right) received the Federal Aviation Administration's highest honor, the Wright Brothers Master Pilot Award on Friday, March 30, at a special ceremony at the Lakeland Airport in Lakeland. Pictured with Brown are, James Minary, FAASTeam Program Manager (left) and John Duncan, Air Transportation Division Manager. Brown began his aviation career in 1935, at the age of 14. Initially, he was a cropduster in Zellwood, then became an airline pilot and flew without major incident for more than 29 years.

U.S. Airline Industry Museum

For the past decade, I have served as president of the U.S. Airline Industry Museum Foundation. Located at Orlando Apopka Airport in Apopka, Florida, we are collecting artifacts and airplanes in hopes of building the first museum in the United States dedicated exclusively to the airline industry. In September 2009, I arranged for the transportation and reassembly of a Convair-240 for display as one of the major attractions. We have repainted it in Pan Am colors.

It has been one of my personal pleasures to interact with fellow retired airline personnel, including pilots, stewardesses, flight engineers, and ground personnel, as we continue our efforts. It is only fitting that I give back something to the industry that has given me so much joy and satisfaction.

Chapter Fifteen
Final Reflections

I always felt that when I retracted the landing gear, I was free from the shackles of the earth and all its problems for a few hours. In this photograph I am launching in one of my Waco's from River Ranch, Florida.

It still fits: wearing my airline captain's uniform.

lying was always a very satisfying occupation to me, whether cruising at 3 feet above the ground or 41,000 feet above the clouds, depending upon the altitude of my airplane's operational limits. While I may have dinged a few personal airplanes, I am proud to say that I never scratched an airliner during the more than 29 years I served as an airline pilot and captain. I flew more than 35,000 flight hours and transported tens of thousands of people safely to their destinations.

Airline transportation involves thousands of workers and is perhaps the largest industry in the United States. It requires food handlers, fuel handlers, aircraft manufacturers, aircraft engine manufacturers, air traffic control, airports, the FAA, and the list goes on and on of people employed by this one transportation system.

The only part I played was flying the airplane with the help of my crewmembers. Besides just flying the airplane, I also had to make sure that the airplane was airworthy and that our route of flight was safe. With the

In my dreams, I still pilot airliners across the country.

help of National Airlines flight control personnel, we studied the weather, computed the optimum fuel supply, calculated the best altitudes for winds, and analyzed many other factors that entered into making a safe flight for passengers and an efficient operation for the airline.

We had to know how to take care of any possible emergency as we alone were in charge once we were airborne. We could not dial 911 and get any help. It was a demanding job for the pilots to make sure we arrived on time and safely. Often overlooked was the hard work of the cabin crew who were there to assist passengers in any way possible to make them comfortable. I always kidded them that they were the only people in the industry who walked across the country on a daily basis. I personally liked all of my assigned cabin crews and I tried mightily to keep everyone happy by making the flight as pleasant as possible for everyone.

I can truthfully say I have never had a flight crew that did not meet high standards. Flight crews live a different life as we fly all around the world, going through many time zones in a few hours, flying all night long, through all kinds of weather, and tolerating often-long separations from our families.

I quite frankly miss seeing some of my old stewardesses, copilots, and

A close friend to this day, Nancy Pace and I flew together many times. She flew as a stewardess for more than 40 years.

flight engineers as we acquired a lasting friendship that is not usually found in any other profession. If we had to fly on Christmas Day or some other major holiday, we always tried to cheer each other up as we would much rather have been home with our families.

I really enjoyed my life as an airline captain and I readily accepted the responsibility that goes with this command position. But I was always comfortable in knowing that I was given an airliner that probably cost anywhere from $50 million to $100 million to build, was very well maintained by expert maintenance personnel, and that I always had a highly trained flight crew with me to face any difficulties. Sometimes people ask me if I have ever had any close calls. I usually reply, "Yes I have." All were on the way to the airport.

Other people ask me what I think of airline deregulation. This happened during the Carter administration when all government control of airline fares, routes, and market entry and exit were removed. I didn't think very much of it then and I think less of it today. I think it destroyed the airlines of old, which as far as I was concerned, was the best transportation system. They not only served big cities but they also served many of the smaller cities that are no longer served. I shared this thought with thousands of others in this business.

However, in my heart, I was forever a crop duster and my dusting experiences were always great and wonderful. This is why I could just about always be found crop dusting

Hand loading my duster on a day off from the airlines.

on my days off from flying the big jets for National Airlines.

One of the reasons I liked crop dusting so much was that I had no outside electronic aids such as a satellite-based global positioning system (GPS) mounted in my cockpit to show me where I was. I flew by pilotage and I loved to fly the old biplanes the way they were designed to be flown, by hand. There were no autopilots, no radios, and no passengers; just I and my open cockpit biplane and I cherished it. Nothing made me happier when passersby's noticed me dusting a field and would actually stop and watch the exhibition. Agricultural aviation is an essential part of our food supply and as you read this, there are crop dusters out there plying their trade to our benefit.

While I always enjoyed hand flying an airplane, today's airline industry modern airliners have so much automated equipment that the pilots are really not flying, but only operating a machine. Their workload has been reduced so much that they probably have a hard time staying awake. I wonder if they are having fun.

But I do have to admit that instant weather information, weather radars, pressurized airplanes, automatic landing systems, and air traffic control surveillance radars have all made flying airliners much easier than it was for me in the old days.

But for me there will always be one special National Airlines employee that I will always love and appreciate. That is, of course, my wife Wanda and we are still in love after 55 years of marriage. As a radio operator, she used to call us on the radio to issue us clearances and as I tell all my friends, she still gives me clearance limits to this day.

After over 60 years of flying which included crop dusting, banner towing, sail plane towing, aerobatic instruction, airline flying, and pleasure flying in all kinds of airplanes and all types of weather, I finally had to walk away from flying. Quite naturally, now that I am part of a group of 90-year-old senior citizens, I can truthfully say that I miss my life as a pilot. But I can also look back and say to myself, "What a wonderful time."

In aviation when a pilot passes away he is said to have gone west where he will have his final check ride given by the man upstairs. I hope I am greeted with a brand new Travel Air and that I have passed this important check ride called life.

Taken from the copilot's seat of a Douglas DC-6 in 1954, every transport pilot in the world has a similar picture in their photo album. You stare out at those big, spinning egg beaters with a mixture of wonder at the miracle of flight and a slight twinge of uneasiness that they might stop. I have the same photograph of jet engines.

We hope you enjoyed Captain Brown's life story. May we suggest some of our other aviation related titles? All are available through www.bluewaterpress.com or by way of other retailers.

Pan American World Airways — Images of a Great Airline

A treasure trove of Pan Am lore. Here is something for everyone — a concise history of the pioneering airline, a rich potpourri of Pan Am memorabilia, and, best of all, a nostalgic journey back to an age when the mighty Pan American ruled the skies.

Pan American World Airways — Aviation History Through the Words of Its People

A tribute to the legacy of one of the world's great airlines and the men and women who for six decades were the soul of the Company. James Baldwin and Jeff Kriendler have created a compelling book, which through the words of its contributors, captures much of the joy, adventure and spirit which was Pan Am.

Shadow Flight

An aviation tale of kidnapping, drug running, and intrigue. The story opens with flight instructor, Kyle Bennett, teaching slow flight and stalls to one of his students, Brooke Roberts, the wife of a surgeon. Brooke's husband, also a pilot, gave his wife flying lessons as a birthday gift. Fast paced and riveting, this is a flying story that winds its way through almost every facet of a flyer's career, from flight instructing to charter work to airline flying.

Wings Over America - The Fact Filled Guide to the Major and Regional Airlines of the USA

A historical, factual, and illustrated overview of the airlines that serve our nation. This book is primarily targeted towards airline enthusiasts, filling a void since the last time a book of this kind had been published nearly two decades ago.

All of these great titles are available online through www.bluewaterpress.com and other online sources.

CPSIA information can be obtained at www.ICGtesting.com
Printed in the USA
LVOW092248170613

339016LV00001B/2/P